Discourse on Social Planning under Uncertainty

Economists have long studied policy choice by social planners aiming to maximize population welfare. Whether performing theoretical studies or applied analyses, researchers have generally assumed that the planner knows enough about the choice environment to be able to determine an optimal action. However, the consequences of decisions are often highly uncertain. *Discourse on Social Planning under Uncertainty* addresses the failure of research to come to grips with this uncertainty. Combining research across three fields – welfare economics, decision theory, and econometrics – this impressive study offers a comprehensive treatment that fleshes out a "worldview" and juxtaposes it with other viewpoints. Building on multiple case studies ranging from medical treatment to climate policy, the book explains analytical methods and how to apply them, providing a foundation on which future interdisciplinary work can build.

Charles F. Manski is Board of Trustees Professor in the Department of Economics and Institute for Policy Research at Northwestern University. He is a member of the National Academy of Sciences and Fellow of the American Academy of Arts and Sciences, the Econometric Society, the American Statistical Association, and the British Academy. His research spans econometrics, judgment and decision, and analysis of public policy.

Discourse on Social Planning under Uncertainty

CHARLES F. MANSKI
Northwestern University

CAMBRIDGE
UNIVERSITY PRESS

Shaftesbury Road, Cambridge CB2 8EA, United Kingdom

One Liberty Plaza, 20th Floor, New York, NY 10006, USA

477 Williamstown Road, Port Melbourne, VIC 3207, Australia

314–321, 3rd Floor, Plot 3, Splendor Forum, Jasola District Centre, New Delhi – 110025, India

103 Penang Road, #05–06/07, Visioncrest Commercial, Singapore 238467

Cambridge University Press is part of Cambridge University Press & Assessment, a department of the University of Cambridge.

We share the University's mission to contribute to society through the pursuit of education, learning and research at the highest international levels of excellence.

www.cambridge.org
Information on this title: www.cambridge.org/9781009556781

DOI: 10.1017/9781009556767

© Charles F. Manski 2024

This publication is in copyright. Subject to statutory exception and to the provisions of relevant collective licensing agreements, no reproduction of any part may take place without the written permission of Cambridge University Press & Assessment.

When citing this work, please include a reference to the
DOI 10.1017/9781009556767

First published 2024

A catalogue record for this publication is available from the British Library

Library of Congress Cataloging-in-Publication Data
Names: Manski, Charles F., author.
Title: Discourse on social planning under uncertainty / Charles F. Manski, Northwestern University, Illinois.
Description: Cambridge, United Kingdom : New York, NY : Cambridge University Press, 2024. | Includes bibliographical references and index.
Identifiers: LCCN 2024019904 | ISBN 9781009556781 (hardback) | ISBN 9781009556767 (ebook)
Subjects: LCSH: Policy sciences. | Social planning. | Welfare economics. | Uncertainty.
Classification: LCC H97 .M3679 2024 | DDC 320.6–dc23/eng/20240815
LC record available at https://lccn.loc.gov/2024019904

ISBN 978-1-009-55678-1 Hardback
ISBN 978-1-009-55675-0 Paperback

Cambridge University Press & Assessment has no responsibility for the persistence or accuracy of URLs for external or third-party internet websites referred to in this publication and does not guarantee that any content on such websites is, or will remain, accurate or appropriate.

*for the General Welfare, and for that of
Lev & Isaac & Grant*

Contents

Preface		*page* xiii
1	Credible Planning under Uncertainty	1
	Organization of the Book	2
1.1	The Prevalent Study of Planning with Incredible Certitude	4
1.2	Uncertainty in Decision Theory	6
	1.2.1 Consequentialist Decision Theory	7
	1.2.2 Axiomatic Decision Theory	8
	Representation Theorems	10
	Is Axiomatic Theory Relevant to Planning?	11
	1.2.3 The Institutional Separation of Research on Planning and Actual Planning	13
1.3	The Structure of Consequentialist Decision Theory	14
	1.3.1 The Choice Set, State Space, and Welfare Function	14
	1.3.2 Decision Criteria	15
	Complete Class Theorems	17
	1.3.3 Statistical Decision Theory	17
	Robust Decisions	18
	1.3.4 Minimax Regret Planning	19
1.4	Uncertainty in Empirical Research	21
	1.4.1 Identification Analysis	21
	Research on Partial Identification	22
	1.4.2 Statistical Imprecision	23
1.5	Perspectives on Social Welfare	24
	1.5.1 The New Welfare Economics	25
	1.5.2 Utilitarian Welfare	25
	Willingness to Pay and Kaldor–Hicks Efficiency	26
	1.5.3 Maximin Welfare	27
	The "Initial Position" Arguments of Harsanyi and Rawls	27
	1.5.4 Optimal Paternalism in Populations with Bounded Rationality	29

	1.5.5 Nonpersonalist Welfare Functions	30
	1.5.6 Pragmatic Welfare	31

PART I CHARACTERIZING UNCERTAINTY

2 Incredible Certitude — 35
- 2.1 Certitude in Religion and Philosophy — 36
- 2.2 Conventional Certitude in Official Economic Statistics — 38
  - 2.2.1 Congressional Budget Office Scoring of Legislation — 38
  - 2.2.2 Economic Statistics Reported by Federal Statistical Agencies — 39
  - 2.2.3 Transitory Uncertainty: Revisions in National Income Accounts — 40
  - 2.2.4 Permanent Uncertainty: Nonresponse in Surveys — 41
  - 2.2.5 Conceptual Uncertainty: Seasonal Adjustment of Official Statistics — 43
  - 2.2.6 Why Do Statistical Agencies Practice Incredible Certitude? — 45
- 2.3 Dueling Certitudes in Criminal Justice Research — 46
  - 2.3.1 The RAND and IDA Studies of Cocaine-Control Policy — 46
  - 2.3.2 The Deterrent Effect of the Death Penalty — 48
  - 2.3.3 How Do Right-to-Carry Laws Affect Crime Rates? — 50
- 2.4 Wishful Extrapolation from Medical Research to Patient Care — 52
  - 2.4.1 Extrapolation from Study Populations to Patient Populations — 52
  - 2.4.2 Extrapolation from Experimental Treatments to Clinical Treatments — 53
  - 2.4.3 Wishful Meta-analyses of Disparate Studies — 54
- 2.5 Sacrificing Relevance for Certitude — 55
  - 2.5.1 The Odds Ratio and Public Health — 56
  - 2.5.2 Randomized Trials and the Primacy of Internal Validity — 58
- 2.6 Psychological Rationales for Incredible Certitude — 59
  - 2.6.1 Intolerance of Uncertainty — 59
  - 2.6.2 Motivated Reasoning Regarding Uncertainty — 60
  - 2.6.3 Expression of Uncertainty in Probability Judgments — 61
- 2.7 As-If Optimization with Incredible Certitude — 62
  - 2.7.1 Using As-If Consensus to Coordinate Collective Decisions: Financial Accounting — 63

3 Identification of Treatment Response — 65
- 3.1 Partial Identification of Mean Treatment Response with Observational Data — 67
  - 3.1.1 Bounding Mean Response with No Knowledge of Counterfactual Outcomes — 67
  - 3.1.2 Sentencing and Recidivism — 69
  - 3.1.3 Instrumental Variables — 72
    - The Mortality Effects of Swan–Ganz Catheterization — 74
  - 3.1.4 Monotone Instrumental Variables — 75

		3.1.5	Monotone Treatment Response	77
	3.2	Partial Identification of Mean Treatment Response with Data from Trials with Limited Internal Validity		78
		3.2.1	Missing Outcome or Covariate Data	78
			Missing Data in a Trial Comparing Treatments for Hypertension	79
		3.2.2	Partial Compliance	81
			The Illinois Unemployment Insurance Experiment	82
			Intention-to-Treat	83
		3.2.3	Identification of Personalized Treatment Response with Trial-Reported Findings on Binary Subgroups	84
			Identification of Long Mean Outcomes Using Short Trial Findings	85
			Bounded-Variation Assumptions	86
	3.3	Identification of Treatment Response with Social Interactions		88
		3.3.1	Basic Concepts and Notation	88
		3.3.2	Constant and Semi-monotone Treatment Response	89
	3.4	Credible Meta-analysis		91
4	Identification of Choice Behavior and Personal Welfare			93
	4.1	Revealed Preference Analysis		94
		4.1.1	Revealing the Preferences of a Classical Consumer	94
			Observation of One Choice Setting	94
			Observation of Several Choice Settings	95
		4.1.2	Random Utility Models of Heterogeneous Decision Makers	96
			Consistency with Utility Theory	97
			Prediction Using Attributes of Alternatives and Decision Makers	98
			Incomplete Data and Conditional Choice Probabilities	98
	4.2	Identification of Income-Leisure Preferences for Evaluation of Income Tax Policy		100
		4.2.1	Taxation and Labor Supply	100
		4.2.2	Basic Revealed Preference Analysis	103
			Predicting Labor Supply under a Proposed Tax Schedule	104
		4.2.3	Restrictions on the Preference Distribution	105
		4.2.4	Implications for Utilitarian Policy Evaluation	107
	4.3	Revealed Preference Analysis of Choices Maximizing Expected Utility		107
		4.3.1	Basic Analysis	108
		4.3.2	Random Expected-Utility Models	108
			Rational Expectations Assumptions	109
			How Do Youth Infer Their Returns to Schooling?	109
	4.4	Analysis of Subjective Data		110
		4.4.1	Measuring Probabilistic Expectations	110
			Using Expectations and Choice Data to Estimate Random Expected-Utility Models	111

	4.4.2 Measuring Imprecise Probabilities	112
	4.4.3 Elicitation of Potential Behavior in Hypothetical Choice Scenarios	113

PART II ANALYSES OF PLANNING PROBLEMS

5 Diversified Treatment under Ambiguity ... 117
  5.1 Treating X-Pox ... 118
  5.2 Utilitarian Allocation to Two Treatments ... 120
    5.2.1 Bayesian Planning ... 121
    5.2.2 Maximin Planning ... 122
    5.2.3 Minimax Regret Planning ... 122
        Choosing Sentences for Convicted Juvenile Offenders ... 122
    5.2.4 Welfare Increasing in Mean Personal Welfare ... 123
  5.3 Diversification and Equal Treatment of Equals ... 124
    5.3.1 Ex Ante and Ex Post Equal Treatment ... 124
    5.3.2 Planning Combining Consequentialism and Deontological Ethics ... 125
  5.4 Adaptive Diversification ... 126
    5.4.1 Adaptive Treatment of a Life-Threatening Disease ... 127
    5.4.2 Adaptive Diversification of Regulatory Approval ... 129

6 Treatment with Data from Statistically Imprecise Trials ... 131
  6.1 Using Hypothesis Tests to Compare Treatments ... 132
  6.2 Using Statistical Decision Theory to Compare Treatments ... 133
    6.2.1 Bayes Decisions ... 134
    6.2.2 Maximin and Minimax Regret Decisions ... 135
  6.3 Treatment Choice with Trial Data ... 137
    6.3.1 Choice between a Status Quo Treatment and an Innovation When Outcomes Are Binary ... 138
  6.4 Setting Sample Size to Enable Near-Optimal Treatment Choice ... 141
  6.5 Treatment with Primary and Secondary Outcomes ... 142
    6.5.1 Reconsidering Choice of Sample Size in the MSLT-II Trial ... 143
  6.6 Covid-19 Treatment with Data from an Imprecise Trial ... 145
  6.7 Managing Uncertainty in FDA Drug Approval ... 147
    6.7.1 The FDA Approval Process ... 147
    6.7.2 FDA Rejection of Formal Decision Analysis ... 148
    6.7.3 Adaptive Partial Drug Approval ... 150

7 Personalized Treatment ... 151
  7.1 Optimal Treatment with Personalized Risk ... 152
    7.1.1 Optimal Choice between Two Treatments ... 153
    7.1.2 The Value of Covariate Information ... 154
    7.1.3 Surveillance or Aggressive Treatment ... 156
    7.1.4 Finding a Defendant Guilty or Not Guilty of a Crime ... 157
        Optimal Conviction Decisions with Frequentist Risk Assessment ... 159
        Legal Precedents ... 159

		7.1.5	Nonutilitarian Arguments to Exclude Race as a Covariate in Medical Risk Prediction	161
		7.1.6	Assessing Benefits, Costs, and Disparate Racial Impacts of Confrontational Proactive Policing	163
			Model	164
	7.2	Separability of Treatment Choice by Covariates under Uncertainty		167
		7.2.1	Treatment Allocation with Partial Identification of Mean Treatment Response	167
			Bayesian Planning	168
			Maximin Planning	168
			MMR Planning	169
		7.2.2	Should a Planner Condition on All Observed Covariates?	170
		7.2.3	Treatment Allocation with Sample Data	171
	7.3	Surveillance or Aggressive Treatment with Partial Knowledge of Personalized Risk		172
	7.4	Diagnostic Testing and Treatment		173
		7.4.1	The Two-Stage Optimization Problem	174
			Optimization with Utilitarian Welfare	175
			Threshold Risk Assessments	177
		7.4.2	Testing and Treatment under Ambiguity	178
			Piecemeal MMR Decision Making	179
8	Vaccination with Unknown Indirect Effects			181
	8.1	Background		181
		8.1.1	Differentiating Epidemic Suppression from Social Cost Minimization	185
	8.2	Choice between Decentralization and a Universal Mandate with a Representative Agent		186
		8.2.1	The Optimization Problem	187
		8.2.2	Policy Choice without Knowledge of the Indirect Effect of a Mandate	188
			Optimization with Partial Knowledge	189
			Planning When the Optimal Policy Is Indeterminate	190
	8.3	Choice between Decentralization and a Universal Mandate in a Heterogeneous Population		191
		8.3.1	The Optimization Problem	192
		8.3.2	Policy Choice without Knowledge of Indirect Effects, Redux	193
			Optimization with Partial Knowledge	193
			Planning When the Optimal Policy Is Indeterminate	193
	8.4	Discussion		195
9	Climate Planning with Uncertainty in Climate Modeling and Intergenerational Discounting			196
	9.1	The Policy Problem		196
	9.2	Prevalent Approaches to Climate and Discount-Rate Uncertainty		198

	9.2.1 Averaging Outputs of Multi-model Ensembles of Climate Models	198
	9.2.2 Uncertainties and Disagreements Regarding the Discount Rate	200
9.3	Minimax Regret Policy Evaluation	202
	9.3.1 The Optimal-Control Problem	202
	9.3.2 The Minimax Regret Decision Rule	203
	9.3.3 Use of Δ to Express Empirical and Normative Uncertainty	204
9.4	Analysis with a Computational Model	205
	9.4.1 Model Details	206
	9.4.2 Findings	209
9.5	Discussion	209

10 Looking Ahead — 212
- 10.1 Strengthening the Foundations for Planning under Uncertainty — 213
  - 10.1.1 Communicating Uncertainty — 213
  - 10.1.2 Specifying Planning Problems — 214
  - 10.1.3 Enhancing the Tractability of Decision Criteria — 215
- 10.2 Pandemic Planning — 216
  - 10.2.1 Incredible Certitude in Epidemiological Modeling of the Covid-19 Pandemic — 217
    - The March 2020 Imperial College Report — 217
    - Combining Epidemiological and Macroeconomic Modeling — 219
  - 10.2.2 Adaptive Diversification of Covid-19 Policy — 219
  - 10.2.3 The Pressing Need for Credible Integrated Assessment of Pandemic Impacts — 220
- 10.3 Planning to Boldly Go — 221

References — 225
Index — 245

Preface

This work has emerged from an intellectual journey that has spanned over fifty years. In retrospect, I see that the long duration was inevitable. I could not have written the book earlier because it combines research and thinking in three fields – welfare economics, decision theory, and econometric analysis of partial identification – that developed separately from one another and in different time periods.

Welfare economic study of social planning began in the late 1700s, was formalized in the mid 1900s, and then progressed for several decades as a central concern of economics, but the subject has more recently become peripheral to the profession. Decision theoretic study of choice under uncertainty has advanced steadily since the mid 1900s, initially focusing on expected-utility maximization, and more recently on approaches to decision making under ambiguity (aka deep uncertainty). Econometric study of partial identification had isolated precursors in the 1930s and 1940s, but it developed into a coherent subject of analysis only from the 1990s onwards.

Different researchers have worked in these fields, so it is not surprising that they developed separately. Of particular importance is that welfare economics has primarily studied deterministic environments, whereas decision theory and econometrics are fundamentally concerned with uncertainty. I began to recognize the cross-field synergies around 2000. Since then, I have sought to build connections and to make the results useful to specific domains of planning. My integration of three disparate fields is unusual, so it may benefit readers if I sketch how my research has evolved.

I was introduced to welfare economics by Jerome Rothenberg, my undergraduate advisor at the Massachusetts Institute of Technology

(MIT) in the late 1960s. I learned directly from him and from his book *The Measurement of Social Welfare* (Rothenberg, 1961). When I began my PhD at MIT in fall 1970, I anticipated that I would do research on public economics. In my second year, I enrolled in the yearlong course sequence, one semester taught by Peter Diamond and the other by E. Cary Brown. The two semesters could not have been more different. Diamond was in the midst of his joint research on optimal income taxation with James Mirrlees, who was visiting MIT at the time. The two gave the lectures, focusing on their work in progress. The presentation was highly technical, to the extent that my difficulty with the math impeded my appreciation of basic concepts. In sharp contrast, Brown exemplified an earlier tradition in public economics whose concerns were closer to real-world public policy but whose methodologies were too heuristic for me to be able to distinguish firm conclusions from conjecture.

Finding myself uncomfortable with both polar approaches, I abandoned public economics as a focus for my research. Instead, I was attracted to econometrics. I learned the classical body of work on identification of simultaneous equations systems from Franklin Fisher. I was intrigued with the central inferential problem, but I was not enamored by the linear algebra brought to bear to study it. I was excited to learn the then brand new subject of discrete choice analysis from Daniel McFadden, who visited for a period and gave lectures. I subsequently wrote my PhD dissertation on the theory and application of discrete choice analysis.

As an econometrician, my research has emphasized analysis of identification much more than statistical inference. From the late 1980s onward, I have almost exclusively studied settings with partial identification. With scattered exceptions, previous econometric research had studied settings with point identification, which combine strong data and assumptions. In these settings, the only source of uncertainty faced in empirical research is the statistical imprecision of inference from finite data samples, which disappears as sample size grows. Research on partial identification studies settings which combine weaker data and assumptions, ones in which uncertainty persists even as sample size grows. Such settings are the norm when realistically available data are combined with credible assumptions. The analysis seeks to determine what one can learn when statistical imprecision disappears. Although one cannot learn the exact value of a population feature of interest, one may be able to learn that the feature lies in an informative set of possible values. The aim is to characterize this set.

Identification has been a central issue in empirical research on treatment response, which seeks to draw conclusions from observational data and from randomized experiments. A core objective of research on treatment response has been to inform decision making by a social planner who chooses treatments for a population of interest. I first connected econometric study of identification to welfare economic study of planning under uncertainty in my article, "Identification Problems and Decisions Under Ambiguity: Empirical Analysis of Treatment Response and Normative Analysis of Treatment Choice" (Manski, 2000). I sketched the basic problem: Combining available data with credible assumptions commonly does not reveal whether one treatment outperforms another in terms of the social welfare it yields. I recognized that, when this occurs, a planner faces a problem of decision making under ambiguity. The statistical imprecision of inference using finite samples adds further uncertainty to social planning. To cope with the latter problem, I brought to bear statistical decision theory in Manski (2004b).

From these beginnings, I have developed a program of research concerned with planning under uncertainty, embodied in numerous articles published in diverse academic journals. Some of this work has been abstract, using modern economics, econometrics, and decision theory to study general conceptual and technical issues. Some has analyzed specific planning problems, including decisions faced in policing, climate policy, and especially medical treatment of patients. I have exposited aspects of my work in two nontechnical books. *Public Policy in an Uncertain World* (Manski, 2013c) aims to make basic themes accessible to policy analysts, journalists, and the educated public. *Patient Care under Uncertainty* (Manski, 2019b) applies the themes to medical decision making, aiming to communicate with clinical researchers, public health analysts, and clinicians engaged in patient care.

Why then this new book? The two earlier books gave elementary discussions of planning under uncertainty. Here I offer a comprehensive treatment, a treatise. I expect the primary readers to be scholars and students who study public and welfare economics, mechanism design and decision theory, econometrics and statistics, operations research and systems analysis, moral philosophy and ethics. These fields of inquiry connect to planning under uncertainty in various ways. Yet they have interacted little with one another, no doubt a consequence of the prevailing siloing of academic disciplines. Research published piecemeal in concise journal articles mainly communicates within fields, not across them. A book provides the opportunity to flesh out a worldview and juxtapose it with other viewpoints. It gives the space to explain analytical methods and show how to apply them. A book provides a foundation on which future work can build.

While writing the book, I benefited from the opportunity to lecture on some of the material in a masterclass at University College London and in my presentation of the Marshall Lectures at the University of Cambridge, both in November 2023. I subsequently used a draft of the book as the primary source material for a PhD field course at Northwestern University in winter 2024. Throughout the entire process of developing the book, I have benefited from stimulating discussions of social planning, both general principles and specific aspects, with my good friend Joram Mayshar.

I

Credible Planning under Uncertainty

A foundational objective of the Constitution of the United States is to "promote the general Welfare." The Preamble states:

We the People of the United States, in Order to form a more perfect Union, establish Justice, insure domestic Tranquility, provide for the common defence, promote the general Welfare, and secure the Blessings of Liberty to ourselves and our Posterity, do ordain and establish this Constitution for the United States of America.

The Constitution does not define "general Welfare."

A century later, Marshall (1890) began his *Principles of Economics* with this sentence (p. 1):

Political economy or economics is a study of mankind in the ordinary business of life; it examines that part of individual and social action which is most closely connected with the attainment and with the use of the material requisites of wellbeing.

The word "wellbeing" may be synonymous with welfare.

In this century, a report on clinical practice guidelines by the US Institute of Medicine (IOM) stated (Institute of Medicine, 2011, p. 4):

Clinical practice guidelines are statements that include recommendations intended to optimize patient care that are informed by a systematic review of evidence and an assessment of the benefits and harms of alternative care options.

The report did not specify what it means to optimize patient care.

The Constitutional premise that the United States should promote the general welfare, Marshall's concern with social action to promote wellbeing, and the IOM premise that clinicians should optimize patient care exemplify broad assertions that entities making societal decisions should aim to maximize social welfare. Such assertions may have rhetorical appeal but they lack substance. They become meaningful only when several questions are answered: What constitutes social welfare? What are the feasible actions? What is known about the welfare consequences of alternative choices?

Maximization of welfare is a well-defined objective if enough is known about the welfare consequences of alternative choices to determine an unambiguous best action. Maximization is ill defined if the consequences are sufficiently uncertain that no action is clearly best. My concern is reasonable societal decision making in such settings.

What are the uncertainties with which planning must cope? They are too many and varied to summarize easily. For now, I will simply list those that I have studied, each of which will be discussed in this book. These include numerous uncertainties in medical risk assessment and prediction of treatment response; see Manski (2019a) for a broad exposition. There is much uncertainty in the epidemiological models used to predict the spread of infectious diseases, which inform choice of vaccination policy (Manski, 2010, 2017). There is also much uncertainty in the physical science climate models used to predict future climate change, which inform choice of climate policy (Manski, Sanstad, and DeCanio, 2021), and in the discount rate used to form a social welfare function (DeCanio, Manski, and Sanstad, 2022).

Challenging uncertainties arise when studying the preferences and behavior of human populations. Knowledge of preferences is essential to policy evaluation when welfare is utilitarian. An ability to predict behavior is required to evaluate policy consequences whatever the welfare function may be. Manski (2007c) provides an abstract analysis. Manski (2014a, 2014b) examined how uncertainties about preferences and behavior complicate evaluation of income tax policies, where a central consideration is the relative preferences of potential workers for consumption goods and for availability of time to enable nonpaid activities. I have shown how uncertainty about the effect of policing on criminal behavior complicates evaluation of proactive policing programs (Manski, 2006).

ORGANIZATION OF THE BOOK

I lay out basic themes in abstraction in this opening chapter and flesh them out in what follows. Part I, constituting Chapters 2 through 4, is concerned with characterization of uncertainty. Part II, being Chapters 5 through 9, describes my research analyzing particular classes of planning problems. Chapter 10 looks ahead to performance of future research on social planning under uncertainty.

In this initial chapter, Section 1.1 calls attention to the prevalent research practice that studies planning with *incredible certitude*. Section 1.2 contrasts the conceptions of uncertainty in consequentialist and axiomatic decision theory. Section 1.3 presents the formal structure of consequentialist theory, which will be used throughout the book. Section 1.4 explains the prevalent econometric characterization of uncertainty, which distinguishes identification problems and statistical imprecision. Section 1.5 discusses the distinct perspectives on social welfare expressed in various strands of research on planning.

In Part I, Chapter 2 demonstrates how incredible certitude harms analysis of planning and assesses explanations that have been suggested for the prevalence of incredible certitude. Chapter 3 considers the central econometric problem of identification of treatment response. Chapter 4 discusses the comparably central problem of identification of choice behavior and the distribution of personal welfare in a society.

In Part II, Chapter 5 presents a core part of my work on treatment of individuals under ambiguity, developing the theme that diversification may be socially beneficial. Chapter 6 shows that use of statistical decision theory can improve treatment choice with data from statistically imprecise randomized trials, replacing the common use of hypothesis testing. Chapter 7 discusses my research on personalized treatment under uncertainty, where the planner wants to condition treatment on observed covariates but does not know how treatment response varies across persons.

Chapter 8 considers an important setting where treatment response has social interactions, this being vaccination to prevent transmission of infectious disease. Moving from treatment of individuals to global planning, Chapter 9 exposits my collaborative research on choice of a greenhouse gas abatement policy to reduce planetary warming when the physics of climate determination and the discount rate used in the social welfare function are uncertain. Chapter 10 looks ahead, calling for work that strengthens the foundations for planning under uncertainty, and touching on certain planning problems that need immediate and long-term attention.

As far as I am aware, only a small body of other research engages any of the themes that I will discuss. In the late 1970s, Johansen (1978) called for research on macroeconomic planning under uncertainty, stating (pp. 263–264): "Uncertainty is not something which should be considered as a theoretically interesting refinement or extension of standard theory and methodology, but a central factor of eminently practical importance. Sometimes uncertainty is itself the heart of the matter when decisions are to be taken." In the early 2000s, Hansen and Sargent initiated a program of work on robust macroeconomic policy, considering certain possible deviations of reality from the assumptions maintained in conventional macroeconomic models; see Hansen and Sargent (2008). Their work uses concepts of robust decision analysis, which I will explain in Section 1.3. Barlevy (2011) reviews work on macroeconomic policy under ambiguity.

1.1 THE PREVALENT STUDY OF PLANNING WITH INCREDIBLE CERTITUDE

Economists have long studied policy choice by an actual or hypothetical social planner who aims to maximize welfare in democracies or other political systems where, in some sense, welfare is intended to express the values of society rather than the preferences of a dictator. The public at large may not be familiar with the formal structure of welfare economics, but basic ideas are familiar through the widespread use of the term *benefit–cost analysis*. Economists often study planning with utilitarian welfare functions. They sometimes specify ones that express a form of paternalism or principles of fairness.

The motivation for studying planning is most transparent when actual planners face specific decision problems. A national government must design an income tax structure and develop a system for national defense. Local governments choose how to maintain roads, perform policing, and organize public education. Planners need not be governmental. Clinicians make medical choices on behalf of patients. Parents act as planners for their families. In these settings and many more, the objective of the planner may be to maximize some idea of social welfare.

Welfare economics has also sought to shed light on noncooperative societal decision processes, where no actual planner exists. In the late 1700s, Adam Smith metaphorically suggested that an *invisible hand* makes decentralized decision making in market economies promote social welfare. Between then and the mid 1900s, economists gradually formalized this notion to develop what have become known as the *fundamental theorems of welfare economics*. These give idealized conditions under which equilibrium outcomes in markets have the desirable welfare property of Pareto efficiency, which would be sought by a planner using a utilitarian or other welfare function that aggregates personal welfare (aka utility).

A central concern of research in public economics has been to study societal outcomes when the idealized conditions of the fundamental theorems of welfare economics do not hold. The social welfare achieved by a hypothetical planner has served as a benchmark in social choice theory, which studies the outcomes produced by voting and other decentralized mechanisms that attempt to aggregate personal preferences. Even when actual societal decisions are made by processes distant from planning, study of hypothetical planning problems has been valuable to clarify the respects in which the members of society agree and to make explicit the nature of disagreements.

I wrote previously that welfare economics has studied maximization of welfare. Whether performing abstract theoretical studies or applied benefit–cost analyses, researchers have generally assumed that the planner knows enough about the choice environment to be able to determine an optimal action. However, the consequences of decisions are often highly uncertain. Aiming to circumvent this difficulty, researchers commonly invoke strong unsubstantiated assumptions and use them to study solvable optimization problems. I have referred to this practice as policy analysis with *incredible certitude* (Manski, 2011b, 2013c).

Planning with incredible certitude can harm society in multiple ways. Most obviously, it seeks to maximize the social welfare that would prevail if untenable assumptions were to hold rather than actual social welfare. If planners incorrectly believe that existing analysis provides an errorless description of the current state of society and accurate predictions of policy outcomes, they may make substantively poor decisions. Moreover, they will not recognize the value of new research aiming to improve knowledge. Nor will they appreciate the potential usefulness of decision strategies that may help society cope with uncertainty and learn. In Chapter 2, I will present a typology of research practices that generate incredible certitude and discuss many specific cases.

The dearth of study of planning under uncertainty is apparent in the comprehensive textbook on public economics of Atkinson and Stiglitz (1980), which mentions uncertainty only a few times and then only in passing. Mongin and Pivato (2016) began their review article with this sentence (p. 711): "PERHAPS surprisingly, uncertainty plays no role whatsoever in the classical works on social welfare."

Addressing the failure of research in welfare economics to come to grips with uncertainty has motivated my research program on credible social planning under uncertainty, which has developed over the past twenty-five years. The word "credible" is inevitably subjective and difficult to pin down, but I use it nonetheless.

1.2 UNCERTAINTY IN DECISION THEORY

A fundamental difficulty with welfare maximization under uncertainty is apparent even in a simple setting with two feasible actions, say A and B, and two possible choice environments, say s_1 and s_2. Suppose that action A yields higher welfare in environment s_1 and action B yields higher welfare in s_2. If it is not known whether s_1 or s_2 is the actual choice environment, it is not known which action is better. Thus, maximization of welfare is logically impossible. At most one can seek a reasonable way to make a choice. A basic issue is how to interpret and justify the word "reasonable."

Research in decision theory has posed and characterized various principles for reasonable decision making under uncertainty. Decision theory is not specifically concerned with societal decisions. It presumes the existence of an abstract decision maker who must choose among a specified set of actions. The decision maker could be an individual, a firm, or another institution. When the decision maker is an entity making societal decisions, it is a social planner. Thus, decision theory provides the formal basis for the study of social planning under uncertainty.

The description of uncertainty in decision theory is abstract. One supposes that outcomes are determined by the chosen action and by some feature of the environment, called the *state of nature*. The decision maker is assumed able to list all states of nature that could possibly occur. This list, called the *state space*, is a primitive concept which provides the most basic expression of uncertainty. The larger the state space, the less the decision maker knows about the consequences of each action. Decision theorists usually describe the state space mathematically, without reference to an actual choice problem. For example, they might describe it as a finite or a convex set.

Much of decision theory adds a secondary expression of uncertainty in the form of a probability distribution over the state space. Some studies view the probability distribution as a cognitive concept, expressing how decision makers might actually perceive uncertainty. Others view it as a mathematical construct, whose existence might be inferred from analysis of choice behavior. Arguing for the psychological realism of subjective probabilities, Tversky and Kahneman (1974) made plain the difference between the two perspectives, writing (p. 1130):

> It should perhaps be noted that, while subjective probabilities can sometimes be inferred from preferences among bets, they are normally not formed in this fashion. A person bets on team A rather than on team B because he believes that team A is more likely to win; he does not infer this belief from his betting preferences. Thus, in reality, subjective probabilities determine preferences among bets and are not derived from them.

Two conceptually distinct but mathematically related approaches have been used to develop criteria for reasonable decision making. Consequentialist theory focuses on the substantive consequences of choices. Axiomatic theory poses choice axioms that characterize consistency of behavior across choice settings and proves *representation theorems* relating choice axioms to consequentialist decision criteria. My research has applied consequentialist rather than axiomatic theory. I explain why in Sections 1.2.1 and 1.2.2.

1.2.1 Consequentialist Decision Theory

Consequentialist decision theory specifies a welfare function and an expression of uncertainty as primitives. It then seeks reasonable criteria to make decisions. The most prevalent recommendation has been maximization of expected utility. One places a probability distribution on the state space and chooses an action that maximizes the expected value of welfare with respect to this distribution.

To assist decision makers who do not find it credible to express uncertainty through a probability distribution, decision theorists have mainly studied criteria that, in some sense, works uniformly well over all of the state space. Two prominent interpretations of this broad idea are the maximin and minimax regret criteria. I will formalize these criteria in Section 1.3 and apply them throughout the book, particularly minimax regret.

The decision theory used in my research on planning is consequentialist. I suppose that the objective is to make substantively good societal decisions in particular settings. To accomplish this, I suppose that a planner specifies a suitable welfare function, expresses uncertainty in a credible manner, and uses these primitives to make a decision. The suitability of a welfare function and the credibility of an expression of uncertainty are context specific. These matters will be discussed in general terms in Sections 1.4 and 1.5 and in specific contexts in Part II.

1.2.2 Axiomatic Decision Theory

Axiomatic decision theory poses principles, called axioms, for consistency of hypothetical behavior across a class of potential choice problems. Researchers introspect and assert it to be reasonable, or rational, that a decision maker should adhere to these choice axioms. The central research activity of axiomatic decision theorists has been to pose and prove representation theorems establishing that adherence to a specified set of axioms is equivalent to acting as if one wants to use some consequentialist decision criterion, coping with uncertainty in some manner.

Perhaps the most famous representation theorems are those of Von Neumann and Morgenstern (1944) and Savage (1954). Both theorems establish that adherence to certain axioms is equivalent to maximization of expected utility. They differ mainly in that the probability distribution on the state space used to form expected utility is pre-specified in the former work and determined within the theory in the latter. Von Neumann and Morgenstern (VN-M) viewed the probability distribution as a primitive concept. Savage viewed the distribution as a construct that may in principle be inferred from analysis of choice behavior. I explain this distinction further on. I emphasize that in neither theorem does the probability distribution have any necessary connection to an objective reality.

Axiomatic theorists have long debated which axioms have normative appeal. Appraisal of normative appeal rests on introspection, so there should be no expectation that consensus will emerge. Indeed, decision theorists exhibit considerable difference in opinion. Binmore (2009) catalogues and assesses a wide spectrum of consistency axioms.

Why should one consider the VN-M, Savage, or other axioms to be compelling? No theorem answers this question. Instead, decision theorists call for introspection. In lecture notes for a Ph.D. course in decision theory, Kreps (1988) counseled a decision maker contemplating application of the VN-M theorem that he must first (p. 5): "Decide that you want to obey the axioms because they seem reasonable guides to behavior."

Considering the matter at length, Savage (1954) put it this way (p. 7):

> I am about to build up a highly idealized theory of the behavior of a "rational" person with respect to decisions. In doing so I will, of course, have to ask you to agree with me that such and such maxims of behavior are "rational." In so far as "rational" means logical, there is no live question; and, if I ask your leave there at all, it is only as a matter of form. But our person is going to have to make up his mind in situations in which criteria beyond the ordinary ones of logic will be necessary. So, when certain maxims are presented for your consideration, you must ask yourself whether you try to behave in accordance with them, or, to put it differently, how you would react if you noticed yourself violating them.

After discussing the positive role of logic in guiding actual human behavior, Savage wrote (p. 20):

> The principal value of logic, however, is in connection with its normative interpretation, that is, as a set of criteria by which to detect, with sufficient trouble, any inconsistencies there may be among our beliefs, and to derive from the beliefs we already hold such new ones as consistency demands. It does not seem appropriate here to attempt an analysis of why and in what contexts we wish to be consistent; it is sufficient to allude to the fact that we often do wish to be so.

Then, addressing his basic axiom P1, which assumes that the decision maker places a complete binary preference ordering on all potential actions, he wrote:

> Pursuing the analogy with logic, the main use I would make of P1 and its successors is normative, to police my own decisions for consistency and, where possible, to make complicated decisions depend on simpler ones. Here it is more pertinent than it was in connection with logic that something be said or why and when consistency is a desideratum, though I cannot say much.

Thus, Savage opined that humans may want their behavior to be consistent beyond the degree required by logic, but he was unable to explain why.

In a famous critique of the Savage axioms, Ellsberg (1961) sharply questioned the Savage conclusion that a rational decision maker must behave as if he places a subjective probability distribution on the state space. He observed that thoughtful persons sometimes exhibit behavioral patterns that violate the Savage axioms in ways implying that they do not hold subjective distributions. Considering this behavior, he wrote (p. 669):

> Are they foolish? It is not the object of this paper to judge that. I have been concerned rather to advance the testable propositions: (1) certain information states can be meaningfully identified as highly ambiguous; (2) in these states, many reasonable people tend to violate the Savage axioms with respect to certain choices; (3) their behavior is deliberate and not readily reversed upon reflection; (4) certain patterns of "violating" behavior can be distinguished and described in terms of a specified decision rule.
>
> If these propositions should prove valid, the question of the optimality of this behavior would gain more interest. The mere fact that it conflicts with certain axioms of choice that at first glance appear reasonable does not seem to me to foreclose this question; empirical research, and even preliminary speculation, about the nature of actual or "successful" decision making under uncertainty is still too young to give us confidence that these axioms are not abstracting away from vital considerations. It would seem incautious to rule peremptorily that the people in question should not allow their perception of ambiguity, their unease with their best estimates of probability, to influence their decision: or to assert that the manner in which they respond to it is against their long-run interest

and that they would be in some sense better off if they should go against their deep-felt preferences. If their rationale for their decision behavior is not uniquely compelling …, neither, it seems to me, are the counterarguments. Indeed, it seems out of the question summarily to judge their behavior as irrational: I am included among them.

In any case, it follows from the propositions above that for their behavior in the situations in question, the Bayesian or Savage approach gives wrong predictions and, by their lights, bad advice. They act in conflict with the axioms deliberately, without apology, because it seems to them the sensible way to behave. Are they clearly mistaken?

When studying consistency axioms of the types posed by VN-M and Savage, decision theorists ordinarily do not differentiate between private entities and social planners. The presumption is that all decision makers should behave consistently in the same manner. However, some theorists have proposed that social planners should adhere to additional ethical axioms that require them, in some sense, to respect the preferences of their populations and/or behave fairly. Review articles include Fleurbaey (2018) and Mongin and Pivato (2016).

Representation Theorems

I now remark further on representation theorems. The staple formalism of axiomatic decision theory considers a collection of hypothetical choice settings and proposes axioms that mandate specific forms of consistency of behavior across settings. A representation theorem proves that adherence to the axioms is necessary and sufficient for behavior across settings to be representable as solution of some consequentialist optimization problem.

Consider the VN-M and Savage representation theorems. Both begin with a basic axiom stipulating that a decision maker has a complete binary preference ordering over a universe A of actions. They then propose further axioms mandating certain consistency properties for the preference ordering. The theorems prove that adherence to the axioms is necessary and sufficient for representation of behavior when facing any hypothetical choice set $D \subset A$ as maximization of expected utility.

Consequentialist decision theory takes the utility function to be a primitive specified by the decision maker to express what he wants to achieve. In contrast, the representation theorems of axiomatic theory view the utility function as a mathematical construct implied by hypothetical choice behavior. In neither the VN-M nor the Savage theorem does the distribution on the state space have any necessary connection to an objective reality. Considering this distribution, Berger (1985) cautioned that (p. 121) "a Bayesian analysis may be 'rational' in the weak axiomatic sense, yet be terrible in a practical sense if an inappropriate prior distribution is used." Berger's comment expresses the consequentialist perspective that a decision maker should express uncertainty in a realistic manner.

Although the VN-M and Savage theorems both represent behavior as maximization of expected utility, they differ in how they view uncertainty. A central primitive of VN-M is an externally specified probability distribution on the state space. This could be a subjective distribution formed by a cognitive process but research in the VN-M tradition often presumes it to be a credible objective distribution.

The Savage theorem does not pre-specify a distribution on the state space. Instead, it proves that a decision maker who adheres to the axioms behaves as if he maximizes expected utility using a (utility function, state-space distribution) pair implied by hypothetical choice behavior. Thus, the utility function and the probability distribution of the Savage theorem are both constructs determined within his representation theorem. The credibility of the implied distribution plays no role in the Savage paradigm.

Axiomatic decision theorists often use language that obscures the distinction between hypothetical and actual choice behavior. They often describe axiomatic theory as revealed preference analysis. Consider, for example, this passage in Savage (1954) concerning two actions labeled f and g (p. 17): "I think it of great importance that preference, and indifference, between f and g be determined, at least in principle, by decisions between acts and not by response to introspective questions." The critical phrase in this sentence is "at least in principle." The enormously rich choice data contemplated in the Savage axioms are essentially never available in practice. This has been pointed out repeatedly over the years, at least as early as Sen (1973). Nevertheless, some theorists continue to describe their subject as revealed preference analysis; see Gul and Pesendorfer (2008).

Is Axiomatic Theory Relevant to Planning?

In Manski (2011a), I argued from a consequentialist perspective that a decision maker facing an actual choice problem is not concerned with the consistency of his behavior across hypothetical choice scenarios. The decision maker wants to make a substantively reasonable choice in the setting that he actually faces. I called this idea *actualist rationality*, stating (p. 196): "Prescriptions for decision making should promote welfare maximization in the choice problem the agent actually faces." The word *actualist* is seldom used in modern English but an old definition captures the idea well. *Webster's Revised Unabridged Dictionary, 1913 Edition* defines an actualist as, "One who deals with or considers actually existing facts and conditions, rather than fancies or theories."

From the perspective of actualist rationality, one need not introspect regarding the normative appeal of choice axioms. Axiomatic theory might become relevant if researchers were to show that adherence to certain axioms promotes substantively good decision making. However, this has not been the objective of axiomatic theory. The representation theorems of the theory are interpretative rather than prescriptive. The decision maker contemplated in axiomatic theory is assumed to know how he would behave when facing any choice set. Hence, he has no need for prescriptions.

Some decision theorists have suggested that axiomatic theory may describe a psychological process in which persons use axioms as a cognitive tool to learn their own preferences. Sugden (1990) alluded to such a process when he wrote (p. 762): "One of the main ways in which we come to know our own preferences is by noting how we in fact choose, or by constructing hypothetical choice problems for ourselves and monitoring our responses." Binmore (2009, section 7.5) interpreted Savage as having in mind a "massaging process," in which a decision maker modifies his hypothetical decisions until he feels comfortable that the implied subjective distribution adequately expresses his beliefs. The idea appears to be that a person holds coherent probabilistic beliefs internally but is psychologically unable to express them directly. Contemplating hypothetical choice problems helps the person discover his internal beliefs.

I find it difficult to reconcile the use of consistency axioms as cognitive tools with the formal structure of axiomatic decision theory. The theory formally contemplates a being who arrives with a complete preference ordering, not a cognitively challenged creature who uses thought experiments with hypothetical choice problems to learn about itself. Thus, efforts to motivate adherence to consistency axioms as tools for cognition lie entirely outside of formal axiomatic theory.

As I see it, a fundamental problem with axiomatic decision theory is that it provides no connection to substantively good decisions. Choice axioms only aim to characterize procedural reasonableness, or rationality, in the sense of consistency of hypothetical behavior across potential choice problems. It is particularly troubling that axiomatic theory is unconcerned with the credibility of a decision maker's expression of uncertainty. Theory in the tradition of VN-M may assume that a decision maker holds objectively accurate probabilistic expectations (aka rational expectations), but it does not explain how this may be accomplished in practice. The accuracy of probabilistic expectations is not germane to theory in the Savage tradition. The realism of expectations should matter to any decision maker. It should matter particularly to a planner who represents a population.

1.2.3 The Institutional Separation of Research on Planning and Actual Planning

Decision theory presumes a unitary setting in which a planner performs his own research to inform policy choice. I observed in Manski (2013c) that modern democratic societies have created an institutional separation between policy analysis and decision making, with professional analysts reporting findings to representative governments. Separation of the tasks of analysis and decision making, the former aiming to inform the latter, appears advantageous from the perspective of division of labor. No one can be an expert at everything. In principle, having researchers study planning problems and provide their findings to law makers and civil servants enables these planners to focus on the challenging task of policy choice, without having to perform their own research.

I also observed that the current practice of policy analysis with incredible certitude does not serve planners well. The problem is that the consumers of policy analysis cannot trust the producers. I argued that, to improve analysis and to increase trust, research on planning should transparently face up to uncertainty rather than hide it.

Some think this idea to be naive or impractical. I have repeatedly heard policy analysts assert that policy makers are either psychologically unwilling or cognitively unable to cope with uncertainty. Some economists with experience in the federal government of the United States have suggested to me that concealment of uncertainty is an immutable characteristic of the American policy environment. Hence, they assert that the prevailing practice of policy analysis with incredible certitude will have to continue as is.

A more optimistic possibility is that concealment of uncertainty is a modifiable social norm. My hope is that salutary change will occur if awareness grows that incredible certitude is harmful. Then I anticipate that the scientific community will reward policy research based on credible analysis more than optimization exercises performed with ill-conceived assumptions. Planners and the public will want researchers to provide reasonable policy recommendations that recognize the subtlety of planning under uncertainty, not unequivocal ones that lack foundation.

1.3 THE STRUCTURE OF CONSEQUENTIALIST DECISION THEORY

1.3.1 The Choice Set, State Space, and Welfare Function

I now deepen the discussion of uncertainty in consequentialist decision theory. The starting point is to suppose that the planner or other decision maker faces a predetermined choice set C and believes that the true state of nature s* lies in a state space S. The welfare function $w(\cdot, \cdot): C \times S \to R^1$ maps actions and states into welfare. The planner wants to maximize $w(\cdot, s^*)$ over C but does not know s*. Hence, maximization is infeasible except in special cases.

The state space S provides the basic decision theoretic expression of uncertainty. In lay language, S is a list of "known unknowns." States of nature that are not elements of S are presumed impossible to occur. Decision theory supposes that the decision maker does not contemplate the possible existence of unlisted "unknown unknowns."

Discussions of the state space often consider it to express uncertainty purely about the physical and social environment within which choice takes place. However, a state space can also express uncertainty about the welfare function that a planner should maximize. This often occurs when the planner is utilitarian. Then the planner must know the preferences of the population to maximize welfare, but this knowledge may not be available. See Chapter 4 for further discussion.

Being a primitive of the decision problem, the state space is necessarily subjective. This does not imply, however, that it is an arbitrary construction. Credibility is a fundamental matter in consequential decision theory in general and in the study of social planning specifically. If planning decisions are to enhance welfare in the real world, the planner should specify a state space that embodies some reasonable sense of credibility. Research seeks to help by providing at least a partially objective basis for specification of the state space. This basis is obtained by combining plausible theory with empirical analysis. I discuss this further in Section 1.4.

1.3.2 Decision Criteria

It is generally accepted that decisions should respect dominance. Action $c \in C$ is weakly dominated if there exists a $d \in C$ such that $w(d,s) \geq w(c,s)$ for all $s \in S$ and $w(d,s) > w(c,s)$ for some $s \in S$. To choose among undominated actions, decision theorists have proposed various ways of using $w(\cdot, \cdot)$ to form functions of actions alone, which can be optimized. In principle, one should only consider undominated actions, but it is often difficult to determine which actions are undominated. Hence, in practice it is common to optimize over the full set of feasible actions. I define decision criteria accordingly.

I initially consider settings without sample data, describing three prominent criteria. I extend these criteria to settings with sample data in Section 1.3.3. Consequentialist decision theory views the welfare function, state space, and decision criterion as meta-choices made by a decision maker. It views these meta-choices as predetermined rather than matters to be studied within the theory. In this sense consequentialist theory requires introspection, as does axiomatic theory.

A familiar idea is to place a subjective probability distribution π on the state space, average state-dependent welfare with respect to π, and maximize subjective expected welfare (SEW) over C. The criterion solves:

$$(1.1) \qquad \max_{c \in C} \int w(c,s) d\pi.$$

Observe that, given a subjective distribution π on S, one need not average over π. Any criterion respecting stochastic dominance has a consequentialist claim to be reasonable. For example, Manski (1988) studied maximization of quantile welfare. However, the prevalent practice has been to average over π.

In the absence of a subjective distribution on S, a prominent idea is to choose an action that, in some sense, works uniformly well over all of S. This yields the maximin and minimax regret (MMR) criteria. The maximin criterion maximizes the minimum welfare attainable across S, solving the problem:

$$(1.2) \qquad \max_{c \in C} \min_{s \in S} w(c,s).$$

The MMR criterion solves:

$$(1.3) \qquad \min_{c \in C} \max_{s \in S} \left[\max_{d \in C} w(d,s) - w(c,s) \right].$$

Here $\max_{d \in C} w(d,s) - w(c,s)$ is the *regret* of action c in state s. The true state being unknown, one evaluates c by its maximum regret over all states and selects an action that minimizes maximum regret. The maximum regret of an action measures its maximum distance from optimality across states. Hence, maximum regret is uniform nearness to optimality.

The maximin and minimax regret criteria are sometimes confused with one another but they yield the same choice only in certain special cases. Whereas the maximin criterion considers only the worst outcome that an action may yield, MMR considers the worst outcome relative to the best achievable in a given state of nature. Hence, the two criteria generically differ. The leading case where the two criteria coincide occurs when the best achievable welfare has the same magnitude in every state of nature; that is, $\max_{d \in C} w(d,s)$ is constant across $s \in S$. Then (1.3) reduces to (1.2) up to this additive constant.

It is also noteworthy that a decision maker who places a subjective probability distribution π on the state space might choose to minimize subjective expected regret rather than maximum regret, subjective expected regret being $\int [\max_{d \in C} w(d,s) - w(c,s)] d\pi$. The expression $\int \max_{d \in C} w(d,s) d\pi$ is constant across the feasible actions $c \in C$. Hence, minimization of subjective expected regret is equivalent to maximization of subjective expected welfare.

I will discuss criteria (1.1) to (1.3) throughout this book. Readers should be aware that these three, which arguably have been the most prominent in decision theory, are not the only criteria that may warrant attention. For example, Hurwicz (1951) suggested modification of the maximin criterion to maximize instead a weighted average of the minimum and maximum welfare attainable across the state space.

Other decision theorists have studied settings intermediate between the polar cases in which a planner asserts either a complete subjective distribution on the state space, or none. A planner might instead assert a partial subjective distribution, placing lower and upper probabilities on states, as in Dempster (1968) or Walley (1991), and then maximize minimum subjective expected welfare or minimize maximum expected regret. These criteria combine elements of averaging across states and concern with uniform performance across states. Statistical decision theorists refer to them as Γ-maximin and Γ-minimax regret (Berger, 1985). The former has drawn attention from axiomatic decision theorists, who call it "maxmin expected utility" (Gilboa and Schmeidler, 1989).

Complete Class Theorems

Complete class theorems show that, in various contexts, an action is weakly undominated only if it would be chosen by a decision maker who maximizes SEW with respect to some subjective probability distribution on S (Wald, 1950). Bayesian decision theorists sometimes cite such theorems as a reason to focus attention on maximization of SEW rather than other decision criteria (Berger, 1985). They say that the action chosen using any alternative criterion would also be chosen by an expected-welfare maximizer with some subjective distribution. Hence, they claim, one might as well think of decision makers as maximizing SEW.

Complete class theorems have proved to be useful analytical devices when studying the properties of alternative consequentialist decision criteria. However, this does not imply that decision makers should be counseled to maximize SEW. To apply the SEW criterion, one must first decide what subjective probability distribution to use and then solve the maximization problem. Complete class theorems provide no guidance on what constitutes a credible subjective distribution. They only state that choice of any undominated action can be represented as the outcome of SEW maximization with some distribution.

1.3.3 Statistical Decision Theory

Abraham Wald, in a series of contributions culminating in Wald (1950), extended consequentialist decision theory to encompass settings where the decision maker observes sample data. Wald's formulation of statistical decision theory supposes that a decision maker observes data generated by a sampling distribution which is a known function of the state of nature. To express this, let the feasible sampling distributions be denoted $(Q_s, s \in S)$. Let Ψ_s denote the sample space in state s; Ψ_s is the set of samples that may be drawn under distribution Q_s. The literature typically assumes that the sample space does not vary with s and is known. I do likewise and denote the sample space as Ψ. A statistical decision function (SDF), $c(\cdot): \Psi \to C$, maps the sample data into a chosen action.

An SDF is a deterministic function after realization of the sample data but it is a random function ex ante. Hence, an SDF generically makes a randomized choice of an action. The only exceptions are SDFs that make almost-surely data-invariant choices. An SDF $c(\cdot)$ is almost-surely data-invariant in state s if there exists a $d \in C$ such that $Q_s[c(\psi) = d] = 1$.

Given that SDFs are random functions, welfare using a specified SDF is a random variable ex ante. Wald's theory evaluates the performance of SDF c(·) in state s by $Q_s\{w[c(\psi),s]\}$, the ex ante distribution of welfare that it yields across realizations ψ of the sampling process. Thus, statistical decision theory is frequentist. In particular, Wald measured the performance of c(·) in state s by its expected welfare across samples; that is, $E_s\{w[c(\psi),s]\} \equiv \int w[c(\psi),s]dQ_s$. Not knowing the true state, a planner evaluates c(·) by the state-dependent expected welfare vector $(E_s\{w[c(\psi),s]\}, s \in S)$, which is computable.

One need not measure the sampling performance of an SDF by its expected welfare across samples. Manski and Tetenov (2023) observe that any criterion respecting stochastic dominance has a claim to be reasonable. In particular, they study measurement of sampling performance by quantile welfare. However, the prevalent practice has been to measure performance by expected welfare across samples.

Statistical decision theory has mainly studied the same decision criteria as has decision theory without sample data. Let Γ denote the set of feasible SDFs, which map $\Psi \to C$. The statistical versions of criteria (1.1), (1.2), and (1.3) are:

$$(1.4) \quad \max_{c(\cdot) \in \Gamma} \int E_s\{w[c(\psi),s]\} d\pi,$$

$$(1.5) \quad \max_{c(\cdot) \in \Gamma} \min_{s \in S} E_s\{w[c(\psi),s]\},$$

$$(1.6) \quad \min_{c(\cdot) \in \Gamma} \max_{s \in S} \left(\max_{d \in C} w(d,s) - E_s\{w[c(\psi),s]\} \right).$$

In settings of choice between two actions, SDFs can be viewed as hypothesis tests. However, evaluation of tests in the Wald theory differs fundamentally from Neyman–Pearson hypothesis testing, which I will discuss in Chapter 6. The Wald theory does not restrict attention to tests that yield a predetermined upper bound on the probability of a Type I error. Nor does it aim to minimize the maximum value of the probability of a Type II error when more than a specified minimum distance from the null hypothesis. Wald proposed for binary choice, as elsewhere, evaluation of the performance of SDF c(·) in state s by the expected welfare that it yields across realizations of the sampling process. See Chapter 6 and Manski (2021a) for further discussion.

Robust Decisions

Research on *robust decisions* includes a statistical literature on robust estimation and prediction (e.g., Huber, 1981; Hampel et. al., 1986) and an engineering literature on robust control (e.g., Zhou, Doyle, and

Glover, 1996). The latter has provided the basis for recent econometric analysis of robust macroeconomic policy (e.g., Hansen and Sargent, 2008).

The study of robust decisions proceeds in a different manner than statistical decision theory. Rather than specify a state space that lists all possible states of nature, the researcher poses a model space. The model specifies a single state or a relatively small set of states, typically a finite-dimensional family. Having posed the model space, a researcher may be concerned that it does not contain the true state; that is, the model may not be correct. To recognize this possibility, the researcher enlarges the model space locally, using some metric to generate a neighborhood thereof. He then acts as if the locally enlarged model space is correct. Watson and Holmes write (2016, p. 465): "We then consider formal methods for decision making under model misspecification by quantifying stability of optimal actions to perturbations to the model within a neighbourhood of [the] model space."

Although research on robust decisions differs procedurally from statistical decision theory, one can subsume the former within the latter if one considers the locally enlarged model space to be the state space. It is unclear how often this perspective characterizes what researchers have in mind. Articles often do not state explicitly whether the constructed neighborhood of the model space encompasses all states that authors deem sufficiently feasible to warrant consideration. The models specified in robust decision analyses often make strong assumptions and generated neighborhoods often relax these assumptions only modestly.

1.3.4 Minimax Regret Planning

Among the decision criteria posed above, maximization of SEW places a subjective distribution on the state space, whereas maximin and MMR do not. Concern with the basis for specification of a subjective distribution motivated Wald (1950) to study the minimax criterion (maximin in my description), writing (p. 18): "a minimax solution seems, in general, to be a reasonable solution of the decision problem when an a priori distribution ... does not exist or is unknown."

I am similarly concerned with decision making with no subjective distribution on states. However, I have mainly measured performance of decisions by maximum regret rather than by minimum welfare. The maximin and MMR criteria both provide ex ante evaluations of the worst result that a decision maker may experience ex post. However, the criteria are equivalent only in special cases, particularly when optimal welfare is invariant across states. They differ more generally. Whereas maximin considers the worst absolute outcome that an action may yield across states, MMR considers the worst outcome relative to what is achievable in a given state.

As I see it, a conceptual appeal of using maximum regret to measure performance is that it quantifies how lack of knowledge of the true state of nature diminishes the quality of decisions. The term "maximum regret" is shorthand for the maximum suboptimality of a decision criterion across the feasible states of nature. A decision with small maximum regret is uniformly near optimal across all states. Introspecting, I think this a desirable property. Each study in Part II of this book applies the MMR criterion. Some consider the maximin criterion as well.

MMR has drawn diverse reactions from axiomatic decision theorists. In a famous early critique, Chernoff (1954) observed that MMR decisions are sometimes inconsistent with the choice axiom known as independence of irrelevant alternatives (IIA). Chernoff considered this a serious deficiency, writing (p. 426):

> A third objection which the author considers very serious is the following. In some examples, the min max regret criterion may select a strategy d_3 among the available strategies d_1, d_2, d_3, and d_4. On the other hand, if for some reason d_4 is made unavailable, the min max regret criterion will select d_2 among d_1, d_2, and d_3. The author feels that for a reasonable criterion the presence of an undesirable strategy d_4 should not have an influence on the choice among the remaining strategies.

This passage is the totality of Chernoff's argument. He introspected and concluded that a reasonable decision criterion should always adhere to IIA, without explaining why he felt this way. He did not argue that minimax regret choices have adverse consequentialist consequences.

Chernoff's view has been endorsed by some modern decision theorists, including Binmore (2009). Indeed, Ken Binmore used picturesque language to express this view in my presence during a conference, declaring that violation of IIA is "Death to minimax regret" (statement made in a presentation at the Kellogg School of Management conference on "Decision Theory and its Discontents," May 1, 2009). On the other hand, Sen (1993) argued that adherence to the IIA axiom does not per se provide a sound basis for evaluation of decision criteria. He asserted that consideration of the context of decision making is essential.

Manski (2011a) argued that adherence to the IIA axiom is not a virtue per se. What matters is how violation of the axiom affects welfare.

The MMR decision is necessarily undominated when it is unique. There generically exists an undominated MMR decision when the criterion has multiple solutions. Hence, I concluded that violation of the IIA axiom is not a sound rationale to dismiss minimax regret.

1.4 UNCERTAINTY IN EMPIRICAL RESEARCH

To characterize uncertainty with enough credibility and concreteness to be useful to the study of planning, I draw heavily on my own study of partial identification in empirical research. I explain in general terms in Section 1.4.1, adding specificity in Chapters 3 and 4 and throughout Part II. Section 1.4.2 addresses how statistical imprecision in research affects planning, with specificity added in Chapter 6.

1.4.1 Identification Analysis

It has become standard in econometrics to specify the state space as a set of objective probability distributions that may possibly describe the system under study. Haavelmo (1944) did so for economic systems when he introduced *The Probability Approach in Econometrics*. Studies of treatment choice do so when they consider the population to be treated to have a distribution of treatment response.

The Koopmans (1949) formalization of identification analysis contemplated unlimited data collection that enables one to shrink the state space, eliminating states that are inconsistent with accepted theory and with the information revealed by observation of data. For most of the twentieth century, econometricians commonly thought of identification as a binary event – a feature of an objective probability distribution (a parameter) is either identified or it is not. Empirical researchers applying econometric methods combined available data with assumptions that yield point identification, and they reported point estimates of parameters. Economists recognized that point identification often requires strong assumptions that are difficult to motivate. However, they saw no other way to perform empirical research.

Yet there is enormous scope for fruitful research using weaker and more credible assumptions that partially identify population parameters. A parameter is partially identified if the sampling process and maintained assumptions reveal that the parameter lies in a set, its *identification region* or *identified set*, that is smaller than the logical range of the parameter but larger than a single point. I explain below.

Research on Partial Identification

Isolated contributions to analysis of partial identification were made as early as the 1930s, but the subject remained at the fringes of econometric consciousness and did not spawn systematic study. A coherent body of research took shape in the 1990s and has since grown rapidly. Reviews of this work include Manski (1995, 2003, 2007a), Tamer (2010), and Molinari (2020).

I first connected identification analysis with decision making under uncertainty in Manski (2000), writing (p. 416):

> This paper connects decisions under ambiguity with identification problems in econometrics. Considered abstractly, it is natural to make this connection. Ambiguity occurs when lack of knowledge of an objective probability distribution prevents a decision maker from solving an optimization problem. Empirical research seeks to draw conclusions about objective probability distributions by combining assumptions with observations. An identification problem occurs when a specified set of assumptions combined with unlimited observations drawn by a specified sampling process does not reveal a distribution of interest. Thus, identification problems generate ambiguity in decision making.

Here I followed Ellsberg (1961) in using the word *ambiguity* to signify uncertainty when one specifies a set of feasible states of nature but does not place a probability distribution on the state space. Synonyms for ambiguity include *deep uncertainty* and *Knightian uncertainty*.

The modern literature on partial identification emerged out of concern with traditional approaches to inference with missing outcome data. Empirical researchers have commonly assumed that missingness is random, in the sense that the observability of an outcome is statistically independent of its value. Yet this and other point-identifying assumptions have regularly been criticized as implausible. It was natural to ask what random sampling with partial observability of outcomes reveals about outcome distributions if nothing is known about the missingness process or if only credible assumptions are imposed.

Studying identification with missing outcome data quickly led to analysis of treatment response. A common objective of empirical research is to predict treatment response conditional on specified covariates, using data from a random sample of the population. Analysis must contend with the fundamental problem that counterfactual outcomes are not observable. At most one can observe the outcomes that have occurred under realized policies. The outcomes of unrealized policies are logically unobservable. Yet determination of an optimal policy requires comparison of all feasible policies. For this and many other reasons, planners usually have only partial knowledge of the welfare achieved by alternative policies.

Findings on partial identification with missing outcome data are directly applicable to analysis of treatment response. Yet analysis of treatment response poses more than a generic missing-data problem. One reason is that observations of realized outcomes, when combined with suitable assumptions, can provide information about counterfactual ones. Another is that practical problems of treatment choice motivate research on treatment response and thereby determine what population parameters are of interest. For these reasons, it has been productive to study partial identification of treatment response as a subject in its own right. See Chapter 3 for further discussion, as well as Part II.

Whatever the specific subject under study, a common theme runs through the literature on partial identification. One first asks what the sampling process alone reveals about the population of interest and then studies the identifying power of assumptions that aim to be credible. This conservative approach to inference makes clear the conclusions one can draw in empirical research without imposing untenable assumptions. It establishes a domain of consensus among analysts who may hold disparate beliefs about what assumptions are appropriate. It also makes plain the limitations of the available data. When identification regions turn out to be large, we should face up to the fact that the available data and credible assumption do not support conclusions as tight as we might like to achieve.

From the perspective of planning, findings on partial identification imply that empirical research may shrink the state space for decision making but not reduce it to a single state of nature. Let S be the state space without observation of the unlimited data assumed in an identification study. Let $S_0 \subset S$ be the shrunken state space using these data. Then decision criteria (1) to (3) posed in Section 1.3.2 have the same forms, but with S_0 replacing S. In (1), the conditional subjective distribution $\pi(s \mid s \in S_0)$ replaces $\pi(s)$.

1.4.2 Statistical Imprecision

Whereas identification analysis contemplates unlimited data collection that enables one to shrink the state space, the data observed in a finite sample generated by a sampling distribution generally are not informative enough to shrink the state space. Nevertheless, Wald's development of statistical decision theory shows how sample data can be informative.

In Wald's paradigm, statistical imprecision is expressed through the state-dependent ex ante distributions $[Q_s\{w[c(\psi),s]\}, s \in S]$ of welfare that an SDF yields across realizations ψ of the sampling process. Wald's concept of an SDF embraces all mappings [data → action]. An SDF need not perform conventional statistical inference; that is, it need not use data to directly draw conclusions about the true state of nature. The prominent decision criteria that have been studied – maximin, minimax regret, and maximization of subjective expected welfare – do not explicitly perform inference on the true state.

Although SDFs need not perform conventional inference, some do. These have the form [data → inference → action], first performing inference and then using the inference to make a decision. There seems to be no accepted term for such SDFs, so I have called them *inference based* (Manski, 2021a).

The general absence of conventional inference in statistical decision theory is striking. Familiar measures of statistical imprecision, such as confidence sets and standard errors, play no role in the Wald theory. On the other hand, statistical imprecision is measured when one computes the maximum regret of an SDF; that is, its maximum distance from optimality. Maximum regret is determined jointly by the identification problem faced and by the statistical imprecision of sample data. When the true state of nature is point identified, maximum regret purely measures statistical imprecision. I will expand on this in Chapter 6 in the context of analysis of randomized trials.

1.5 PERSPECTIVES ON SOCIAL WELFARE

Given a specified choice set and welfare function, analysis of optimal planning is straightforward in abstraction, even if solution of the optimization problem may be difficult in practice. The fundamental subtleties in research on planning are conceptual rather than mathematical. If analysis is to be useful in practice, the welfare function should express normative properties acceptable to some meaningful part of the relevant society. The specified choice set should be realistic, expressing options that may actually be available. Throughout this book, I stress that analysis should appropriately recognize uncertainty in policy outcomes. To conclude this opening chapter, I comment on specification of the welfare function.

Specification of the welfare function has vexed economists and philosophers in broad terms, as well as policy analysts in particular contexts. Most research by economists, and some by philosophers and others, has supposed that the social welfare function should somehow aggregate the personal welfares of the individuals who compose society. Yet it has long been understood that, in general, a heterogeneous society cannot develop a consensus social welfare function. The Arrow (1950) Possibility Theorem nullified the residual hope that a heterogeneous society might be able to devise a coherent non-dictatorial welfare function. How then should research on planning proceed? The literature is vast and varied.

1.5.1 The New Welfare Economics

One route was taken in the 1930s and 1940s by the economists who initiated the study of the *new welfare economics*, a term apparently first used by Hicks (1939). Wary of any criterion to choose among policies that benefit some people but harm others, they retreated to the study of Pareto efficiency with extension to the fictional redistributions proposed by Kaldor (1939) and Hicks (1939). However, this restriction on their domain of concern drastically limited their ability to study actual planning problems. This led Chipman and Moore (1978) to write (p. 548): "In this paper we shall argue that, judged in relation to its basic objective of enabling economists to make welfare prescriptions without having to make value judgments and, in particular, interpersonal comparisons of utility, the New Welfare Economics must be considered a failure." Efficiency in the fictional Kaldor–Hicks sense has become at most a peripheral topic in economic theory, but it continues to be used in applied benefit–cost analysis, as I explain below.

1.5.2 Utilitarian Welfare

Within the body of economic research that studies planning when policies benefit some people but harm others, it has been common to specify a utilitarian welfare function. The standard theory of rational individual behavior under certainty requires only an ordinal personal concept of welfare. A utilitarian social welfare function specifies interpersonally comparable cardinal personal welfares and sums them. This gives formal expression to what Bentham (1776) may have had in mind when he wrote (p. ii): a "fundamental axiom, it is the greatest happiness of the greatest number that is the measure of right and wrong."

In utilitarian welfare analysis, concern with equity is expressed through specification of the personal welfare functions, measured on a commensurate scale, that are summed to compute social welfare. A prominent example is the Mirrlees (1971) analysis of optimal income taxation. There, personal welfare was taken to be a concave function of income, thus expressing "diminishing marginal utility of money." It follows that, all else equal, transferring a dollar from a wealthy person to a poor one increases social welfare. In the Mirrlees analysis, this motivates progressive income tax schedules that impose higher tax rates on persons with higher incomes and lower (or negative) rates on those with lower incomes. Mirrlees showed that the structure of an optimal tax schedule is complex because the schedule generally affects the amount of labor that persons choose to supply. This consideration affects how much redistribution a society is able to accomplish in practice.

Willingness to Pay and Kaldor–Hicks Efficiency

Rather than sum interpersonally comparable personal welfare values, economists performing benefit–cost analysis often sum monetary "willingness to pay" values across persons. Willingness-to-pay analysis seeks to measure the monetary amount that each member of a population would be willing to pay for a specified change in policy relative to a given status quo or, alternatively, the amount that each member would be willing to pay to preserve the status quo. Thus, willingness to pay may be positive or negative, depending on how a change in policy would affect an individual. The methodology aggregates willingness to pay across the population and uses the result to evaluate a policy change.

To justify this approach to planning, economists cite the Kaldor–Hicks argument that concerns with equity could in principle be addressed by redistribution of money, even if the redistribution is not accomplished in practice. However, if redistribution is not actually performed, the practical outcome is to choose policies that weight the welfare of the wealthy more than that of the poor.

I commented critically on willingness-to-pay analysis in Manski (2015a), responding to an article on benefit–cost analysis of criminal justice policy by Dominguez-Rivera and Raphael (2015). I find it instructive to summarize what these authors wrote, not to single them out for scrutiny, but because their discussion illustrates how economists have sought to justify the willingness-to-pay approach to planning.

Dominguez-Rivera and Raphael called attention to some unpalatable features of the methodology. They cautioned that it (p. 589): "provides a specific weighting (or social accounting) of the relative welfare of alternative groups in society that often conflicts with widely held beliefs regarding fairness and equity." They observed that willingness to pay is positively associated with ability to pay and stated that (p. 596): "This positive relationship between income and benefit and/or cost valuation ultimately results in greater weight being placed on the welfare of the well-to-do in cost-benefit calculations." They subsequently wrote that (p. 597): "the systematic tendency to place greater weight on the welfare of the wealthy is certainly of concern."

Nevertheless, they wrote that (p. 601): "there is a strong case to make for cost-benefit analysis as a principal input for policy making, equity concerns notwithstanding." Referring to the Kaldor–Hicks idea of fictional redistribution, they wrote that (p. 601): "any policy choice with net positive monetary benefits provides what economists call a potential Pareto improvement." They suggested that society consider equity and fairness separately from benefit–cost analysis, writing (p. 590): "Responsible analysis requires ... a careful parallel analysis of the equity implications of policy alternatives." Yet they did not provide guidance on how society might combine willingness-to-pay analysis with equity considerations so as to make sensible policy decisions.

Economists often use willingness-to-pay analysis to evaluate policy quantitatively, paying only qualitative lip service to equity. This is concerning. As I see it, direct specification of interpersonally comparable personal welfares, in the manner of Mirrlees, better expresses utilitarian policy choice.

1.5.3 Maximin Welfare

One need not sum cardinal personal welfares to develop social welfare functions that respect Pareto efficiency. Among alternatives, the work of Rawls (1971) has received considerable attention outside of economics. He recommended evaluation of policy by the minimum value of interpersonally comparable ordinal personal welfares. He argued that society should evaluate social welfare in this manner, rather than the utilitarian one.

The "Initial Position" Arguments of Harsanyi and Rawls

To reach his conclusion, Rawls argued that the welfare function should be determined by a social contract. Attempting to circumvent the deep problem of aggregating heterogeneous personal welfares, he maintained that the social contract should express a consensus that he argued all rational people would accept in an *initial position*, characterized by a *veil of ignorance*. He wrote (p. 10): "the guiding idea is that the principles of justice for the basic structure of society are the object of the original agreement. They are the principles that free and rational persons concerned to further their own interests would accept in an initial position of equality." He declared that he knew what principles free and rational persons would accept, writing (p. 13):

> I shall maintain instead that the persons in the initial situation would choose two rather different principles: the first requires equality in the assignment of basic rights and duties, while the second holds that social and economic inequalities, for example inequalities of wealth and authority, are just only if they result in compensating benefits for everyone, and in particular for the least advantaged members of society.

Thus, Rawls assumed that personal welfares are ordinally comparable across individuals and argued that social welfare should be the minimum personal welfare of all members of society.

Rawls did not originate the idea that all rational people would agree on a unique social welfare function in a hypothetical original position under a veil of ignorance. Earlier, Harsanyi (1955) posed a thought experiment of this type and reached a different conclusion than Rawls. Harsanyi argued that, not knowing their positions in society, individuals in the original position would place equal probability on realizing each possible position and would maximize expected utility. He thus concluded that all rational persons would accept a utilitarian social welfare function.

Rawls barely acknowledged the precedent Harsanyi argument, mentioning Harsanyi by name only briefly in a footnote. Nevertheless, he sharply attacked utilitarianism, writing (p. 13):

> It may be observed, however, that once the principles of justice are thought of as arising from an original agreement in a situation of equality, it is an open question whether the principle of utility would be acknowledged. Offhand it hardly seems likely that persons who view themselves as equals, entitled to press their claims upon one another, would agree to a principle which may require lesser life prospects for some simply for the sake of a greater sum of advantages enjoyed by others. Since each desires to protect his interests, his capacity to advance his conception of the good, no one has a reason to acquiesce in an enduring loss for himself in order to bring about a greater net balance of satisfaction. In the absence of strong and lasting benevolent impulses, a rational man would not accept a basic structure merely because it maximized the algebraic sum of advantages irrespective of its permanent effects on his own basic rights and interests. Thus it seems that the principle of utility is incompatible with the conception of social cooperation among equals for mutual advantage. It appears to be inconsistent with the idea of reciprocity implicit in the notion of a well-ordered society. Or, at any rate, so I shall argue.

Critics have questioned how one could know that all free and rational persons would accept either the Harsanyi or Rawls principles. In his review of the Rawls book, Arrow (1973a) wrote(p. 247): "How do we know other peoples' welfare enough to apply a principle of justice?" ... "the criterion of universalizability may be impossible to achieve when people are really different, particularly when different life experiences mean that they can never have the same information." He concluded his review by writing (p. 263):

> To the extent that individuals are really individual, each an autonomous end in himself, to that extent they must be somewhat mysterious and inaccessible to each other. There cannot be any rule that is completely acceptable to all. There must, or so it now seems to me, be the possibility of unadjudicable conflict, which may show itself logically as paradoxes in the process of social decision-making.

This conclusion reminds one of Arrow's Possibility Theorem.

1.5.4 Optimal Paternalism in Populations with Bounded Rationality

The norm in the study of utilitarian planning has been to assume that members of the population maximize their personal welfare. However, the realism of this assumption has long been questioned. Simon (1955) put it this way in the article that spawned the modern literature in behavioral economics (p. 101): "Because of the psychological limits of the organism (particularly with respect to computational and predictive ability), actual human rationality-striving can at best be an extremely crude and simplified approximation to the kind of global rationality that is implied, for example, by game-theoretical models." This idea has come to be called *bounded rationality*. Simon put forward this mission for research on behavior (p. 99):

> Broadly stated, the task is to replace the global rationality of economic man with a kind of rational behavior that is compatible with the access to information and the computational capacities that are actually possessed by organisms, including man, in the kinds of environments in which such organisms exist.

A recent development in the field of public economics has been the initiation of research on utilitarian planning in populations with bounded rationality. Behavioral economists have suggested that planners should limit the choice options available to individuals to ones deemed beneficial from a utilitarian perspective or, less drastically, should frame the options in a manner thought to influence choice in a positive way. Thaler and Sunstein (2003) evocatively wrote that such policies express (p. 175): "libertarian paternalism." However, here and elsewhere, their discussion has been verbal rather than formal.

An early expression of formal analysis was given by O'Donoghue and Rabin (2003), who began their article as follows (p. 186):

> The classical economic approach to policy analysis assumes that people always respond optimally to the costs and benefits of their available choices. A great deal of evidence suggests, however, that in some contexts people make errors that lead them not to behave in their own best interests. Economic policy prescriptions might change once we recognize that humans are humanly rational rather than superhumanly rational, and in particular it may be fruitful for economists to study the possible advantages of *paternalistic policies* that help people make better choices.
>
> We propose an approach for studying optimal paternalism that follows naturally from standard assumptions and methods of economic theory: Write down assumptions about the distribution of rational and irrational types of agents, about the available policy instruments, and about the government's information about agents, and then investigate which policies achieve the most efficient outcomes. In other words, economists ought to treat the analysis of optimal paternalism as a mechanism-design problem when some agents might be boundedly rational.

Economists have subsequently performed a growing set of analyses of the type sought by O'Donoghue and Rabin, addressing different classes of policy choices and assuming various distributions of preferences and deviations from utility maximization.

Research in the developing field of behavioral public economics has thus far assumed that the planner understands bounded rationality in the population well enough to be able to optimize social welfare. Thus, authors have assumed that, while members of the population are boundedly rational, the planner is globally rational. However, detailed knowledge of population preferences and deviations from global rationality is rare. Manski and Sheshinski (2023) argue that a utilitarian planner with limited knowledge should not seek to optimize policy invoking assumptions that lack credibility. Instead, the planner should use a reasonable criterion to plan under uncertainty.

1.5.5 Nonpersonalist Welfare Functions

I have so far discussed research that assumes the social welfare function somehow aggregates personal welfare across society. Sen (1977) called such research *welfarism*, writing (p. 1559): "The general approach of making no use of any information about the social states other than that of personal welfares generated in them may be called 'welfarism.'" He then wrote that (p. 1559): "welfarism as an approach to social decisions is very restrictive." Sen's perspective warrants serious attention, but it seems to me that the word "welfarism" does not express his concern well. I shall instead use the word "personalism."

Nonpersonalist welfare functions place direct societal value on certain ethical concepts, beyond their possible manifestations as determinants of personal welfare. These concepts have been given many appealing names, including justice, fairness, and equity. However, they are devilishly difficult to interpret. Moreover, interpretations vary across the persons who use the concepts. See Backhouse et al. (2021) for multiple discussions.

Economists have long sought to pose and analyse concepts of fairness. For example, Tobin (1970) posed a concept of "specific egalitarianism." This idea moves away from utilitarianism, which concerns itself with the overall utility that a person experiences, instead supposing that society desires that (p. 264): "certain specific scarce commodities should be distributed less unequally than the ability to pay for them." Tobin discussed medical care as a leading case of such a specific commodity.

Foley (1967) and Varian (1974) formalized concepts of *envy-free* and *fair* allocations of resources within a population. Manski, Mullahy, and Venkataramani (2023) formalized concepts of *disparity aversion*. In this book, Chapter 5 discusses welfare functions that formalize the idea of *equal treatment of equals*. Considering policing in Chapter 7, I specify welfare functions that value the personal welfare of law-abiding citizens but do not similarly value the preferences of criminals.

1.5.6 Pragmatic Welfare

Research in welfare economics and moral philosophy has mainly been abstract. In contrast, studies of realistic classes of planning problems have specified pragmatic welfare functions. I use the word "pragmatic" to mean that researchers motivate their welfare functions by some combination of conjecture regarding societal values, empirical study of population preferences, and concern for analytical tractability.

For example, the literature on optimal taxation stemming from Mirrlees (1971) has assumed a utilitarian welfare function and has placed various restrictions on the population distribution of labor–leisure preferences; see Chapter 4 for further discussion. Research on government spending to optimize macroeconomic growth has assumed utilitarian welfare and a representative infinite-lived household, as in Barro (1990). Integrated assessment studies of optimal climate policy has assumed that the objective is to maximize present-discounted gross world product, as in Nordhaus (2008); see Chapter 9 for further discussion. Analysis of optimal medical care may assume that the objective is to maximize a population survival rate or mean quality-adjusted life years (QALYS) net of treatment cost; see Chapters 5 through 8. Benefit–cost analyses of transportation projects quantify and weigh an array of societal project benefits and costs; see US Department of Transportation (2023).

When academic researchers specify pragmatic welfare functions, they may believe that these functions have sufficient social acceptability to make them worthy of study. However, they usually do not argue that actual planners should necessarily use these welfare functions to make decisions. The less ambitious goal is to learn what decisions would be optimal if specified welfare functions were to be used. This perspective is maintained throughout my own work. Research should be distinct from advocacy.

PART I

CHARACTERIZING UNCERTAINTY

2

Incredible Certitude

Analyses of public policy regularly express certitude about the consequences of alternative policy choices. Expressions of uncertainty are rare. Yet predictions are often fragile. Conclusions may rest on critical unsupported assumptions or on leaps of logic. Then the certitude of policy analysis is not credible.

One can illuminate the tension between the credibility and power of assumptions by posing assumptions of varying strength and determining the conclusions that follow. In practice, policy analysis tends to sacrifice credibility in return for strong conclusions. Why?

Analysts and policy makers respond to incentives. The scientific community rewards strong novel findings. The public wants unequivocal policy recommendations. These incentives make it tempting to maintain assumptions far stronger than can be persuasively defended, in order to draw strong conclusions.

My concern with incredible certitude originated at a 1988 conference on evaluation of income tax policy, where I first presented in public my early findings on partial identification with missing data. Responding to my remarks, the econometrician Jerry Hausman stated: "You can't give the client a bound. The client needs a point." In the early 1990s, my colleague and friend Daniel McFadden relayed to me a story he had heard about an economist's attempt to describe uncertainty about a forecast to US President Lyndon B. Johnson. The economist is said to have presented the forecast as a likely range of values for the quantity under discussion. Johnson is said to have replied, "Ranges are for cattle. Give me a number."

In Manski (2011b), I introduced a typology of practices that contribute to incredible certitude. I have since elaborated in Manski (2013c, 2015a, 2019a, 2020e). The typology is:

- conventional certitude: A prediction that is generally accepted as true but is not necessarily true.
- dueling certitudes: Contradictory predictions made with alternative assumptions.
- conflating science and advocacy: Specifying assumptions to generate a predetermined conclusion.
- wishful extrapolation: Using untenable assumptions to extrapolate.
- illogical certitude: Drawing an unfounded conclusion based on logical errors.
- media overreach: Premature or exaggerated public reporting of policy analysis.

Most of this chapter documents the prevalence of incredible certitude. Section 2.1 calls attention to the core role that certitude has played in major streams of religion and philosophy. Section 2.2 describes conventional certitude in official economic statistics reported by federal statistical agencies in the United States. Section 2.3 discusses dueling certitudes in research on criminal justice. Section 2.4 documents wishful extrapolation from medical research to patient care. Section 2.5 remarks on the complementary practice of sacrificing relevance for certitude, again using medical research to illustrate.

The closing part of the chapter poses and assesses arguments that seek to explain incredible certitude. Section 2.6 discusses psychological arguments asserting that expression of incredible certitude in policy analysis is necessary because the public is unable to cope with uncertainty. Section 2.7 considers arguments asserting that incredible certitude is useful or necessary as a device to simplify collective decision making.

2.1 CERTITUDE IN RELIGION AND PHILOSOPHY

While my concern is incredible certitude in modern policy analysis, it is worth keeping in mind that expression of uncertainty is an ancient human issue. Religious dogma provides extreme manifestations of incredible certitude. Hebrew prayers asserting the existence and power of God end with the congregation stating, "Amen," which is variously interpreted in English to mean "certainty," "truth," or "I believe." The Apostles' Creed of Christianity asserts that the speaker believes in basic tenets of the faith and concludes: "I believe in the Holy Spirit, the holy Catholic Church, the communion of saints, the forgiveness of sins, the resurrection of the body, and the life everlasting. Amen." No proof of these tenets is given, and no space is left for uncertainty. The faith asks that one simply believe.

Religious dogma is a conventional certitude in a society with a consensus faith. Dueling certitudes occur when people hold different faiths whose dogmas are inconsistent with one another. It is sometimes said that dueling certitudes may be useful as a device to promote learning. The ancient idea of dialectic proposes that debating contradictory perspectives can be an effective way to determine truth. However, history presents numerous examples of bitter conflicts that result from dueling religious certitudes.

Classical and Enlightenment philosophers manifest a spectrum of views about uncertainty. Some assert that they know basic truths while others express uncertainty. I will focus on one persistent idea in the philosophy of science, namely that a scientist should choose one hypothesis among those that are consistent with the available data.

Researchers often refer to *Occam's Razor*, the medieval philosophical declaration that: "Plurality should not be posited without necessity." Duignan (2023) gives the usual modern interpretation of this cryptic statement, remarking that: "The principle gives precedence to simplicity; of two competing theories, the simplest explanation of an entity is to be preferred." The philosopher Richard Swinburne wrote (Swinburne, 1997, p. 1):

> I seek to show that – other things being equal – the simplest hypothesis proposed as an explanation of phenomena is more likely to be the true one than is any other available hypothesis, that its predictions are more likely to be true than those of any other available hypothesis, and that it is an ultimate a priori epistemic principle that simplicity is evidence for truth.

The choice criterion offered here is as imprecise as the one given by Occam. What do Duignan and Swinburne mean by "simplicity"?

Among economists, Milton Friedman expressed the Occam perspective in an influential methodological essay. Friedman (1953) placed prediction as the central objective of science, writing (p. 5): "The ultimate goal of a positive science is the development of a 'theory' or 'hypothesis' that yields valid and meaningful (i.e. not truistic) predictions about phenomena not yet observed." He later wrote (p. 10): "The choice among alternative hypotheses equally consistent with the available evidence must to some extent be arbitrary, though there is general agreement that relevant considerations are suggested by the criteria 'simplicity' and 'fruitfulness,' themselves notions that defy completely objective specification."

Thus, Friedman counseled scientists to choose one hypothesis, even though this may require the use of "to some extent ... arbitrary" criteria. He did not explain why scientists should choose one hypothesis from many. He did not entertain the idea that scientists might offer predictions under a range of plausible hypotheses that are consistent with the available evidence.

However one tries to operationalize the Occam perspective, its relevance to planning is not evident. In policy analysis, knowledge is instrumental to the objective of making good decisions. Discussions of Occam's Razor do not pose this objective. Does use of a criterion such as "simplicity" to choose one hypothesis promote good decision making? As far as I am aware, philosophers have not addressed this essential question.

2.2 CONVENTIONAL CERTITUDE IN OFFICIAL ECONOMIC STATISTICS

2.2.1 Congressional Budget Office Scoring of Legislation

Conventional certitude is exemplified by US Congressional Budget Office (CBO) scoring of federal legislation. The CBO was established in the Congressional Budget Act of 1974. The Act has been interpreted as mandating the CBO to provide point predictions (*scores*) of the budgetary impact of legislation. CBO scores are conveyed in letters that the Director writes to leaders of Congress, unaccompanied by measures of uncertainty. CBO scores exemplify conventional certitude because they have achieved broad acceptance. They are used by both Democratic and Republican members of Congress. Media reports largely take them at face value.

A well-known example is the scoring of the Patient Protection and Affordable Care Act of 2010, commonly known as Obamacare or the ACA. In March of 2010, the CBO and the Joint Committee on Taxation (JCT) together scored the combined consequences of the ACA and the Reconciliation Act of 2010 and reported (Elmendorf, 2010, p.2) that "enacting both pieces of legislation ... would produce a net reduction of changes in federal deficits of $138 billion over the 2010–2019 period as a result of changes in direct spending and revenue." Media reports largely accepted the CBO score as fact without questioning its validity, the hallmark of conventional certitude.

A simple approach to avoid incredible certitude would be to provide interval forecasts of the budgetary impacts of legislation. The CBO would produce two scores for a bill, a low score and a high score, and report both. Or it could present a full probabilistic forecast in a graphical fan chart such as the one used by the Bank of England to predict gross domestic product (GDP) growth. If the CBO must provide a point prediction, it could continue to do so, with some convention used to locate the point within the interval forecast.

In 2010, when I became concerned about the incredible certitude expressed by the CBO when scoring Obamacare, I spoke with Douglas Holtz-Eakin, a former director of the CBO. He told me that he expected Congress would be highly displeased if the CBO were to express uncertainty when scoring pending legislation. I gave a seminar at the CBO and talked with staff members. They agreed that there is enormous uncertainty when attempting to predict the impact on the federal debt of complex legislation such as Obamacare. Yet they shared the perspective expressed by Holtz-Eakin, that they could not express this uncertainty in their official reports to Congress.

2.2.2 Economic Statistics Reported by Federal Statistical Agencies

Further leading cases of conventional certitude are evident in the official statistics published by federal statistical agencies in the United States, including the Bureau of Economic Analysis, Bureau of Labor Statistics, and Census Bureau. These agencies respectively report point estimates of GDP growth, unemployment, and household income. Agency staff know that official statistics suffer from sampling and non-sampling errors. Yet the practice has been to report statistics with only occasional measurement of sampling errors and no measurement of non-sampling errors. The media and the public generally accept the estimates as reported, making them instances of conventional certitude.

Government agencies communicate official economic statistics in news releases that make little if any mention of uncertainty in the reported estimates. Technical publications documenting data and methods acknowledge that official statistics are subject to error. They may use standard errors or confidence intervals to measure sampling errors; that is, the statistical imprecision that occurs with finite samples of the population. However, they generally do not attempt to quantify the many forms of non-sampling errors that generate identification problems. Neglect of non-sampling errors may reflect the fact that statistical theory has mainly focused on sampling error, making strong assumptions that imply point identification.

Reporting official statistics as point estimates without adequate attention to error manifests conventional certitude: The point estimates may be viewed as true but they are not necessarily true. In the absence of agency guidance, some users of official statistics may naively assume that errors are small and inconsequential. Persons who understand that the statistics are subject to error must fend for themselves and conjecture the error magnitudes. Thus, users of official statistics – economists, government officials, firm managers, and citizens – may misinterpret the information that the statistics provide.

Considering error from the perspective of users of statistics rather than of statisticians, I think it essential to refine the general problem of conventional certitude in official statistics, distinguishing errors in measurement of well-defined concepts from uncertainty about the concepts themselves. I also think it useful to distinguish transitory and permanent measurement problems. To highlight these distinctions, Manski (2015a) discussed transitory statistical uncertainty, permanent statistical uncertainty, and conceptual uncertainty. In what follows, I define these ideas and give illustrative examples.

2.2.3 Transitory Uncertainty: Revisions in National Income Accounts

Transitory statistical uncertainty arises because data collection takes time. Agencies may release a preliminary statistic with incomplete data and revise it as new data arrives. Uncertainty diminishes as data accumulates. A leading example is the Bureau of Economic Analysis's (BEA) initial measurement of GDP and revision of the estimate as new data arrives. The BEA reports multiple vintages of quarterly GDP estimates. An "advance" estimate combines data available one month after the end of a quarter with trend extrapolations. "Second" and "third" estimates are released after two and three months, when new data become available. A "first annual" estimate is released in the summer, using data collected annually. There are subsequent annual and five-year revisions. Yet the BEA reports GDP estimates without quantitative measures of uncertainty.

A publication by BEA staff explains the practice of reporting estimates without measures of error as a response to the presumed wishes of the users of GDP statistics. Fixler et al. (2014) state (p. 2): "Given that BEA routinely revises its estimates during the course of a year, one might ask why BEA produces point estimates of GDP instead of interval estimates ... Although interval estimates would inform users of the uncertainty surrounding the estimates, most users prefer point estimates, and so they are featured." BEA analysts have provided an upbeat perspective on the accuracy of GDP statistics (Fixler et al., 2011).

In contrast, Croushore (2011) offers a more cautionary perspective, writing (p. 73): "Until recently, macroeconomists assumed that data revisions were small and random and thus had no effect on structural modeling, policy analysis, or forecasting. But real-time research has shown that this assumption is false and that data revisions matter in many unexpected ways."

Communication of the transitory uncertainty of GDP estimates should be relatively easy to accomplish. The historical record of revisions has been made accessible for study in two "real-time" data sets maintained by the Philadelphia and St. Louis Federal Reserve Banks; see Croushore (2011) for a definition of "real time." Measurement of transitory uncertainty in GDP estimates is straightforward if one finds it credible to assume that the revision process is time stationary. Then historical estimates of the magnitudes of revisions can credibly be extrapolated to measure the uncertainty of future revisions. The BEA could communicate uncertainty as a probability distribution via a fan chart, as the Bank of England does regularly. See Aikman et al. (2011) for commentary on the thinking underlying the Bank's use of fan charts to communicate uncertainty.

2.2.4 Permanent Uncertainty: Nonresponse in Surveys

Permanent statistical uncertainty arises from incompleteness or inadequacy of data collection that is not resolved over time. Sources include sampling error due to finite sample size and non-sampling error due to nonresponse and misreporting. I focus here on nonresponse to employment and income questions in the Current Population Survey (CPS).

Each year the US Census Bureau reports statistics on the household income distribution based on data collected in a supplement to the CPS. The Census Bureau's annual *Current Population Report* provides statistics characterizing the income distribution and measures sampling error by providing 90-percent confidence intervals for various estimates. The report does not measure non-sampling errors. A supplementary document describes some sources of non-sampling error but does not quantify them.

Each month, the BLS issues a news release reporting the unemployment rate for the previous month based on data collected in the monthly CPS. A "technical note" issued with the release contains a section on "Reliability of the Estimates" that acknowledges the possibility of errors (U.S. Bureau of Labor Statistics, 2023). The note describes the use of standard errors and confidence intervals to measure sampling error. It states that non-sampling errors "can occur for many reasons, including the failure to sample a segment of the population, inability to obtain information for all respondents in the sample, inability or unwillingness of respondents to provide correct information on a timely basis, mistakes made by respondents, and errors made in the collection or processing of the data." The Note does not measure the magnitudes of non-sampling errors.

When the Census Bureau and BLS report point estimates of statistics on household income and employment, they assume that nonresponse is random conditional on specified observed covariates of sample members. This assumption, which implies the absence of non-sampling error, is implemented as weights for unit nonresponse and imputations for item nonresponse. CPS documentation of its imputation approach offers no evidence that the method yields a distribution for missing data that is close to the actual distribution. Another Census document describing the American Housing Survey is revealing. The US Census Bureau (2011) states: "The Census Bureau does not know how close the imputed values are to the actual values." Indeed, lack of knowledge of the closeness of imputed values to actual ones is common. Manski (2024) critiques imputation from the perspective of partial identification analysis.

Research on partial identification shows how to measure potential non-sampling error due to nonresponse without making assumptions about the nature of the missing data. One contemplates all values that the missing data can take. Then the data yield interval estimates of official statistics. The literature derives intervals for population means and quantiles. The intervals have simple forms, their lower and upper bounds being the values that the estimate would take if all missing data were to take the smallest or largest logically possible value. The literature shows how to form confidence intervals that jointly measure sampling and non-response error. See Manski (2007a) for a textbook exposition.

To illustrate, Manski (2016) used CPS data to form interval estimates of median household income and the fraction of families with income below the poverty line in 2001–2011. There was considerable nonresponse to the income questions. During 2002–2012, 7 to 9 percent of the sampled households yielded no income data due to unit nonresponse and 41 to 47 percent of the interviewed households yielded incomplete income data due to item nonresponse. One set of estimates recognizes item nonresponse alone and another recognizes unit response as well. The interval estimate for the family poverty rate in 2011 is [0.14, 0.34] if one makes no assumptions about item response but assumes that unit nonresponse is random. The interval is [0.13, 0.39] if one drops the assumption that unit nonresponse is random.

Interval estimates of official statistics that place no assumptions on the values of missing data are easy to understand and simple to compute. One might therefore think that it would be standard practice for government statistical agencies to report them, but official statistics are not reported this way. It is sometimes said that such interval estimates are "too wide to be informative." Nevertheless, I recommend that statistical agencies report them.

Wide bounds reflect real data uncertainties that cannot be washed away by assumptions lacking credibility. Even when wide, interval estimates making no assumptions on nonresponse are valuable for three reasons: (a) They are easy to compute and understand. (b) They are maximally credible in the sense that they express all logically possible values of the statistic of interest. (c) They make explicit the fundamental role that assumptions play in inferential methods that yield tighter findings.

The above does not imply that statistical agencies should refrain from making assumptions about nonresponse. Interval estimates making no assumptions may be excessively conservative if agency analysts have some understanding of the nature of nonresponse. There is much middle ground between interval estimation with no assumptions and point estimation assuming that nonresponse is conditionally random. The middle ground obtains interval estimates using assumptions that may include random nonresponse as one among various possibilities. Manski (2016) posed some alternatives that agencies may want to consider.

2.2.5 Conceptual Uncertainty: Seasonal Adjustment of Official Statistics

Conceptual uncertainty arises from incomplete understanding of the information that official statistics provide about economic concepts or from lack of clarity in the concepts themselves. Conceptual uncertainty concerns the interpretation of statistics rather than their magnitudes.

A leading example is seasonal adjustment of statistics. Viewed from a sufficiently high altitude, the purpose of seasonal adjustment appears straightforward to explain. It is less clear from ground level how one should perform seasonal adjustment.

The prevalent X-12-ARIMA method was developed by Census and is used by BLS and BEA. X-12, along with its predecessor X-11 and successor X-13, may be a sophisticated and successful algorithm for seasonal adjustment. Or it may be an unfathomable black box containing a complex set of operations that lack economic foundation. Wright (2013) noted the difficulty of understanding X-12, writing (p. 67): "Most academics treat seasonal adjustment as a very mundane job, rumored to be undertaken by hobbits living in holes in the ground. I believe that this is a terrible mistake, but one in which the statistical agencies share at least a little of the blame." He states that understanding the practice of seasonal adjustment matters because (p. 65): "Seasonal adjustment is extraordinarily consequential."

There presently exists no clearly appropriate way to measure the uncertainty associated with seasonal adjustment. X-12 is a standalone algorithm, not a method based on a specified dynamic theory of the economy. It is not obvious how to evaluate the extent to which it accomplishes the objective of removing the influences of predictable seasonal patterns. One might perhaps juxtapose X-12 with other seemingly reasonable algorithms, perform seasonal adjustment with each one, and view the range of resulting estimates as a measure of conceptual uncertainty. More principled ways to evaluate uncertainty may open up if agencies were to use a seasonal adjustment method derived from a specified model of the economy. One could then assess the sensitivity of seasonally adjusted estimates to variation in the parameters and the basic structure of the model.

A more radical departure from present practice would be to abandon seasonal adjustment and leave it to the users of statistics to interpret unadjusted statistics. Publication of unadjusted statistics should be particularly valuable to users who want to make year-to-year rather than month-to-month comparisons of statistics. Suppose that one wants to compare unemployment in March 2013 and March 2014. It is arguably more reasonable to compare the unadjusted estimates for these months than to compare the seasonally adjusted estimates. Comparison of unadjusted estimates for the same month each year sensibly removes the influences of predictable seasonal patterns, and compares data collected in the two months of interest.

2.2.6 Why Do Statistical Agencies Practice Incredible Certitude?

The concerns that I have expressed about incredible certitude in official economic statistics are not new. Simon Kuznets (1948), the father of national income accounting, called for publication of "margins of error" with these official statistics. Soon after, Oskar Morgenstern wrote a book that urgently argued for regular measurement of error in all official economic statistics Morgenstern (1950, 1963). He was well placed to influence the status quo, being famous for his contribution to game theory. Yet his efforts did not bear fruit. More recently, agencies have not adhered to the National Research Council (2013) call for "Openness about Sources and Limitations of the Data Provided" in the document, *Principles and Practices for a Federal Statistical Agency*.

Why is it that statistical agencies do so little to communicate uncertainty in official statistics? I am not aware of any valid professional reason that would explain the failure of the BLS and Census to report measures of sampling error in their news releases of employment and income statistics. Agency administrators could task their research staffs to develop measures of non-sampling error. While I cannot conjure a valid professional explanation for the status quo, I do see a possible political explanation.

Federal statistical agencies may perceive a political incentive to express incredible certitude about the state of the economy when they publish official economic statistics. Morgenstern (1963) commented cogently on the political incentives facing statistical agencies, writing (p. 11):

Finally, we mention a serious organizational difficulty in discussing and criticizing statistics. These are virtually always produced by large organizations, government or private; and these organizations are frequently mutually dependent upon each other in order to function normally. Often one office cannot publicly raise questions about the work of another, even when it suspects the quality of the work, since this might adversely affect bureaucratic-diplomatic relations between the two and the flow of information from one office to another might be hampered. A marked esprit de corps prevails. All offices must try to impress the public with the quality of their work. Should too many doubts be raised, financial support from Congress or other sources may not be forthcoming. More than once has it happened that Congressional appropriations were endangered when it was suspected that government statistics might not be 100 percent accurate. It is natural, therefore, that various offices will defend the quality of their work even to an unreasonable degree.

2.3 DUELING CERTITUDES IN CRIMINAL JUSTICE RESEARCH

Dueling certitudes – contradictory predictions made with alternative assumptions – are common in research on controversial policy questions. Research on criminal justice policy provides many illustrations. I describe three controversies here.

2.3.1 The RAND and IDA Studies of Cocaine-Control Policy

In the mid 1990s, two studies of cocaine-control policy played prominent roles in discussions of federal policy towards illegal drugs. One was performed by analysts at RAND (Rydell and Everingham, 1994) and the other by analysts at the Institute for Defense Analyses (IDA) (Crane, Rivolo, and Comfort, 1997). The two studies posed similar hypothetical objectives for cocaine-control policy, namely reduction in cocaine consumption in the United States by 1 percent. Both studies predicted the cost of using certain policies to achieve this objective. However, the RAND and IDA authors used different assumptions and data to reach dramatically different policy conclusions.

The RAND study specified a model of the supply and demand for cocaine that aimed to characterize the interaction of producers and users and the process through which alternative cocaine-control policies may affect consumption and prices. It used this model to evaluate various demand-control and supply-control policies and concluded that drug treatment, a demand-control policy, is much more effective than any supply policy. The IDA study examined the time series association between source-zone interdiction activities and retail cocaine prices. It concluded that source-zone interdiction, a supply-control policy, is at least as effective as is drug treatment.

When they appeared, the RAND and IDA studies drew attention to the ongoing struggle over federal funding of drug-control activities. The RAND study was used to argue that funding should be shifted towards drug-treatment programs and away from activities to reduce drug production or to interdict drug shipments. The IDA study, undertaken in part as a response to the RAND findings, was used to argue that interdiction activities should be funded at current or higher levels.

At a congressional hearing, Lee Brown, then director of the Office of National Drug Control Policy (ONDCP), used the RAND study to argue for drug treatment (Subcommittee on National Security, International

Affairs, and Criminal Justice, 1996, p. 61): "Let me now talk about what we know works in addressing the drug problem. There is compelling evidence that treatment is cost- effective and provides significant benefits to public safety. In June 1994, a RAND Corporation study concluded that drug treatment is the most cost effective drug control intervention."

In a subsequent hearing specifically devoted to the IDA study, Subcommittee Chair William Zeliff used the study to argue for interdiction (Subcommittee on National Security, International Affairs, and Criminal Justice 1998, p. 1):

We are holding these hearings today to review a study on drug policy, a study we believe to have significant findings, prepared by an independent group, the Institute for Defense Analysis, at the request of Secretary of Defense Perry in 1994.... The subcommittee has questioned for some time the administration's strong reliance on treatment as the key to winning our Nation's drug war, and furthermore this subcommittee has questioned the wisdom of drastically cutting to the bone interdiction programs in order to support major increases in hardcore drug addiction treatment programs. The basis for this change in strategy has been the administration's reliance on the 1994 RAND study.

At the request of the ONDCP, the National Research Council Committee on Data and Research for Policy on Illegal Drugs assessed the RAND and IDA studies; see National Research Council (1999). After examining the two studies, the committee concluded that neither constitutes a persuasive basis for the formation of cocaine-control policy. Specifically, the committee concluded that neither the RAND nor the IDA study provides a credible estimate of what it would cost to use alternative policies to reduce cocaine consumption in the United States.

I chaired the National Research Council Committee. When I think now about the RAND and IDA studies, I consider their many specific differences to be less salient than their shared lack of credibility. Each study may have been coherent internally, but each rested on such a fragile foundation of weak data and unsubstantiated assumptions as to undermine its findings. To its great frustration, the committee had to conclude that the nation should not draw even the most tentative policy lessons from either study. Neither yields usable findings.

What troubles me most about both studies is their injudicious efforts to draw strong policy conclusions. It is not necessarily problematic for researchers to try to make sense of weak data and to entertain unsubstantiated conjectures. However, the strength of the conclusions drawn in a study should be commensurate with the quality of the evidence. When researchers overreach, they not only give away their own credibility, but they diminish public trust in science more generally. The damage to public trust is particularly severe when researchers inappropriately draw strong conclusions about matters as contentious as drug policy.

2.3.2 The Deterrent Effect of the Death Penalty

American society has long debated the deterrent effect of the death penalty as a punishment for murder. Disagreement persists because research has not been able to settle the question. Researchers have used data on homicide rates and sanctions across states and years to examine the deterrent effect of the death penalty. The fundamental difficulty is that the outcomes of counterfactual policies are unobservable. Data alone cannot reveal what the homicide rate in a state without (with) a death penalty would have been had the state (not) adopted a death penalty statute. Data must be combined with assumptions to predict homicides under counterfactual deterrence policies.

A large body of work has addressed deterrence and the death penalty, yet the literature has not achieved consensus. Researchers studying the question have used much the same data, but have maintained different assumptions and have consequently reached different conclusions. Rather than acknowledge uncertainty about the realism of its maintained assumptions, each published article touts its findings as accurate. The result is dueling certitudes across articles.

Two committees of the National Research Council have documented the substantial variation in research findings and have investigated in depth the problem of inference on deterrence; see Blumstein, Cohen, and Nagin (1978) and National Research Council (2012). The latter committee, reiterating a basic conclusion of the former one, wrote (p. 2): "The committee concludes that research to date on the effect of capital punishment on homicide is not informative about whether capital punishment decreases, increases, or has no effect on homicide rates."

To illustrate in a simple setting how research that uses the same data, but different assumptions, can reach very different findings, Manski and Pepper (2013) examined data from the critical 1970s period when the Supreme Court decided the constitutionality of the death penalty. The 1972 Supreme Court case *Furman* v. *Georgia* resulted in a multi-year moratorium on the application of the death penalty, while the 1976 case *Gregg* v. *Georgia* ruled that the death penalty could be applied subject to certain criteria. We examined the effect of death penalty statutes on homicide rates in two years: 1975, the last full year of the moratorium, and 1977, the first full year after the moratorium was lifted. In 1975, the death penalty was illegal throughout the country. In 1977, thirty-two states had statutes legalizing the death penalty. For each state and year, we observe the homicide rate and whether the death penalty is legal.

We computed three simple estimates of the effect of death penalty statutes on homicide. A *before-and-after* analysis compares homicide rates in the treated states in 1975 and 1977. The 1975 homicide rate in these states, when none had the death penalty, was 10.3 per 100,000. The 1977 rate, when all had the death penalty, was 9.7. The before-and-after estimate is the difference between the 1977 and 1975 homicide rates; that is 9.7 – 10.3 = –0.6. This is interpretable as the average effect of the death penalty on homicide in the treated states if one assumes that nothing germane to homicide occurred in these states between 1975 and 1977 except for legalization of capital punishment.

Alternatively, one might compare the 1977 homicide rates in the treated and untreated states. The 1977 rate in the treated states, which had the death penalty, was 9.7. The 1977 rate in the untreated states, which did not have the death penalty, was 6.9. The estimate is the difference between these homicide rates; that is, 9.7 – 6.9 = 2.8. This is interpretable as the nationwide average effect of the death penalty on homicide in 1977 if one assumes that persons living in the treated and untreated states have the same propensity to commit murder in the absence of the death penalty and respond similarly to enactment of the death penalty. With this assumption, the observed homicide rate in the treated states reveals what the rate would have been in the untreated states if they had enacted the death penalty and vice versa.

Yet a third way to use the data is to compare the temporal changes in homicide rates in the treated and untreated states. Between 1975 and 1977, the homicide rate in the treated states fell from 10.3 to 9.7, while the rate in the untreated states fell from 8.0 to 6.9. The so-called *difference-in-difference* (*DID*) estimate is the difference between these temporal changes; that is, (9.7 – 10.3) – (6.9 – 8.0) = 0.5. This is interpretable as the nationwide effect of the death penalty on homicide if one assumes that all states experience a common time trend in homicide and that enactment of the death penalty has the same effect in all states.

These three estimates yield different empirical findings regarding the effect of the death penalty on homicide. The before-and-after estimate implies that enactment of a death penalty statute reduces the homicide rate by 0.6 per 100,000. The other two estimates imply that having the death penalty raises the homicide rate by 2.8 or 0.5 per 100,000. The idea that capital punishment may increase the homicide rate is contrary to the traditional view of punishment as a deterrent. However, some researchers have argued that the death penalty shows a lack of concern for life that brutalizes society into greater acceptance of commission of murder.

Which estimate is correct? Given certain assumptions, each appropriately measures the effect of the death penalty on homicide. However, the assumptions that justify this interpretation differ across estimates. One may be correct, or none of them. If three researchers were to each maintain a different one of the assumptions and report one of the three estimates, they would exhibit dueling certitudes.

The antidote to dueling certitudes about the deterrent effect of capital punishment is to recognize uncertainty by generating a set of estimates under alternative assumptions. To formalize this idea in a flexible manner, Manski and Pepper (2013) studied the conclusions implied by relatively weak *bounded-variation* assumptions that restrict variation in treatment response across places and time. See Chapter 3 for a formal description of such assumptions.

The results are findings that bound the deterrent effect of capital punishment. By successively adding stronger identifying assumptions, we sought to make transparent how assumptions shape inference. We performed empirical analysis using state-level data in the United States in 1975 and 1977. Under the weakest restrictions, there is substantial ambiguity: we cannot rule out the possibility that having a death penalty statute substantially increases or decreases homicide. This ambiguity is reduced when we impose stronger assumptions, but inferences are sensitive to the maintained restrictions. Combining the data with some assumptions implies that the death penalty increases homicide, but other assumptions imply that the death penalty deters it.

2.3.3 How Do Right-to-Carry Laws Affect Crime Rates?

A considerable body of research on crime in the United States has used data on county or state crime rates to evaluate the impact of laws allowing individuals to carry concealed handguns – so called right-to-carry (RTC) laws. Theory alone cannot predict even the direction of the impact. The knowledge or belief that potential victims may be carrying weapons may deter commission of some crimes but may escalate the severity of criminal encounters. Ultimately, how allowing individuals to carry concealed weapons affects crime is an empirical question.

Lott (2010) described some of this empirical research in a book with the provocative and unambiguous title *More Guns, Less Crime*. Yet, despite dozens of studies, the full body of research provides no clear insight on whether more guns yield less crime. Some studies find that RTC laws reduce crime, others find that the effects are negligible, and still others find that such laws increase crime. In a series of papers starting in 1997, Lott and co-authors have argued forcefully that RTC laws have important deterrent effects which can play a role in reducing violent crime. Lott and Mustard (1997) and Lott (2010), for example, found that RTC laws reduce crime rates in every violent crime category by between 5 and 8 percent. Using different models and revised/updated data, however, other researchers have found that RTC laws either have little impact or may increase violent crime rates. See, for example, Black and Nagin (1998), Duggan (2001), Aneja et al. (2011), and Durlauf et al. (2016).

This sharp disagreement may seem surprising. How can researchers using similar data draw such different conclusions? In fact, it has long been known that inferring the magnitude and direction of treatment effects is inherently difficult due to the unobservability of counterfactual outcomes. Suppose that one wants to learn how crime rates would differ with and without a RTC law in a given place and time. Data cannot reveal what the crime rate in a RTC state would have been if the state had not enacted the law. Nor can data reveal what the crime rate in a non-RTC state would have been if an RTC law had been in effect. To identify the law's effect, one must somehow "fill in" the missing counterfactual observations. This requires making assumptions that cannot be tested empirically. Different assumptions may yield different inferences, hence dueling certitudes.

Empirical research on RTC laws has struggled to find consensus on a set of credible assumptions. Reviewing the literature, the National Research Council Committee to Improve Research Information and Data on Firearms concluded that it is not possible to infer a credible causal link between RTC laws and crime using the current evidence (National Research Council, 2005). Indeed, the committee concluded that (National Research Council, 2005, p. 150), "additional analysis along the lines of the current literature is unlikely to yield results that will persuasively demonstrate" this link. The committee observed that findings are highly sensitive to model specification. Yet there is no solid foundation for specific assumptions and, as a result, no obvious way to prefer specific results. Hence, drawing credible precise findings that lead to consensus about the impact of RTC laws has been impossible.

The antidote to dueling certitudes about the effect on crime of RTC laws is to recognize uncertainty by generating a set of estimates under alternative assumptions. To formalize this idea in a flexible manner, Manski and Pepper (2018) studied the conclusions implied by relatively weak bounded-variation assumptions that restrict variation in treatment response across places and time. The methodology extended that used in the Manski and Pepper (2013) analysis of the deterrent effect of capital punishment, discussed above. The results were findings that bound the crime effect of RTC laws. Considering alternative assumptions makes transparent how assumptions shape inference.

2.4 WISHFUL EXTRAPOLATION FROM MEDICAL RESEARCH TO PATIENT CARE

Extrapolation is essential to policy analysis. A central objective is to inform policy choice by predicting the outcomes that would occur if past policies were to be continued or alternative ones were to be enacted. Researchers often use untenable assumptions to extrapolate. I have called this manifestation of incredible certitude *wishful extrapolation*. To illustrate, I will discuss extrapolation from randomized trials in medicine to inform patient care, drawing on Manski (2019b).

Trials have long enjoyed a favored status within medical research on treatment response. They are often called the "gold standard" for such research. The appeal of trials is that, with sufficient sample size and complete observation of outcomes, they deliver credible findings on treatment response in the study population. However, extrapolation of findings from trials to clinical practice can be difficult. Researchers and guideline developers often use untenable assumptions to extrapolate.

2.4.1 Extrapolation from Study Populations to Patient Populations

Study populations in trials often differ from patient populations. It is common to perform trials studying treatment of a specific disease only on subjects who have no comorbidities. Another source of difference between study and patient populations is that a study population consists of persons with specified demographic attributes who volunteer to participate in a trial. Participation in a trial may be restricted to persons in certain age categories who reside in certain locales. Among such persons, volunteers are those who respond to financial and medical incentives to participate. It may be wishful extrapolation to assume that treatment response in trials performed on volunteers with specified demographic attributes who lack comorbidities is the same as what would occur in actual patient populations.

To justify trials performed on study populations that may differ substantially from patient populations, researchers often cite Donald Campbell, who distinguished between the internal and external validity of studies of treatment response (Campbell and Stanley, 1963). A study is said to have *internal validity* if it has credible findings for the study population. It has *external validity* if an invariance assumption permits credible extrapolation. The appeal of randomized trials is their internal validity. Wishful extrapolation is an absence of external validity.

Campbell argued that studies should be judged primarily by their internal validity and secondarily by their external validity. This perspective has been used to argue for the primacy of experimental research over observational studies, whatever the study population may be. The Campbell position is well grounded if treatment response is homogeneous. Then researchers can learn about treatment response in easy-to-analyze study populations and clinicians can confidently extrapolate findings to patient populations. However, homogeneity of treatment response may be the exception rather than the rule. Hence, it may be wishful to extrapolate from a study population to a patient population. See Section 2.5.2 for further discussion of the distinction between internal and external validity.

2.4.2 Extrapolation from Experimental Treatments to Clinical Treatments

Treatments in trials often differ from those that occur in clinical practice. This is particularly so in trials comparing drug treatments. Drug trials are commonly double-blinded, neither the patient nor the clinician knowing the assigned treatment. A double-blinded drug trial reveals the distribution of response in a setting where patients and clinicians are uncertain what treatment a patient is receiving. It does not reveal what response would be when patients and clinicians know what drug is being administered and can react to this information.

Consider drug treatments for hypertension. Patients may react heterogeneously to the various drugs available for prescription. A clinician treating a specific patient may sequentially prescribe alternative drugs, trying each for a period in an effort to find one that performs satisfactorily. Sequential experimentation is not possible in a blinded trial. The standard protocol prohibits the clinician from knowing what drug a subject is receiving and from using judgment to modify the treatment. Blinding is also problematic for interpretation of noncompliance with assigned treatments.

2.4.3 Wishful Meta-analyses of Disparate Studies

The problems discussed above concern extrapolation of findings from a single trial. Further difficulties arise when one attempts to combine findings from multiple trials.

It is easy to understand the impetus for combination of findings. Decision makers must somehow interpret the mass of information provided by empirical research. The hard question is how to interpret this information sensibly. Combination of findings is sometimes performed by *systematic review* of a set of studies. This is a subjective process similar to the exercise of clinical judgment.

Statisticians have proposed *meta-analysis*, attempting to provide an objective methodology for combining the findings of multiple studies. Meta-analysis was originally developed to address a purely statistical problem. Suppose that multiple trials have been performed on the same population, each drawing an independent random sample. The best way to use the data combines them into one sample.

Suppose that the raw data are unavailable. Instead, multiple parameter estimates are available, each computed with the data from a different sample. Meta-analysis proposes methods to combine the estimates. A common proposal computes a weighted average, weighting estimates by sample size.

The original concept of meta-analysis is uncontroversial, but its applicability is limited. It is common to have multiple disparate studies. The studies may examine distinct patient populations, whose members may have different risk of disease or different distributions of treatment response. Administration of treatments and measurement of outcomes may vary. Gene Glass, who introduced the term *meta-analysis*, wrote (Glass, 1977, p. 358): "The tough intellectual work in many applied fields is to make incommensurables commensurable, in short, to compare apples and oranges."

Meta-analysis is performed often in such settings, computing weighted averages of estimates for distinct study populations and trial designs. Specifically, meta-analyses often use a *random-effects* model

(DerSimonian and Laird, 1986). The model considers trials to be drawn at random "from a population of possible studies." Then each trial estimates a parameter drawn at random from a population of possible parameters. A weighted average estimates the mean of these parameters.

The relevance to clinical practice is obscure. DerSimonian and Laird do not explain what is meant by a population of possible studies, nor why published studies should be considered a random sample from this population. They do not explain how a population of possible studies connects to what matters to a clinician – the distribution of health outcomes across the relevant population of patients.

Manski (2020f) draws on econometric research on partial identification to propose principles for patient-centered meta-analysis. One specifies a prediction of concern and determines what each available study reveals. Given common imperfections in internal and external validity, studies typically yield credible set-valued rather than point predictions. Thus, a study may enable one to conclude that a probability of disease, or mean treatment response, lies within a range of possibilities. Patient-centered meta-analysis would combine the findings of multiple studies by computing the intersection of the set-valued predictions that they yield. See Chapter 3 for further discussion.

2.5 SACRIFICING RELEVANCE FOR CERTITUDE

Researchers often are aware that they cannot form a credible point prediction or estimate of a quantity of interest. They could face up to uncertainty and determine what they can credibly infer about the quantity, perhaps obtaining a bound. However, the lure of incredible certitude being strong, they often respond differently. They change the objective and focus on another quantity that is not of substantive interest but that can be predicted or estimated credibly. Thus, they sacrifice relevance for certitude.

Notable scientists have critiqued this practice. The statistician John Tukey wrote (Tukey, 1962, pp. 13–14): "Far better an approximate answer to the right question, which is often vague, than an exact answer to the wrong question, which can always be made precise." Many cite some version of the joke about the drunk and the lamppost. Noam Chomsky has been quoted as putting it this way (Barsky, 1998, p. 95): "Science is a bit like the joke about the drunk who is looking under a lamppost for a key that he has lost on the other side of the street, because that's where the light is."

Sacrificing relevance for certitude does not imply incredible certitude if everyone understands that the quantity being estimated or predicted is not of substantive interest. The problem is that authors may not be forthright about this, or readers may misinterpret findings. I provide two illustrations, focusing on medical research.

2.5.1 The Odds Ratio and Public Health

In a well-known text on epidemiology, Fleiss (1981) stated that retrospective studies of disease do not yield policy-relevant predictions and so are (p. 92), "necessarily useless from the point of view of public health." Nevertheless, he went on to say that "retrospective studies are eminently valid from the more general point of view of the advancement of knowledge." What Fleiss meant in the first statement is that retrospective studies do not provide data that enable credible point estimation of *attributable risk*, a quantity of substantive interest in public health. The second statement means that retrospective studies enable credible point estimation of the *odds ratio*, a quantity that is not of substantive interest but that is widely reported in epidemiological research. I explain here, drawing on Manski (2007a, Chapter 5).

The term *retrospective studies* refers to a sampling process that is also known to epidemiologists as *case-control* sampling and to econometricians studying behavior as *choice-based* sampling (Manski and Lerman, 1977). I call it *response-based* sampling here, as in Manski (2007a). Formally, consider a population each of whose members is described by covariates x and a response (or outcome) y. Consider inference on the response probabilities $P(y | x)$ when the population is divided into response strata and random samples are drawn from each stratum. This is response-based sampling.

In a simple case prevalent in epidemiology, y is a binary health outcome and x is a binary risk factor. Thus, y = 1 if a person becomes ill and y = 0 otherwise, while x = 1 if the person has the risk factor and x = 0 otherwise. In a classic example, y denotes the presence of lung cancer and x denotes whether a person is a smoker. Response-based sampling draws random samples of ill and healthy persons. This reveals the distributions of the risk factor among those who are ill and healthy; that is, $P(x | y = 1)$ and $P(x | y = 0)$. It does not reveal $P(y | x)$.

A basic concern of research in public health is to learn how the probability of illness varies across persons who do and who do not have a risk factor. Attributable risk is the difference in illness probability between these groups; that is, $P(y = 1 | x = 1) - P(y = 1 | x = 0)$. Another measure of the variation of illness with the risk factor is the ratio $P(y = 1 | x = 1) / P(y = 1 | x = 0)$, called *relative risk*.

Texts on epidemiology discuss both relative and attributable risk, but empirical research has focused on relative risk. This focus is hard to justify from the perspective of public health. The health impact of a risk factor presumably depends on the number of illnesses affected; that is, on attributable risk times the size of the population. The relative risk statistic is uninformative about this quantity.

For example, consider two scenarios. In one, the probability of lung cancer conditional on smoking is 0.12 and conditional on nonsmoking is 0.08. In the other, these probabilities are 0.00012 and 0.00008. The relative risk in both scenarios is 1.5. Attributable risk is 0.04 in the first scenario and 0.00004 in the second. The first scenario is clearly much more concerning to public health than the second. The relative risk statistic does not differentiate the scenarios, but attributable risk does.

Given that attributable risk is more relevant to public health, it seems odd that epidemiological research has emphasized relative risk rather than attributable risk. Indeed, the practice has long been criticized; see Berkson (1958), Fleiss (1981, Section 6.3), and Hsieh, Manski, and McFadden (1985). The rationale, such as it is, rests on the widespread use in epidemiology of response-based sampling.

The data generated by response-based sampling do not point-identify attributable risk. Fleiss (1981) remarked that (p. 92) "retrospective studies are incapable of providing estimates" of attributable risk. Manski (2007a) proved that these data do yield a bound.

Cornfield (1951) showed that the data from response-based sampling point-identify the odds ratio, defined as $[P(y = 1 | x = 1) / P(y = 0 | x = 1)] / [P(y = 1 | x = 0) / P(y = 0 | x = 0)]$. He also observed that when $P(y = 1)$ is close to zero, a condition called the "rare-disease" assumption, the odds ratio approximately equals relative risk. The rare-disease assumption is credible when considering some diseases. In such cases, epidemiologists have used the odds ratio as a point estimate of relative risk.

Cornfield's finding motivates the widespread epidemiological practice of using response-based samples to estimate the odds ratio and then invoking the rare-disease assumption to interpret the odds ratio as relative risk. Fleiss' (1981) statement that retrospective studies are (p. 92) "valid from the more general point of view of the advancement of knowledge" endorses this practice. Thus, use of the odds ratio to point-estimate relative risk sacrifices relevance for certitude.

2.5.2 Randomized Trials and the Primacy of Internal Validity

As discussed earlier, randomized trials of treatment response have long enjoyed a favored status in medical research. They have increasingly acquired this status in the social sciences. However, as discussed earlier, the treatment response studied in a trial may differ considerably from the response that a clinician or other planner would find of substantive interest.

Seeking to justify the estimates obtained in trials, researchers in public health and the social sciences often cite Donald Campbell, who distinguished between the internal and external validity of studies of treatment response (Campbell and Stanley, 1963; Campbell, 1984). The appeal of randomized trials is their internal validity. Campbell argued that studies of treatment response should be judged first by their internal validity and secondarily by their external validity.

In practice, researchers commonly neglect external validity. Analyses of trials focus on the outcomes measured with the treatments assigned in the study population. Research articles may offer verbal conjectures on external validity in the discussion sections of their papers, but they do not assess external validity quantitatively. Thus, relevance is sacrificed for certitude.

The doctrine of the primacy of internal validity has been extended from randomized trials to observational studies. When considering the design and analysis of observational studies, Campbell and his collaborators recommended that researchers aim to emulate as closely as possible the conditions of a randomized experiment, even if this requires focus on a study population that differs materially from the population of interest.

Among economists, this perspective on observational studies has been championed by those who advocate study of a *local average treatment effect* (LATE). This is defined as the average treatment effect within the subpopulation of persons whose received treatment would be modified by altering the value of an instrumental variable; see Imbens and Angrist (1994) and Angrist, Imbens, and Rubin (1996). Local average treatment effects generally are not quantities of substantive interest; see Manski (1996, 2007a), Deaton (2009), and Heckman and Urzua (2009). Their study has been motivated by the fact that they are point-identified given certain assumptions that are sometimes thought credible.

2.6 PSYCHOLOGICAL RATIONALES FOR INCREDIBLE CERTITUDE

I have repeatedly heard colleagues who advise policy makers assert that expression of incredible certitude is necessary because the consumers of their research are psychologically unable or unwilling to cope with uncertainty. They contend that, if they were to express uncertainty, policy makers would either misinterpret findings or not listen at all.

Colleagues sometimes state that "psychologists have shown" that humans cannot deal with uncertainty, without providing citations. What has research in psychology and related fields shown about the ability and willingness of humans to deal with uncertainty? I will discuss several literatures that relate to this question. They do not provide a basis to conclude that expression of incredible certitude is a psychological necessity.

2.6.1 Intolerance of Uncertainty

Clinical psychologists have studied "intolerance of uncertainty" (IU) as a phenomenon associated with the clinical disorder called "generalized anxiety disorder" (GAD). Buhr and Dugas (2009) define IU as follows (Buhr and Dugas, 2009, p. 216):

> Research has shown that intolerance of uncertainty is a fundamental cognitive process involved in excessive worry and GAD. Intolerance of uncertainty can be viewed as a dispositional characteristic that results from a set of negative beliefs about uncertainty and its implications ... and involves the tendency to react negatively on an emotional, cognitive, and behavioral level to uncertain situations and events.... More specifically, individuals who are intolerant of uncertainty find uncertainty stressful and upsetting, believe that uncertainty is negative and should be avoided, and experience difficulties functioning in uncertainty – inducing situations ... These individuals find many aspects of life difficult to tolerate given the inherent uncertainties of daily living. They tend to feel threatened in the face of uncertainty and engage in futile attempts to control or eliminate uncertainty.

If IU as defined here were a common occurrence, researchers might have good reason to think that expression of incredible certitude is a psychological necessity. However, it does not appear to be common. I am unaware of estimates of the prevalence of IU, but Kessler and Witchen (2002) and Craske and Stein (2016) give estimates of the prevalence of GAD, a disorder that encompasses IU and much else. Relying on epidemiological surveys from various countries, they respectively report that 4–7 or 3–5 percent of persons suffer from GAD at some point in their lives. These estimates, to the extent they are accurate, give upper bounds on the lifetime prevalence of IU. If the lifetime prevalence of IU is no more than 4–7 or 3–5 percent, the disorder is too rare for researchers to conclude that incredible certitude is a psychological necessity.

Moreover, it may be that IU is a treatable disorder. Clinical psychologists have developed "intolerance of uncertainty therapy" (IUT) as a treatment. IUT is defined by Van der Heiden, Muris, and van der Molen (2012) as follows (Van der Heiden et al., 2012, p. 103): "IUT focuses on decreasing anxiety and the tendency to worry by helping patients develop the ability to tolerate, cope with, and even accept uncertainty in their everyday lives." Reporting on a randomized trial comparing IUT with other treatments for GAD, these authors report that IUT yields clinically significant reduction in patient experience of the symptoms of GAD.

2.6.2 Motivated Reasoning Regarding Uncertainty

Now consider the general population; that is, the 93 percent or more of persons who do not have diagnosable IU disorder. Economists studying the general population have commonly maintained a sharp distinction between preferences and beliefs. This distinction is expressed cleanly in the expected utility model. A utility function evaluates the desirability of an action in a specified state of nature. A subjective probability distribution expresses belief about the likelihood of each feasible state.

In contrast, social psychologists commingle preferences and beliefs in various ways. They sometimes use the term *motivated reasoning*; see Kunda (1990). Some closing of the gap between economic and social psychological thinking is evident in recent economic work that formalizes the notion of motivating reasoning. See Akerlof and Dickens (1982), Caplin and Leahy (2001), Brunnermeier and Parker (2005), Gollier and Muermann (2010), and Bénabou and Tirole (2016).

A subset of the work by social psychologists focuses on uncertainty as a motivating force per se. Bar-Anan, Wilson, and Gilbert (2009) put it this way (p. 123): "Uncertainty has both an informational component (a deficit in knowledge) and a subjective component (a feeling of not knowing)." The idea of "a feeling of not knowing" has no interpretation in the expected utility model.

While social psychologists embrace the notion that uncertainty engenders feelings, they have not attained consensus about the nature of the feelings. Citing earlier research, Bar-Anan, Wilson, and Gilbert (2009) initially write that (p. 123), "uncertainty is generally viewed as an aversive state that organisms are motivated to reduce." This view, if accurate, might give researchers an incentive to express certitude to mitigate the negative feelings that persons obtain from uncertainty. However, these authors go on to question the general view, stating (Bar-Anan, Wilson, and Gilbert, 2009, p. 123): "In contrast, we propose an *uncertainty intensification hypothesis*, whereby uncertainty makes unpleasant events more unpleasant (as prevailing theories suggest) but also makes pleasant events more pleasant (contrary to what prevailing theories suggest)." The theme that uncertainty may sometimes be pleasurable is developed further in other papers, including Wilson et al. (2005) and Whitchurch, Wilson, and Gilbert (2011).

2.6.3 Expression of Uncertainty in Probability Judgments

Possible evidence for the psychological view that persons are motivated to reduce uncertainty exists within a body of empirical research that asks subjects to place subjective probabilities on the truth of objectively verifiable statements and subjective distributions on the values of objectively measurable quantities. Some studies have reported findings of overconfidence. Combining evidence across multiple experiments, psychologists have found that reported subjective probabilities that statements are true tend to be higher than the frequency with which they are true. Confidence intervals for real-valued quantities tend to be too narrow. The phenomenon has come to be called "overconfidence bias." Tversky and Kahneman (1974) and Fischhoff and MacGregor (1982) view overconfidence bias as a well-established and widespread phenomenon.

Nevertheless, the literature on overconfidence bias does not provide a rationale for policy analysts to express incredible certitude. Experimental subjects typically do not manifest bias so extreme as to give responses of 0 or 1 when asked to state subjective probabilities of uncertain events. They commonly give responses that express uncertainty, albeit not as much uncertainty as warranted. Moreover, Gigerenzer, Hoffrage, and Kleinbölting (1991) and others argue that research findings on overconfidence bias are fragile. They report that subjects often express more uncertainty when they are asked questions with different wording than psychologists have traditionally used.

Further reason to question the prevalence of overconfidence appears in the large body of economic research that elicits subjective probabilities of future personal events from survey respondents. This literature finds substantial heterogeneity in the expectations that persons hold, including the degree to which they express uncertainty. It does not find that respondents are generally overconfident. Review articles by Manski (2004a, 2018b) describe the emergence of this field and summarize a range of applications. Review articles by Hurd (2009), Armantier et al. (2013), Delavande (2014), and Schotter and Trevino (2014) focus on work measuring probabilistic expectations of older persons, inflation, populations in developing countries, and subjects making decisions in lab experiments. See Chapter 4 for further discussion of economic research measuring probabilistic expectations.

2.7 AS-IF OPTIMIZATION WITH INCREDIBLE CERTITUDE

A possible rationale for incredible certitude is that it may be useful as a device to simplify decision making under uncertainty. The broad idea, following Simon (1955), is that humans are boundedly rational, in the sense of having computational limitations in cognition. Simon argued that it may be burdensome or infeasible for people to make choices with the decision criteria studied in standard decision theory. He suggested that people use approximations or heuristics to reduce decision effort. He called these approximations "satisficing."

As discussed in Chapter 1, standard consequentialist decision theory assumes that a decision maker determines the set of undominated actions and use a reasonable decision criterion to make a choice. However, these tasks may require substantial computational effort. The feasibility of applying these criteria depends on the setting, but they often become less tractable as the sizes of the choice set C and the state space S grow. Maximization of expected utility requires integration of welfare over S and then maximization over C. The maximin and minimax regret criteria require solution of saddle point problems in S and C. The literature in applied decision analysis encounters many cases in which it is infeasible to find exact solutions to these problems, even with modern computers and software. Researchers use numerical or analytical approximations to simplify.

Expressing incredible certitude enables a more extreme simplification than is typically performed in applied decision analysis. One selects a single state of nature, say s^*, and optimizes "as if" this is the actual state. Thus, one solves the problem $\max_{c \in C}(c, s^*)$. This is much simpler than the criteria discussed above.

The question is the quality of the decision yielded by as-if optimization. When it yields a unique solution, the choice is necessarily undominated.

However, it does not seem possible to say anything further without placing more structure on the decision problem. Depending on the circumstances, as-if optimization may yield relatively high or low expected welfare, minimum welfare, or maximum regret.

As-if optimization cannot yield some choices that may be attractive if one recognizes uncertainty. In particular, it cannot yield a choice that involves costly information acquisition. If one acts as if the actual state is s*, there exists no relevant information to acquire.

As-if optimization also cannot yield diversification. As will be discussed in Chapter 5, Manski (2009) studied allocation of two treatments to a population and showed that the minimax regret criterion always yields a diversified allocation under uncertainty. In contrast, as-if optimization does not diversify. It allocates the entire population to the treatment that gives the higher welfare in state s*.

2.7.1 Using As-If Consensus to Coordinate Collective Decisions: Financial Accounting

An idea similar to as-if optimization is to use "as-if consensus" to simplify collective decision making. As-if consensus means that the members of a community agree to accept a conventional certitude, which asserts that some specified state of nature holds. The motivation is that this eliminates coordination failures that may arise if persons recognize uncertainty and deal with it in different ways. I am aware of one context with a compelling argument for as-if consensus. This is in establishment of rules for financial accounting.

The literature on accounting has long been aware of uncertainties in the estimates that accounting systems make; see Brief (1975) for a historical perspective. The question has been how to deal with uncertainty. The answer has been to propose conventions for producing point estimates and seek to have them widely accepted, the result being as-if consensus.

As-if consensus seems essential when formulating rules for transactions. Without it, parties may not agree on the amounts to be transacted. Consider, for example, the use by the federal government of decennial state-by-state Census population estimates in apportionment of the U.S. House of Representatives and allocation of federal funds across the states. It is recognized that Census population estimates may have various forms of error; see, for example, Seeskin and Spencer (2015). Nevertheless, apportionment and fund allocation require that the Census Bureau use some convention to produce a point estimate of each state's population.

The use of point estimates in accounting may be inevitable, but such use does not imply that the producers of these estimates should act as if they are errorless. The conceptual framework for accounting promulgated in Financial Accounting Standards Board (2018) is instructive. The framework calls for accountants to provide a "faithful representation" of financial information, writing (Financial Accounting Standards Board, 2018, p. 4):

> Faithful representation does not mean accurate in all respects. Free from error means there are no errors or omissions in the description of the phenomenon, and the process used to produce the reported information has been selected and applied with no errors in the process. In this context, free from error does not mean perfectly accurate in all respects. For example, an estimate of an unobservable price or value cannot be determined to be accurate or inaccurate. However, a representation of that estimate can be faithful if the amount is described clearly and accurately as being an estimate, the nature and limitations of the estimating process are explained, and no errors have been made in selecting and applying an appropriate process for developing the estimate.

I find admirable the way the board defines "free from error." It does not ask that a financial estimate or prediction be "perfectly accurate in all respects," which would require incredible certitude. It asks the accountant to describe without error "the process used to produce the reported information" and to explain "the limitations of the estimating process." Thus, the board calls on accountants to describe uncertainty transparently rather than hide it.

3

Identification of Treatment Response

Chapter 1 introduced the problem of identification of objective probability distributions. Statistical imprecision in empirical analysis is also relevant to planning, but identification is generally the deeper and more profound source of uncertainty. With the exception of Chapter 6, this book addresses identification problems that arise in planning. Combining available data with credible assumptions rarely yields point identification of social welfare functions in realistic settings. Partial identification is the norm.

Theoretical analysis of identification may become sterile unless it engages actual planning problems. The uncertainties that planners face become most evident when studying realistic decisions. This chapter focuses on identification of treatment response. Chapters 5, 7, 8, and 9 confront identification problems in specific settings of treatment choice.

Readers who want to obtain further understanding of partial identification analysis may draw on multiple sources. I have written three books on the subject. Manski (1995) is intended broadly for social scientists. Manski (2003) is meant for econometric theorists and mathematical statisticians. Intermediate in technical level is Manski (2007a), developed as the text for a first-year PhD course in econometrics that I taught for many years. I also recommend the informative review articles of Tamer (2010) and Molinari (2020).

Before discussing specific identification problems, I explain here some basic concepts of identification analysis. Research on identification studies the conclusions about population features (parameters) of interest that hold when available data are combined with specified assumptions. The generic result is a determination that a feature of interest lies within a set of possibilities, called its *identification region* or *identified set*. The literature has characterized identification regions for various parameters, under alternative assumptions. Those analyzed include means, quantiles, and spread parameters. The assumptions considered aim to be credible when combined with available observational or trial data.

A central theme of my research has been to characterize how the conclusions drawn in empirical research vary with the strength of the assumptions maintained. One may be tempted to maintain strong assumptions, in order to draw strong conclusions. However, there is a tension between the strength of assumptions and their credibility, described in Manski (2003, p. 1) as:

The Law of Decreasing Credibility: The credibility of inference decreases with the strength of the assumptions maintained.

This "Law" implies that analysts face a dilemma as they decide what assumptions to maintain. Stronger assumptions yield conclusions that are more powerful but less credible.

I have called attention to the distinction between refutable and non-refutable assumptions. An assumption is not refutable if the identification region obtained with the evidence obtained in a specified manner is necessarily non-empty. Leading examples are assumptions on distributions of missing data. Missing data being unobserved, available evidence logically cannot refute any assumptions regarding the values of missing data. Assumptions are refutable if combining them with the evidence could conceivably imply an empty identification region. If this occurs, one should conclude that the assumption is incorrect.

I have emphasized that one should not confuse the refutability of an assumption with its credibility. Refutability is a matter of logic. Credibility is a subjective matter. An assumption is refutable if it is inconsistent with some possible configuration of the empirical evidence. It is non-refutable otherwise. Credibility is a property of an assumption and the person contemplating it. An assumption is credible to the degree that someone thinks it so.

The body of research studying identification of treatment response is vast, so I cannot provide a comprehensive description here. I only consider research that aims to inform planning, maintaining credible assumptions. This focus motivates analysis of partial identification of treatment response. I do not discuss research on local average treatment effects, mentioned in Chapter 2. As noted there, this concept sacrifices relevance for certitude. Local average treatment effects generally do not inform

Identification of Treatment Response

planning. Their study has been motivated by the fact that they are point-identified given certain assumptions that are sometimes thought credible.

Section 3.1 presents key findings on partial identification of mean treatment response with observational data, with accompanying illustrations. Section 3.2 considers identification problems that arise with data from randomized trials, focusing on an important practical issue that has escaped notice until recently. Section 3.3 discusses the difficult problem of identification of treatment response with social interactions. Section 3.4 revisits the subject of meta-analysis discussed in Chapter 2, now offering an alternative to the manner in which meta-analysis has been performed to date.

3.1 PARTIAL IDENTIFICATION OF MEAN TREATMENT RESPONSE WITH OBSERVATIONAL DATA

Consider a planner choosing treatments for each member of a population. Let a population member under consideration have observed covariates x. Let T denote a set of alternative treatments. For each $t \in T$, let y(t) denote a real-valued outcome that the person would experience with treatment t. Let treatment be individualistic; that is, the treatment received by one person does not affect the outcomes experienced by others.

Probabilistic prediction of treatment response means that the planner wants to know the conditional distributions $P[y(t)|x]$, $t \in T$. These are distributions of outcomes among persons with covariates x. Utilitarian planners want to learn mean welfare outcomes. Then the quantities of interest are $E[y(t)|x]$, $t \in T$. This section examines identification with observational data. Identification problems that arise with trial data will be discussed later.

3.1.1 Bounding Mean Response with No Knowledge of Counterfactual Outcomes

Manski (1990) derived nonparametric bounds on mean treatment response obtained from an observational study. The bounds suppose that the study examines data from the relevant population, who receive the treatments of interest. Hence, there is no issue of external validity.

I began by asking what conclusions one can draw without any knowledge of counterfactual outcomes. The findings are obtained by contemplating all logically possible values of the counterfactual outcomes. This quantifies what one can learn from observational data without assuming random treatment assignment or any other restriction on treatment selection in the study population.

Suppose that the planner wants to learn E[y(t)|x], t being a treatment of interest. Let z denote the treatment received by a member of the study population. Let P(z = t | x) be the fraction of persons in the study population who receive t, among those with covariates x. Let y denote a person's observed outcome, which is y(t) when z = t. The Law of Iterated Expectations and the fact that y(t)=y when z = t give:

$$(3.1) \quad E\big[y(t)|x\big] = E(y|x, z = t) \cdot P(z = t|x) + E\big[y(t)|x, z \neq t\big] \cdot P(z \neq t|x).$$

Here E[y(t) | x, z = t] = E(y | x, z = t) is mean treatment response within the group who have covariates x and who receive treatment t, whereas E[y(t) | x, z ≠ t] is mean response for those who receive another treatment. Abstracting from statistical imprecision with finite-sample data, an observational study reveals P(z = t | x) and E[y(t) | x, z = t]. E[y(t) | x, z ≠ t] is counterfactual, hence unlearnable from observation.

An informative bound emerges if y(t) has a known bounded range. For simplicity, scale the outcome so that the smallest and largest feasible values are 0 and 1. Then, making no assumptions about treatment selection in the study population, we can conclude that E[y(t) | x] lies in the interval:

$$(3.2) \quad E(y|x, z=t) \cdot P(z=t|x) \leq E\big[y(t)|x\big] \leq E(y|x, z=t) \cdot P(z=t|x) + P(z \neq t|x).$$

The lower and upper bounds are obtained by inserting the polar possibilities for the counterfactual E[y(t) | x, z ≠ t], which are that it equals 0 or 1, respectively. The width of the bound is the fraction of persons in the study population who do not receive treatment t; that is, the fraction for whom y(t) is counterfactual.

An important special case is when y(t) is a binary outcome, taking the value 0 or 1. Then the objective is to learn the conditional probability E[y(t) | x] = P[y(t) = 1 | x]. The bound is:

$$(3.3) \quad P(y=1|x, z=t) \cdot P(z=t|x) \leq P\big[y(t)=1|x\big] \leq P(y=1|x, z=t) \cdot P(z=t|x) + P(z \neq t|x).$$

Suppose that y(t) measures personal welfare with treatment t and that the planner is utilitarian. Then the planner ideally would choose the

Identification of Treatment Response

treatment with the highest mean treatment response. This motivates the planner to determine the signs of the average treatment effects (ATEs) E[y(t)|x] − E[y(t′)|x], where t and t′ are distinct treatments. The lower (upper) bound on this ATE is the lower (upper) bound on E[y(t)|x] minus the upper (lower) bound on E[y(t′)|x]. The width of the ATE bound is the sum of the fractions of the study population for whom each treatment is counterfactual. This width is necessarily at least one, so the lower (upper) bound on the ATE is necessarily less (greater) than or equal to zero. Hence, in the absence of assumptions that restrict counterfactual outcomes, a utilitarian planner cannot determine which treatment is best.

Although observational data alone cannot reveal the optimal treatment, the data yield informative bounds on ATEs. Consider two treatments, say A and B. The bound on the ATE is:

(3.4)
$$E(y \mid x, z = B) \cdot P(z = B \mid x) - E(y \mid x, z = A) \cdot P(z = A \mid x)$$
$$- P(z = A \mid x)$$
$$\leq E[y(B) \mid x] - E[y(A) \mid x] \leq$$
$$E(y \mid x, z = B) \cdot P(z = B \mid x) + P(z = B \mid x)$$
$$- E(y \mid x, z = A) \cdot P(z = A \mid x).$$

When A and B are the only treatments, $P(z = A \mid x) + P(z = B \mid x) = 1$. Hence, the width of bound (3.4) is one. This width is half the width of the logical bound [−1, 1] that would hold if the study data were not available.

3.1.2 Sentencing and Recidivism

To illustrate, I use the Manski and Nagin (1998) analysis of sentencing and recidivism of juvenile offenders in the state of Utah. Judges act as planners, making multiple decisions in the criminal justice system. The question of how judges should sentence convicted juvenile offenders has long been of interest to policy makers and criminologists. We compared the impacts on recidivism of the two main sentencing options available to judges: confinement in residential treatment facilities and diversion to nonresidential treatment.

From its inception, the juvenile justice system has been philosophically different from the adult justice system. Departing from the legal model of the adult system, with its principles of criminal responsibility, punishment, and deterrence, the juvenile justice system has been predicated on a medical model of deviance. The medical model rejects notions of criminal responsibility in favor of the view that deviance/delinquency is symptomatic of an underlying pathology that requires treatment. Reflecting the different purposes of the two systems, the juvenile justice system abandoned the goal of separating the guilty from the innocent and punishing only the former in favor of the goal of determining the needs of the child and directing the treatment resources of the state to ameliorating those needs.

Although the intention of juvenile justice has been the provision of regenerative care for its clients rather than punishment, there has been skepticism as to whether such care was actually being delivered. Critics have contended that in spite of benevolent intentions and therapeutic rhetoric, the juvenile justice system has delivered much the same kinds of punishment and coercion as the adult system. This skepticism was given theoretical guidance in the 1960s with the emergence of the labeling or social reaction school of deviance. According to the labeling school of deviance, there is a constellation of negative consequences that may flow from official processing of an actor as deviant, even with a therapeutic intent. For example, confinement in a residential facility may make it more likely that the juvenile thinks of himself as deviant and may exclude the person from the normal routines of life and normal opportunities.

Hence, there has been controversy as to whether residential confinement tends to reduce or exacerbate juvenile deviant behavior. Tittle (1980, p. 259) concluded that "not a single good test of either of the major propositions of labeling theory exists in the literature." Researchers have generally found that offenders who are subjected to formal judicial processing tend to have higher recidivism rates than ones who are treated informally (Smith and Paternoster, 1990). While this finding accords with the prediction of labeling theory, it may also be an artifact of treatment selection. Smith and Paternoster (1990, p. 1111) observed: "high risk youth are more likely to receive more severe dispositions. Thus, those individuals assigned more severe sanctions would be more likely to commit new offenses whether or not any relationship existed between juvenile court disposition and future offending."

With this background, Manski and Nagin (1998) examined the outcomes of juvenile sentencing in Utah. We took the outcome of interest to be recidivism; that is, future offending. Recidivism may not be the only outcome that a judge considers when making sentencing decisions, but it usually is a key consideration.

Identification of Treatment Response

The feasible treatments were alternative sentencing options. Judges in Utah have had the discretion to order various sentences for juvenile offenders. Some offenders have been given sentences with no residential confinement (treatment A) and others have been sentenced to confinement (treatment B). A possible alternative policy would be to replace judicial discretion with a mandate that all offenders in Utah be confined. Another would be to mandate that no offenders be confined.

We defined the outcome of interest to be whether an offender commits a new offense in the two-year period following sentencing. This is a binary outcome, with no new offense indicating that treatment succeeds and commission of a new offense indicating that it fails. The average treatment effect is the difference between treatments A and B in their probabilities of success.

We obtained data on the sentences received and the recidivism outcomes realized by all male offenders in Utah who were born from 1970 through 1974 and who were convicted of offenses before they reached age sixteen. The Utah data reveal that 11 percent of the offenders were sentenced to confinement and that 23 percent of these persons did not offend again in the two years following sentencing. The remaining 89 percent were sentenced to non-confinement and 41 percent of these persons did not offend again.

If one were to assume that judges randomly sentence offenders to the two treatments, the observed outcome data would imply that the success probability for confinement is 0.23 and for non-confinement is 0.41. Hence, the ATE would be −0.18, indicating that non-confinement is superior to confinement. However, it is not credible to assume that judges sentence randomly. Moreover, no other assumption about judicial sentencing behavior is widely accepted by criminologists. This motivates our computation of bounds that assume no knowledge of counterfactual outcomes.

The lower bound on the success probability for treatment B is 0.03 and the upper bound is 0.92. The bound has width 0.89 because 0.89 of the offenders in the study population were not confined. We do not know what the recidivism of these persons would have been if they had been confined. Analogously, the lower bound on the success probability for treatment A is 0.36 and the upper bound is 0.47, a bound of width 0.11. Thus, the data reveal much more about recidivism with mandatory non-confinement than with mandatory confinement. The bound on the ATE is [−0.44, 0.56], whose width must be 1 as explained earlier.

3.1.3 Instrumental Variables

Assuming nothing about counterfactual outcomes provides a logical starting point for research on treatment response. Yet researchers understandably would like to draw stronger conclusions than those implied by the data alone. For most of the twentieth century, econometric research brought to bear assumptions that are strong enough to point-identify average treatment effects and other features of treatment response. But the cost in credibility was high.

Research on partial identification explores the vast middle ground between making no assumptions and ones that yield point identification. The goal is to illuminate the trade-off alluded to in the *Law of Decreasing Credibility*: Stronger assumptions yield conclusions that are more powerful but less credible. Manski (2007a, Chapters 7 and 9) presents findings on the identifying power of a spectrum of middle-ground assumptions.

An especially prominent subject of study has been the identifying power of assumptions that use an *instrumental variable* (IV). An IV is an observable covariate whose value varies across a study population. The term *instrumental variable* originated with Reiersol (1945), who thought of such a covariate as an instrument or tool that may help to identify an object of interest. Reiersol and other econometricians of his time used IVs in combination with other assumptions to point-identify linear structural equation systems. See Goldberger (1972) for an informative review of the early literature.

Modern econometric research uses IVs to help address many identification problems, including identification of treatment response. Whatever the application may be, it is important to understand that observation of an IV does not per se carry any implications for inference. It is useful only when combined with an assumption that has identifying power. Empirical researchers often ask whether some covariate is or is not a "valid instrument" in an application of interest. The expression "valid instrument" is imprecise because it focuses attention on the covariate used as the IV, without reference to the accompanying assumption. It would be better to ask whether an assumption using an instrumental variable is credible.

A particularly common assumption using an IV supposes that different subpopulations of a study population experienced different processes of treatment selection but share the same distribution of treatment response, or at least the same mean response. For example, when studying patient care, one might assume that patient subpopulations treated by different groups of clinicians have the same distribution of treatment response, or at least the same mean response. This assumption may be credible in some studies of geographic variation in clinical practice. Then the IV is the geographic area in which a patient is treated.

A similar example arose in the Manski and Nagin (1998) study of juvenile sentencing. In that setting, treatment selection may vary across judges in the state of Utah. The Utah juvenile justice system is divided into districts composed of geographically contiguous counties. Each district has different judges and, perhaps, different sentencing norms. One might assume that treatment response does not vary from district to district. That is, one might assume that if all districts were to have policies of mandatory residential (or nonresidential) treatment, all districts would experience the same recidivism probability. This assumption may or may not be realistic.

Whatever the application may be, an assumption that different subpopulations of a study population share the same distribution of treatment response, or the same mean response, generates what is now called an *intersection bound* on treatment response. The basic idea is straightforward. Consideration of each subpopulation separately yields a bound that uses no knowledge of treatment allocation, as described earlier. The assumption of a common distribution of treatment response across subpopulations implies that the common distribution must simultaneously lie in each of these no-assumptions bounds. In other words, it must lie in the intersection of the bounds. The same reasoning applies if one assumes only the same mean response across subpopulations.

Study of intersection bounds obtained with observational data was initiated in Manski (1990), where I assumed that mean treatment response is common across subpopulations. Then the lower intersection bound is the maximum of the lower bounds obtained using no assumptions and the upper bound is the minimum of the upper bounds obtained this way. Intersection bounds are more complex if one assumes that the entire distribution of treatment response is common across subpopulations. Study of this case was initiated by Balke and Pearl (1997), with subsequent contributions by Manski (2003) and Kitagawa (2021).

It is instructive to formalize the simple bound assuming common mean treatment response across subpopulations. Let the IV be denoted v and let it take one of K values, denoted $v_1, \ldots, v_K$. Then the assumption applied to treatment t is:

(3.5) $$E[y(t) | x] = E[y(t) | x, v_k], \quad k = 1, \ldots, K.$$

The resulting intersection bound based on Equation (3.2) is:

$$(3.6) \quad \max_{k=1,\ldots,K} E(y \mid x, v_k, z = t) \cdot P(z = t \mid x, v_k) \le E\big[y(t) \mid x\big] \le$$
$$\min_{k=1,\ldots,K} E(y \mid x, v_k, z = t) \cdot P(z = t \mid x, v_k)$$
$$+ P(z \ne t \mid x, v_k).$$

The identifying power of assuming common mean treatment response can range from point identification of $E[y(t)|x]$ to no power at all, depending on the specifics of the case. An obvious sufficient condition for point identification holds if, for some value of k, all persons with IV value v_k receive treatment t; thus, $P(z = t \mid x, v_k) = 1$. This case occurs in a classical trial, where subjects are randomly assigned to treatments, and all comply with the assignment. Let the treatments be labelled t = 1, ..., K. Then v = z and $P(z = t \mid x, v_t) = P(z = t \mid x, z = t) = 1$.

Assumption (3.5) has no identifying power if v is statistically independent of the pair [y(t), z], conditional on x. Then the quantities maximized (minimized) on the left-hand (right-hand) side of (3.6) are all the same. Hence, their intersection is the same as the bound obtained using the data alone. This happens when one uses a random number generator to assign a value of v to each member of the population. A covariate generated by drawing random numbers is necessarily statistically independent of [y(t), z] and, thus, has no identifying power.

Bound (3.6) may be empty. That is, the lower bound may be larger than the upper bound. If this occurs, one can conclude that the assumption of common mean treatment response is incorrect. Hence, the assumption is refuted.

The Mortality Effects of Swan–Ganz Catheterization

I use a study by Bhattacharya et al. (2012) to illustrate a setting in which an IV was informative. The Swan–Ganz catheter is a sensory device placed in an artery of cardiac patients in the intensive care unit (ICU), the aim being to guide therapy. Catheterization has been a standard practice since the 1970s. However, a series of observational studies from the 1980s onward have reported that its use increases patient mortality, a matter of much clinical importance. An influential study by Connors et al. (1996) examined data on mortality outcomes among a population of patients admitted to the ICU and concluded that patients who receive Swan–Ganz catheterization during their first day in the ICU are more likely to die a week or a half year after their admission.

Identification of Treatment Response 75

To point-identify treatment response, Connors et al. (1996) assumed that patients are assigned randomly to catheterization or non-catheterization, conditional on certain patient attributes. The credibility of this assumption is questionable. Clinicians in the ICU select which patients do and do not receive catheterization. Clinicians may base their decisions on mortality-relevant patient attributes that they observe but that were not considered in the Connors et al. study.

With this concern in mind, Bhattacharya et al. (2012) re-analyzed the Connors et al. data, using an IV and other assumptions to bound the effect of Swan–Ganz catheterization on mortality outcomes. Their analysis permitted the possibility of unobserved differences across patients who do and do not receive catheterization.

The authors used period during the week (weekday v. weekend) as an IV for administration of catheterization. They observed that clinician propensity to catheterize patients varies during the week, with catheterization occurring less frequently on weekends. They assumed that mean treatment response is the same for patients admitted to the ICU on a weekday or during the weekend.

Applying the IV identification analysis of Manski (1990), they found that the IV assumption yields an informative bound on the average effect of catheterization on mortality. However, the bound was not narrow enough to reveal the sign of the average effect. To achieve a tighter bound, the authors also assumed a nonparametric selection model that jointly explains clinician choice of treatment and patient mortality. Combining the IV assumption with the selection model, they found that catheterization increases mortality at thirty days after catheterization and beyond. This finding is clinically informative if one finds credible the IV assumption and the selection model that the authors used in their analysis.

3.1.4 Monotone Instrumental Variables

The IV assumptions discussed so far assert equality of distributions or means across different values of the instrumental variable. Empirical researchers often find these equalities too strong to be credible. There is therefore reason to consider weakening them in ways that may enhance credibility while preserving some identifying power. One way to do this is to change the equalities into weak inequalities. I continue to focus on mean treatment response for simplicity. I discuss monotone instrumental variable assumptions here and generalize further to bounded variation assumptions in Section 3.2.

Manski and Pepper (2000) posed and studied the identifying power of *monotone instrumental variable* (MIV) assumptions. An MIV assumption takes the IV to be a real-valued or otherwise ordered variable, say with ordering $v_k \leq v_{k+1}$, $k = 1, \ldots, K-1$. One replaces the equalities in assumption (3.5) by the weak inequalities:

(3.7) $\quad E[y(t) \mid x, v_k] \leq E[y(t) \mid x, v_{k+1}]$, $k = 1, \ldots, K-1$.

We showed that the resulting identification region for $E[y(t) \mid x]$ is the interval:

(3.8)
$$\sum_{k=1,\ldots,K} P(v = v_k) \max_{k' \leq k} E(y \mid x, v_{k'}, z = t) \cdot P(z = t \mid x, v_{k'})$$
$$\leq E[y(t) \mid x] \leq$$
$$\sum_{k=1,\ldots,K} P(v = v_k) \min_{k' \geq k} E(y \mid x, v_{k'}, z = t) \cdot P(z = t \mid x, v_{k'})$$
$$+ P(z \neq t \mid x, v_{k'}).$$

This bound is a subset of the one obtained using the data alone and is a superset of the one obtained under assumption (3.5).

Recall the special case of assumption (3.5) that occurs in a classical trial, where $v = z$. This assumption is rarely credible in observational studies, where treatments are self-selected or otherwise purposefully chosen rather than randomly assigned. However, it sometimes is credible to assume *monotone treatment selection* (MTS); that is, treatments are ordered $(1, \ldots, K)$ and persons who receive larger treatments have weakly larger mean treatment response. Formally, the MTS assumption is:

(3.9) $\quad E[y(t) \mid x, z = k] \leq E[y(t) \mid x, z = k+1]$, $k = 1, \ldots, K-1$.

Manski and Pepper (2000) showed that bound (3.8) then reduces to the simple inequality:

(3.10)
$$E(y \mid x, z = t) \cdot P(z \geq t \mid x) \leq E[y(t) \mid x]$$
$$\leq E(y \mid x, z = t) \cdot P(z \leq t \mid x) + P(z > t \mid x).$$

To illustrate, we considered the response of wages to schooling. In this setting, assumption (3.5) asserts that persons who select different levels of schooling have the same mean wage functions. The MTS assumption asserts that persons who select higher levels of schooling have weakly higher mean wage functions than do those who select lower levels of schooling. Many economic models of schooling choice and wage determination predict that persons with higher ability have higher mean wage functions and choose higher levels of schooling than do persons with lower ability. The MTS Assumption is consistent with these models, but assumption (3.5) is not.

3.1.5 Monotone Treatment Response

Another monotonicity assumption, different from MTS, is *monotone treatment response* (MTR), posed and studied in Manski (1997). Here treatments are ordered, say from smaller to larger values, and one assumes that for each person j and all treatment pairs (s, t),

(3.11) $$t \geq s \implies y_j(t) \geq y_j(s).$$

Assumption MTR permits each person to have a distinct response function. It only requires that all response functions be weakly monotone. While (3.11) supposes that response functions are weakly increasing, an analogous assumption obviously may suppose response is weakly decreasing. Considering the increasing version (3.11), I showed that the assumption implies this sharp bound on mean treatment response for each treatment t:

(3.12) $$E(y \mid x, z \leq t) P(z \leq t \mid x) \leq E[y(t) \mid x] \\ \leq E(y \mid x, z \geq t) P(z \geq t \mid x) + P(z < t \mid x).$$

It is easy to see that an MTR assumption is not refutable. For each person j, only one point on the response function $y_j(\cdot)$ is observable, namely $y_j \equiv y_j(z_j)$. Hence, the empirical evidence is necessarily consistent with the hypothesis that $y_j(\cdot)$ is weakly increasing. For example, the evidence is consistent with the hypothesis that every response function is flat, with $\{y_j(t) = y_j, t \in T, \text{all } j\}$.

There are many settings in which one may be confident that response is monotone. Consumer theory suggests that, ordinarily, the demand for a product weakly decreases as a function of the product's price. The theory of production holds that the output of a product weakly increases as a function of each input into the production process. Human capital theory conjectures that the wage that a worker earns weakly increases as a function of the worker's years of schooling. In Chapter 8, I will use an MTR assumption when studying vaccination, as it is credible to assume that the population rate of illness with an infectious disease falls as the rate of vaccination rises.

It is important to understand that the MTS and MTR assumptions differ from one another but are not mutually exclusive. Consider the variation of wages with schooling. It is common to hear the verbal assertion that "wages increase with schooling." The MTS and MTR assumptions interpret this statement in different ways. The MTS interpretation is that persons who select higher levels of schooling have weakly higher mean wage functions than do those who select lower levels of schooling. The MTR interpretation is that each person's wage function is weakly increasing in potential years of schooling. Thus, the MTS and MTR interpretations of the statement "wages increase with schooling" are distinct and both are credible. Manski and Pepper (2000) showed that combining the two assumptions has considerable identifying power.

3.2 PARTIAL IDENTIFICATION OF MEAN TREATMENT RESPONSE WITH DATA FROM TRIALS WITH LIMITED INTERNAL VALIDITY

Performance and analysis of randomized trials has been strongly recommended as a methodology to point-identify treatment response, particularly in medical research. Yet many identification problems arise when research attempts to interpret trial evidence and use it in planning. In Chapter 2, I called attention to wishful extrapolation from clinical trials to patient care; that is, unwarranted assertions of external validity. Trials also often have limited internal validity, implying further identification problems. I discuss three prominent problems here.

3.2.1 Missing Outcome or Covariate Data

One well-appreciated difficulty is missing outcome or covariate data. Outcomes are missing when subjects drop out of trials before their outcomes are recorded. Covariate data may be missing because subjects may report their backgrounds incompletely or due to incompleteness in administrative records.

Researchers commonly assume that data are missing at random, in the sense that the observability of an outcome or covariate is statistically independent of its value. This done, researchers often report findings only for trial subjects with complete data, discarding those with incomplete data. Or they impute missing values and report findings for all subjects, acting as if the imputed values of missing data are actual values. It is rare for researchers to discuss the credibility of the assumptions they make.

Horowitz and Manski (2000) analyzed the identification problem stemming from missing outcome or covariate data. We focused on cases in which outcomes are binary (success or failure) and derived sharp bounds on success probabilities without imposing any assumptions about the distribution of the missing data. To illustrate, we applied the findings to data from a trial comparing treatments for hypertension. I summarize here.

Missing Data in a Trial Comparing Treatments for Hypertension

Materson et al. (1993) reported on a trial comparing treatments for hypertension sponsored by the U.S. Department of Veteran Affairs (DVA). Male veteran patients at fifteen DVA hospitals were randomly assigned to one of six antihypertensive drug treatments or to placebo. The trial had two phases. In the first, the dosage that brought diastolic blood pressure (DBP) below 90 mm Hg was determined. In the second, it was determined whether DBP could be kept below 95 mm Hg for a period. Treatment was defined to be successful if DBP < 90 mm Hg on two consecutive measurement occasions in the first phase and DBP ≤ 95 mm Hg in the second. Treatment was deemed unsuccessful otherwise. Thus, the measured outcome was binary, with y = 1 if the criterion for success was met and y = 0 otherwise. The authors recommended that clinicians treating hypertension should consider this outcome as well as patient's quality of life and the cost of treatment.

Materson et al. examined how treatment response varies with the race and age of the patient. There were no missing data on these attributes. We obtained the trial data and used them to examine how treatment response varies with another covariate that did have missing data. This was the biochemical indicator renin response, taking the values (low, medium, high), which had previously been studied as a factor that might be associated with successful treatment. Renin-response was supposed to be measured at the time of randomization, but data were missing for some subjects in the trial.

Materson et al. interpreted attrition from the trial as lack of success; that is, in the absence of outcome data they imputed the value y = 0. We instead viewed subjects who leave the trial as having unknown outcomes. We computed sharp bounds on the success probabilities for the seven treatments without imposing assumptions on the distribution of missing data. Rather than report the bounds on the success probabilities directly, we reported the implied bounds on average treatment effects, which measure the efficacy of each treatment relative to the placebo. Manski (2008) reported the estimates of the bounds on the success probabilities themselves. Tables 3.1 and 3.2 respectively present the pattern of

TABLE 3.1 *Missing Data in the DVA Hypertension Trial*

Treatment	Number Randomized	Observed Successes	None Missing	Missing Only y	Missing Only x	Missing (y, x)
1	188	100	173	4	11	0
2	178	106	158	11	9	0
3	188	96	169	6	13	0
4	178	110	159	5	13	1
5	185	130	164	6	14	1
6	188	97	164	12	10	2
7	187	57	178	3	6	0

TABLE 3.2 *Bounds on Success Probabilities Conditional on Renin Response*

Renin Response	Treatment						
	1	2	3	4	5	6	7
Low	[0.54, 0.61]	[0.52, 0.62]	[0.43, 0.53]	[0.58, 0.66]	[0.66, 0.76]	[0.54, 0.65]	[0.29, 0.32]
Medium	[0.47, 0.62]	[0.60, 0.74]	[0.53, 0.68]	[0.50, 0.69]	[0.68, 0.85]	[0.41, 0.65]	[0.27, 0.32]
High	[0.28, 0.50]	[0.64, 0.86]	[0.56, 0.75]	[0.63, 0.84]	[0.55, 0.78]	[0.34, 0.59]	[0.28, 0.40]

missing covariate and outcome data and the estimated bounds on success probabilities.

To focus on the identification problem, ignore sampling imprecision in the estimates of the bounds. Observe that even though the findings are bounds rather than precise success probabilities, many bounds are sufficiently narrow to enable one to conclude that certain treatments are dominated; that is, surely inferior to others. For patients with low renin response, treatments 1, 2, 3, 4, 6, and 7 are all dominated by treatment 5, which has the greatest lower bound (0.66). For patients with medium renin response, treatments 1, 3, 6, and 7 are dominated by treatment 5, which again has the greatest lowest bound (0.68). For patients with high renin response, treatments 1, 6, and 7 are dominated by treatment 2, which has the greatest lowest bound (0.64). Thus, without imposing any assumptions on the distribution of missing data, a clinician can reject treatments 1, 6, and 7 for all patients, reject treatment 3 for patients with medium renin response, and determine that treatment 5 is optimal for patients with low renin response.

The analysis of Horowitz and Manski (2000) showed that missing data in the DVA trial lowers its internal validity but does not eliminate it. Materson et al. (1993) may or may not have been correct to assume that treatment failed for all patients with missing outcomes. Data on renin response may or may not have been missing at random. The bounds on success probabilities give the conclusions that hold without making these or other assumptions about the missing data. Thus, the bounds quantify the degree to which the trial was internally valid, despite the fact that some data were missing.

3.2.2 Partial Compliance

Another well-appreciated difficulty is interpretation of trial data when some subjects do not comply with randomly assigned treatments. A participant in a trial is said to comply with treatment assignment if the treatment received is the same as the treatment assigned. Noncompliance occurs otherwise.

Researchers often assume that the groups of subjects who do and do not comply have the same distribution of treatment response. Compliance is then said to be random. Given this assumption, the observable outcome distribution for subjects who comply with a particular treatment assignment is the same as the outcome distribution that would occur if the entire population were to receive this treatment. However, the credibility of this assumption is often suspect. Compliance is ordinarily a choice. There is often reason to think that persons who choose to comply and not comply have different distributions of treatment response.

To understand the implications of noncompliance for identification of treatment response, it is useful to conceptualize a trial with K treatment arms as research in which K observational studies have been performed and the outcomes observed. For each $k = 1, \ldots, K$, study k is intended to yield evidence on the outcomes of subjects who are randomly assigned to treatment k. If all subjects comply with treatment, then observation of the outcomes in study k point-identifies the distribution of treatment response with this treatment. Observation of the outcomes in the other $K - 1$ studies yields no information about treatment response with treatment k.

If some subjects do not comply, the situation is more complex. When a subject assigned to treatment k does not comply, his outcome with treatment k is missing but his outcome with a different treatment is observed. When a subject assigned to a treatment other than k does not comply and this person actually receives treatment k, his outcome with treatment k is observed. Despite the presence of noncompliance, randomization of treatment assignment makes it credible to view treatment assignment as an instrumental variable when studying identification of treatment response.

Robins (1989) initiated study of this identification problem, assuming equality of mean treatment response across groups of subjects assigned to different treatments. Thus, he posed and studied the same assumption (3.5) as in Manski (1990), but he applied it to trial data with partial compliance rather than to observational data. Balke and Pearl (1997) examined the compliance problem afresh and recognized that random assignment of treatments implies restrictions not only on mean treatment response but on the joint distribution of treatment response; that is, on $P[y(k), k = 1, ..., K | x]$. Considering the special case with a binary outcome and two treatments, they showed that the identification region for mean treatment response using the full force of randomized assignment is sometimes smaller than the bound obtained by Robins. This is a subtle finding, subsequently generalized by Kitagawa (2021).

The Illinois Unemployment Insurance Experiment

To illustrate partial compliance, I will describe the Illinois Unemployment Insurance Experiment carried out in 1984–1985. Newly unemployed persons were randomly assigned to conventional unemployment insurance (UI) or to UI augmented by a wage subsidy paid to the employer if the unemployed person should find a full-time job within eleven weeks. An outcome of interest was whether an unemployed person found a full-time job within this time period.

Compliance was an issue because participation in the subsidy-augmented version of UI could not be compelled. On the other hand, participation in conventional UI could be compelled, as the subsidy-augmented version was not available to these subjects. In practice, 32 percent of those assigned UI with the wage subsidy did not comply, choosing instead to receive conventional UI. See Dubin and Rivers (1993).

Suppose that the objective is to predict the outcomes that would occur if all unemployed persons were to receive the version of UI with the wage subsidy. The outcome of policy interest is binary, being success or failure in finding a new job within eleven weeks. The experiment revealed these outcomes for the 68 percent of subjects who complied with assignment to UI with the wage subsidy. It did not reveal the relevant outcomes for the 32 percent who chose not to comply. All subjects assigned to conventional UI had to comply. Hence, in the absence of assumptions about the nature of noncompliance, the experimental data yield an interval prediction of success in job search that has width 0.32.

Researchers analyzing experiments with partial compliance often assume that compliance is random. There is reason to question the assumption's credibility in the Illinois UI setting. It has been suggested that unemployed workers may have viewed the wage subsidy as stigmatizing. Hence, among subjects assigned the wage subsidy, those believing that they could find a job without the subsidy would choose to comply less often than those thinking their job prospects were dim.

Intention-to-Treat
Researchers analyzing data from trials with partial compliance sometimes do not attempt to predict outcomes for a policy that mandates a particular treatment. Instead, they specify study objectives that make noncompliance logically impossible.

Consider the common situation where A is a status quo treatment available to anyone in the population, while B is an innovation available only to experimental subjects assigned to this treatment. Rather than predict the outcomes of a policy that mandates treatment B, researchers sometimes seek to predict the outcomes of a policy offering persons the option to choose B. They then interpret randomized assignment to treatment B as giving a subject an offer of B rather than mandating this treatment. This makes noncompliance logically impossible. The term *intention-to-treat* is used to describe an offer of a treatment.

Viewing treatment group B as receiving an offer rather than a mandate does not solve the original prediction problem but rather dismisses it by redefining the study objective. The original objective was to learn the outcomes that would occur if everyone were to actually receive treatment B. The redefined objective is to learn the outcomes that would occur if everyone were to receive an offer of this treatment, which they may either accept or reject.

To illustrate, consider again the Illinois UI experiment. Woodbury and Spiegelman (1987) described the experiment as randomly assigning unemployed persons to conventional UI or to an offer of UI with a wage subsidy, allowing the unemployed person to choose between conventional UI and the wage-subsidy augmented UI. Hence, they were unconcerned with compliance and analyzed the experimental data in the classical manner. This contrasts with the Dubin and Rivers (1993) study mentioned above, which paid considerable attention to noncompliance.

The findings reported by Woodbury and Spiegelman differ from those reported by Dubin and Rivers. In part, this is because the authors had different objectives. Woodbury and Spiegelman wanted to predict the outcomes that would occur if unemployed persons were permitted to choose between conventional UI and a program with a wage subsidy. Dubin and Rivers wanted to predict the outcomes that would occur if conventional UI were replaced by a program with a wage subsidy.

3.2.3 Identification of Personalized Treatment Response with Trial-Reported Findings on Binary Subgroups

I now summarize the study by Li, Litvin, and Manski (2023) of another identification problem with trial data. This one stems from conventions in reporting findings rather than difficulties in the performance of trials.

Medical journals have adhered to a reporting practice that seriously limits the usefulness of published trial findings. Clinicians commonly observe many patient covariates and seek to use this information to personalize treatment choices. Yet standard summaries of trial findings only partition subjects into broad subgroups, typically into binary categories.

Illustration: Zinman et al. (2015) studied the effects of the drug empagliflozin on cardiovascular morbidity and mortality in patients with type 2 diabetes at high cardiovascular risk. The investigators randomly assigned subjects to receive empagliflozin or placebo once daily and compared the between-group incidence of the primary composite outcome, which included cardiovascular death from cardiovascular causes, nonfatal myocardial infarction, and nonfatal stroke. Following convention, the authors reported multiple subgroup analyses defined by categorical covariates, most of which were binary. These included sex, age, and high or low glycated hemoglobin. In practice, a diabetologist knows values for many patient covariates. Learning the probability of the outcome for a patient with a specified combination of covariates would facilitate decision making. However, the journal article only reported findings on the frequency of the outcome in each covariate category separately. ∎

Concerned with the standard reporting practice, Li, Litvin, and Manski (2023) studied the problem of identification of mean treatment outcomes $E[y(t)|x]$. In our work, t is a treatment administered in a randomized trial and y(t) is a bounded real-valued treatment outcome, whose range is normalized to take values in the interval [0, 1]. The covariate vector

$x = (x_1, x_2, \ldots, x_K)$ has length K, each component being a binary categorical variable.

The trial findings reported in research articles commonly provide estimates of the conditional mean outcomes $E[y(t) | x_k = 0]$ and $E[y(t) | x_k = 1]$, $k = 1, \ldots, K$. Adapting the regression terminology of Goldberger (1991) and Cross and Manski (2002), we referred to $E[y(t) | x]$ and $E[y(t) | x_k]$ as *long* and *short* mean outcomes. Articles commonly also report the fraction of the study sample having each covariate value. These fractions provide estimates of $P(x_k)$, $k = 1, \ldots, K$.

Identification of Long Mean Outcomes Using Short Trial Findings

The identification problem is to determine what can be deduced about $E[y(t) | x]$ and $P(x)$, given knowledge of $[E[y(t) | x_k = 0], E[y(t) | x_k = 1], P(x_k)]$, $k = 1, \ldots, K$. To focus on identification, we abstracted from sampling imprecision and supposed that reported trial estimates are accurate.

To begin, we listed inequalities satisfied by $E[y(t) | x]$ and $P(x)$. A covariate vector may be relevant to treatment only if it occurs with positive probability. Hence, $E[y(t) | x]$ satisfy the inequalities:

(3.13a) $$0 \le E\big[y(t) | x = \xi\big] \le 1, \; \xi \in \{0, 1\}^K,$$

and we supposed that:

(3.13b) $$0 < P(x = \xi), \; \xi \in \{0, 1\}^K.$$

Next consider the relationship between short and long mean treatment outcomes. Let x_{-k} be the $(K-1)$-dimensional sub-vector of x that excludes x_k. The Law of Iterated Expectations and Bayes Theorem give 2K equations relating short to long mean outcomes:

(3.14a) $$\begin{aligned} & E\big[y(t) | x_k = 0\big] \cdot P(x_k = 0) \\ & = \sum_{\xi_{-k} \in \{0, 1\}^{K-1}} E\big[y(t) | x_k = 0, \; x_{-k} = \xi_{-k}\big] P(x_k = 0, \; x_{-k} = \xi_{-k}), \end{aligned}$$

(3.14b) $$\begin{aligned} & E\big[y(t) | x_k = 1\big] \cdot P(x_k = 1) \\ & = \sum_{\xi_{-k} \in \{0, 1\}^{K-1}} E\big[y(t) | x_k = 1, \; x_{-k} = \xi_{-k}\big] P(x_k = 1, \; x_{-k} = \xi_{-k}). \end{aligned}$$

The Law of Total Probability gives K equations relating marginal to joint probabilities of covariate values and one more from the fact that joint probabilities sum to one. These equations are:

$$P(x_k = 1) = \sum_{\xi_{-k} \in \{0,1\}^{K-1}} P(x_k = 1, x_{-k} = \xi_{-k}), \quad (3.15a)$$

$$1 = \sum_{\xi \in \{0,1\}^K} P(x = \xi). \quad (3.15b)$$

Reported summaries of trial findings reveal the left-hand sides of Equations (3.14–3.15). The quantities $E[y(t) \mid x]$ and $P(x)$ on the right-hand sides are not reported in journal articles. Inequalities (3.13) and Equations (3.14–3.15) express all of the available information about $E[y(t) \mid x]$ and $P(x)$. Thus, the identification region for $\{E[y(t) \mid x], P(x)\}$ is the set of values that solve (3.13–3.15). Equations (3.14–3.15) comprise $3K + 1$ equations in 2^{K+1} unknowns.

Analysis of identification of long average treatment effects is a simple extension of the above. Whereas we stated inequalities (3.13a) and Equations (3.14) for a specified treatment t, analogous conditions hold for any other treatment t'. Inequalities (3.13b) and Equations (3.15) hold as stated when considering t'. Thus, the feasible values of $E[y(t) \mid x] - E[y(t') \mid x]$ are those that solve (3.13–3.15) and the analogous versions applied to t'.

Although the above identification analysis is logically simple, computation of identification regions is complex. Equations (3.14a–3.14b) are nonlinear, with multiplicative terms $E[y(t) \mid x = \xi] \cdot P(x = \xi)$, $\xi \in \{0,1\}^K$. It follows that the identification region for $\{E[y(t) \mid x], P(x)\}$ is not convex. Rather than take on the formidable problem of computing the joint identification region for $\{E[y(t) \mid x = \xi], P(x) = \xi\}$ for all values of (t, ξ), we specified a value of (t, ξ) and addressed the still challenging but more tractable problem of computing sharp lower and upper bounds for the scalar $E[y(t) \mid x = \xi]$. This task entails minimizing and maximizing $E[y(t) \mid x = \xi]$ subject to the constraints imposed by (3.13–3.15).

Bounded-Variation Assumptions

We performed computations with a spectrum of short trial findings and found that the implied bounds on long mean outcomes are typically very wide. Sometimes they are so wide as to be essentially uninformative. We therefore strongly cautioned against wishful extrapolation from reported short trial findings to long mean outcomes. Nevertheless, we did not conclude that short findings are useless to medical decision making.

The bounds on long mean outcomes can be tightened if one combines reported trial findings with credible assumptions having identifying power. Such assumptions may take many forms. We brought to bear *bounded-variation* assumptions. These are types of IV assumptions that have previously been used to add identifying power in other settings, including Manski (2018a), Manski and Pepper (2018), and Manski, Tambur, and Gmeiner (2019). Whereas IV assumptions have traditionally supposed that mean treatment response is equal across subpopulations, bounded variation assumptions weaken this requirement and suppose that the means lie within a specified distance. The MIV assumptions discussed earlier are a type of bounded-variation assumption.

The simplest bounded-variation assumptions place a priori bounds directly on long mean treatment outcomes, expressing expert judgment about the potential range in which they may take values. Formally, one may think it credible to assume that:

(3.16) $\quad a(t, \xi) \leq E[y(t) | x = \xi] \leq b(t, \xi),$

where $a(t, \xi)$ and $b(t, \xi)$ are specified constants.

Or one may think it credible to bound the degree to which mean outcomes vary across persons with different covariates. One may express this as a bound on the absolute or relative difference between mean outcomes. Such bounds have the form:

(3.17) $\quad c(t, \xi, \xi') \leq E[y(t) | x = \xi] - E[y(t) | x = \xi'] \leq d(t, \xi, \xi'),$

(3.18) $\quad e(t, \xi, \xi') \leq E[y(t) | x = \xi] / E[y(t) | x = \xi'] \leq f(t, \xi, \xi'),$

where (ξ, ξ') are distinct covariate values and $[c(t, \xi, \xi'), d(t, \xi, \xi'), e(t, \xi, \xi'), f(t, \xi, \xi')]$ are specified constants.

Or one may think it credible to bound the degree to which mean outcomes vary across treatments, expressing this as a bound on ATEs or on relative risks across treatments. Such bounds have the form:

(3.19) $\quad g(t, t', \xi) \leq E[y(t) | x = \xi] - E[y(t') | x = \xi] \leq h(t, t', \xi),$

(3.20) $\quad i(t, t', \xi) \leq E[y(t) | x = \zeta] / E[y(t') | x = \xi] \leq j(t, t', \xi).$

Here (t, t') are distinct treatments and $[g(t, t', \xi), h(t, t', \xi), i(t, t', \xi), j(t, t', \xi)]$ are specified constants.

Bounded-variation assumptions of forms (3.16–3.20) are not mutually exclusive. One may think it credible to assert a set of such assumptions, depending on the context. Adding assumptions of forms (3.16–3.18) to the information available in (3.13–3.15) does not complicate the problem of computing identification regions for long mean outcomes. We found that our computational approach works well in practice when these inequalities are imposed. Adding assumptions of forms (3.19–3.20) complicates computation substantially. One must now jointly apply Equations (3.14) to both treatments t and t'. This increases the dimensionality and complexity of the problem of searching for sharp lower and upper bounds.

We combined the short trial findings reported in Zinman et al. (2015) with various bounded-variation assumptions to compute bounds on long mean outcomes for treatment of diabetic patients with or without empagliflozin. The widths and locations of the bound depend on the particular assumptions used. When presenting these bounds, we did not assert that clinicians considering treatment of diabetes should believe it credible to assert the specific versions of the assumptions that we posed. Our objective was only to illustrate partial identification analysis using bounded-variation assumptions.

3.3 IDENTIFICATION OF TREATMENT RESPONSE WITH SOCIAL INTERACTIONS

This section considers identification of treatment response in settings with social interactions, where personal outcomes vary with the treatment of others. Social interactions are common in households, schools, workplaces, and communities. Yet research on treatment response has mainly assumed that a person's outcome may vary only with his own treatment, not with those of other members of the population. Cox (1958) called this "no interference between units." Rubin (1978) called it the Stable Unit Treatment Value Assumption. I have called it *individualistic treatment response* (ITR), to mark it as an assumption that restricts the form of treatment response functions.

Manski (2013b) studied the general problem of identification of treatment response with social interactions. Specifying basic concepts and notation requires only a modest extension of the setup used in research on identification of individualistic treatment response. However, the broad spectrum of forms that social interactions may take inevitably makes identification analysis much more complex. I summarize key points here, without diving into the technical analysis.

3.3.1 Basic Concepts and Notation

Let T be a finite set of feasible treatments. Recall that, when response is individualistic, each member j of population J has a response function $y_j(\cdot): T \to Y$ mapping $t \in T$ into outcomes $y_j(t) \in Y$. If J is an observable

Identification of Treatment Response 89

study population who have received treatments, each person j has an observed realized treatment $z_j \in T$ and realized outcome $y_j \equiv y_j(z)$.

Observation of $(y_j, z_j; j \in J)$ reveals $P(y, z)$, the joint distribution of realized outcomes and treatments. As discussed earlier, a common research objective is to learn about the outcome distribution $P[y(t)]$ that would occur if all persons were to receive a specified treatment t. Interest in $P[y(t)]$ may be motivated by a scenario in which a planner has the power to mandate treatment t. Then the planner wants to learn the outcome distribution $P[y(t)]$ that would occur if t were to be mandated.

Now remove assumption ITR, so each person's outcome may vary with the treatments received by all members of the population. To express this, one extends the domain of the response function from T to the Cartesian product of T across the population; that is, T^J. The response function becomes $y_j(\cdot): T^J \to Y$, mapping treatment vectors $t^J \in T^J$ into outcomes $y_j(t^J) \in Y$. Here $t^J \equiv (t_k, k \in J)$ denotes a potential treatment vector specifying the treatment to be received by every member of the population. Now person j has observable realized outcome $y_j \equiv y_j(z^J)$, where $z^J \equiv (z_k, k \in J)$. A planner with the power to mandate treatments wants to learn the outcome distribution $P[y(t^J)]$ that would occur if the planner were to mandate treatment vector t^J.

Comparison of the setup with and without assumption ITR makes plain that identification without the assumption presents a much more severe challenge than with it. Given assumption ITR alone, the identification region for $P[y(t)]$ is the set of distributions $[P(y \mid z = t)P(z = t) + \gamma \cdot P(z \neq t), \gamma \in \Gamma_Y]$, where Γ_Y denotes the space of all probability distributions on Y. The size of this region grows with $P(z \neq t)$, the fraction of the study population who do not receive treatment t. Without assumption ITR or another assumption restricting social interactions, the identification region for $P[y(t^J)]$ is $[P(y \mid z^J = t^J)P(z^J = t^J) + \gamma \cdot P(z^J \neq t^J), \gamma \in \Gamma_Y]$. However, $P(z^J \neq t^J) = 0$ when $z^J = t^J$ and $P(z^J \neq t^J) = 1$ when $z^J \neq t^J$. It follows that observation of $P(y, z)$ is uninformative about $P[y(t^J)]$ when $z^J \neq t^J$. Thus, no prediction of counterfactual treatment response is possible.

3.3.2 Constant and Semi-monotone Treatment Response

Given assumption ITR, research on treatment response has highly valued performance of a classical randomized trial, which point-identifies the distribution $P[y(t)]$ of outcomes under a potential mandate of treatment t. With unrestricted social interactions, a randomized trial only reveals the distribution $P[y(z^J)]$ for the particular treatment vector z^J generated by the random assignment process. It reveals nothing about $P[y(t^J)]$ when $z^J \neq t^J$.

Informative study of $P[y(t^J)]$ becomes feasible only when the empirical evidence, whether from observational or trial data, is combined with assumptions that restrict the distribution $P[y(\cdot)]$ of response functions. Manski (2013b) studied identification under the assumption of *constant treatment response* (CTR) and *semi-monotone treatment response* (SMTR).

Assumption CTR posits that a person's outcome remains constant when t^J varies within specified subsets of T^J. Leading cases are assumptions asserting that interactions may occur within but not across known subpopulations, commonly called *reference groups*. A CTR assumption asserts that a person's outcome remains constant when treatment varies outside his reference group. Assumption ITR is the polar case where each person is his own reference group.

Going further, Manski (2013b) studied the identifying power of the assumption that a social interaction is *anonymous*. This asserts that the outcome of person j is invariant with respect to permutations of the treatments received by other members of his reference group. Consider, for example, vaccination of some children in a community. When considering illness from an infectious disease, one might think it credible to take each child's reference group to be the set of children who attend the same school. One might additionally think it credible to assume that each child's illness outcome depends on his own vaccination treatment and on the number of children vaccinated in his school, but not on the identities of the other schoolmates vaccinated.

Assumption SMTR states that set T is partially ordered and that outcomes vary monotonically across ordered pairs of treatment vectors. Important subcases are *reinforcing* and *opposing* interactions. A reinforcing interaction occurs when a person's outcome increases both with the value of his own treatment and with the values of the treatments received by others in the reference group. An opposing interaction occurs when a person's outcome increases with the value of his own treatment but decreases with the values of the treatments received by others. SMTR assumptions generalize the individualistic monotone-treatment-response assumptions discussed in Section 3.1.5. Reinforcing interactions will be considered further in Chapter 8, where I discuss my research on vaccination planning under uncertainty.

3.4 CREDIBLE META-ANALYSIS

To conclude this chapter, I revisit meta-analysis of disparate studies, which I critiqued sharply in Chapter 2. Manski (2020f) recommended that meta-analysis be viewed through the lens of partial identification analysis. I explain here.

Recall that meta-analysis aims to aggregate findings across multiple studies. Suppose that M studies have been performed, each partially identifying a parameter of interest. The studies may use observational or trial data. A potential value of the parameter is consistent with everything learned in the M studies if and only if it lies within each of the M identification regions. Thus, the identification region combining the studies is the intersection of the regions obtained with each study. I have previously discussed the simple logic of set intersection when considering IV assumptions.

Set intersection is easy to perform when the parameter is real-valued and the M identification regions are intervals. Then the intersection is itself an interval, whose lower bound is the greatest lower bound of the study-specific intervals and whose upper bound is the least upper bound of these intervals. For example, let three studies of patient survival be available. Suppose that their identification regions for the probability of survival are [0.4, 0.7], [0.2, 0.6], and [0.5, 1]. Set intersection yields [0.5, 0.6] as the bound on survival probability obtained by combining the studies.

This example is interesting because it demonstrates a subtlety in the operation of set intersection. One might intuit that when M studies yield identification regions of different sizes, the studies yielding the smallest identification regions would play the most prominent role when combining findings. The example shows that this need not be the case. The lengths of the three study-specific intervals are 0.3, 0.4, and 0.5, respectively. Yet the set intersection is determined entirely by the second and third intervals. The lesson is that the result of set intersection depends on the joint positioning of the sets, not only by their sizes.

Intersecting identification regions for a parameter of interest differs markedly from use of random-effects models in conventional meta-analysis. Applications of the random-effects model of Dersimonian and Laird (1986) make assumptions strong enough to point-identify the parameter value that pertains to each study. They then focus attention on the mean parameter value across studies.

Combining findings from observational studies and trials has long been a concern in medical research. The influential *Cochrane Handbook*

(Higgins and Green, 2011) views trials as qualitatively superior to observational studies. The *Handbook* discusses the GRADE approach to rating the certainty of a body of evidence, the four rating levels being (high, moderate, low, very low). GRADE recommends that the high rating should be reserved for evidence from certain randomized trials. The Cochrane authors write (Section 12.2.1): "Review authors will generally grade evidence from sound observational studies as low quality." Developers of clinical practice guidelines often act accordingly, valuing trial evidence more than observational studies. Indeed, guideline developers sometimes use only trial evidence, excluding observational studies from consideration.

The discussion in this chapter makes clear that it is misguided to prima facie favor trials over observational studies. Jointly considering internal and external validity, observational studies and trials may each credibly bound but not point-identify a quantity of interest. The truth must lie within the intersection of the bounds obtained with each type of data.

4

Identification of Choice Behavior and Personal Welfare

In principle, identification of choice behavior and personal welfare are distinct subjects of concern to planning. Choice behavior matters when planning decisions influence the behavior of population members or others in ways that affect social welfare. This makes identification of choice behavior a class of problems within the broad domain of identification of treatment response. Personal welfare matters when the social welfare function is personalist. Then identification of personal welfare is essential to evaluate social welfare, regardless of how planning decisions influence behavior.

Viewing choice behavior as treatment response may not be obvious, so I will explain. Let A be a universe of potential actions. Let Γ be the set of all non-empty subsets of A. Then each element of Γ, that is each $D \subset A$, is a potential choice set. Let $y_j(D)$ denote the action that person j would choose if he were to face choice set D. In the terminology of analysis of treatment response, Γ is a set of feasible treatments, D is a treatment in Γ, and $y_j(D)$ is treatment response.

In economic research, identification of choice behavior and personal welfare have long been closely connected. Economists have commonly assumed that behavior results from maximization of personal welfare. Hence, identification of personal welfare has been studied both to enable prediction of behavior and to evaluate personalist social welfare.

This chapter mainly discusses *revealed preference analysis*, which assumes that choice results from maximization of personal welfare. Section 4.1 discusses revealed preference analysis in some generality. Section 4.2 focuses on identification of income-leisure preferences for evaluation of income tax policy. Whereas Sections 4.1 and 4.2 concern behavior in deterministic settings, Section 4.3 considers identification when it is assumed that individuals cope with uncertainty by maximizing expected utility. Going beyond revealed preference analysis, Section 4.4 discusses identification using subjective data in place of or in addition to observations of actual choices.

In principle, I would want to also discuss identification when choices are made under ambiguity or with bounded rationality. However, there has been little research on these topics. Hence, their consideration must be deferred.

4.1 REVEALED PREFERENCE ANALYSIS

Revealed preference analysis combines data on choices made by a population with assumptions about their decision processes. The core assumption is that choice results from maximization of personal welfare, but this per se has weak identifying power. The practice of revealed preference analysis has combined the core assumption with assumptions about the structure of preferences.

Two literatures have developed. The work discussed in Section 4.1.1 analyzes data from a single decision maker or, equivalently, from a group of decision makers who are assumed to behave homogeneously. The research discussed in Section 4.1.2 studies the choices of members of a heterogeneous population of decision makers. My presentation draws substantially on Manski (2007a, Chapter 13).

4.1.1 Revealing the Preferences of a Classical Consumer

The original form of revealed preference analysis, introduced by Samuelson (1938, 1948), considered the classical economic problem of predicting the commodity demands of a person with a given income when commodities have given prices. Samuelson supposed that a researcher observes the consumption bundles that a person chooses in various income-price settings. He showed that the observed consumption outcomes, when combined with standard assumptions of consumer theory, enables partial predictions regarding the consumption bundles that this person would choose in some other income-price scenarios.

Observation of One Choice Setting
Suppose that one observes a person's consumption in a single choice setting. Let there be K commodities, with prices $p \equiv (p_k, k = 1, ..., K)$.

Suppose that the person has income m and that he chooses the commodity bundle $c \equiv (c_k, k = 1, ..., K)$; thus, the person purchases c_k units of commodity k. Let $d \equiv (d_k, k = 1, ..., K)$ denote any non-chosen commodity bundle that costs strictly less than m at the prevailing prices.

Now consider a counterfactual scenario in which the price vector and the person's income are (p^0, m^0) rather than (p, m). Suppose that commodity bundles c and d both remain feasible in this scenario; that is, both bundles cost no more than m^0 when the price vector is p^0. Might the person choose bundle d in this scenario?

This prediction question calls for extrapolation from an observed choice setting to a counterfactual scenario. One's ability to answer depends on what one is willing to assume. Standard consumer theory assumes that persons are rational and that preferences do not exhibit satiation. *Rationality* in this context means that a person orders all commodity bundles in terms of preference and chooses one that is ranked highest among those that are feasible. *Non-satiation* means that a person strictly prefers a larger commodity bundle to a smaller one. Bundle d' is larger than d if $d'_k \geq d_k$ for all commodities k and $d'_k > d_k$ for some k.

These assumptions and observation that the person chooses bundle c in income-price setting (p, m) imply that the person strictly prefers c to d. To see this, note that rationality and the observed choice of c imply that d is not strictly preferred to c, but leave open the possibility of indifference between c and d. Non-satiation and the presumption that d costs less than m eliminates the possibility of indifference. Thus, revealed preference analysis predicts that the person would not choose d in any scenario where both c and d are feasible choices.

The non-satiation assumption enables further predictions as well. Consider any bundle c' that is larger than c and any bundle d' that is smaller than d. Non-satiation, combined with preference of c over d, implies that the person strictly prefers c' to d'.

Observation of Several Choice Settings

With observation of only one choice setting, one can only perform extrapolations of the above kind. More powerful applications of revealed preference analysis are possible if one observes the consumption bundles that a person chooses in several income-price settings. The key is application of the transitivity property of preferences.

Consider three commodity bundles, say c, d, and e. Suppose that observation of behavior in one income-price setting shows that a person strictly prefers bundle c to d, while observation of another setting shows that this person strictly prefers bundle d to e. Transitivity of preferences implies that this person strictly prefers bundle c to e. Thus, transitivity enables one to form chains of inference across choice settings. Afriat (1967) and Varian (1982) have characterized these chains of inference.

Samuelsonian revealed preference analysis is admirable for its objective of predicting choice behavior with weak assumptions. The assumption of rationality has enjoyed high credibility among economists, although it has been criticized in research on behavioral economics.

A severe practical problem with application of the transitivity assumption is the need to observe individual behavior in several choice settings. The mutual exclusivity of treatments makes this a logical impossibility at a point in time. If a person is observed to have income m and face prices p, then this person does not have another income or face other prices. Hence, the literal form of Samuelsonian analysis is more a thought experiment than a practical prescription for prediction.

Aiming to exploit the identifying power of transitivity, a researcher might observe choices made by a person over time in different choice settings and assume that preferences are time invariant. Or the researcher might observe choices by several persons who face different choice sets and assume that these persons have the same preferences. Then the researcher may act as if he observes several choices by one person. However, the ensuing analysis rests critically on the maintained assumption of preference time invariance or homogeneity, which may lack foundation.

A researcher might also ask a single person to state the choices the person would make when facing several hypothetical choice scenarios. Analysis of such subjective data will be discussed in Section 4.4.

4.1.2 Random Utility Models of Heterogeneous Decision Makers

Whereas Samuelsonian revealed preference analysis aims to predict the choice behavior and learn the welfare function of an individual, the form of revealed preference analysis developed by McFadden (1974) seeks to predict the distribution of choices made by the members of a population and learn their distribution of personal welfare functions. The McFadden approach supposes that a researcher observes the decisions made by a population of heterogeneous persons, each of whom faces one discrete choice problem. McFadden showed that these data, combined with strong assumptions on the population distribution of preferences, enable point identification and estimation of parametric probabilistic

Identification of Choice Behavior and Personal Welfare

choice models. He showed how such probabilistic choice models may be used to predict population choice behavior in counterfactual settings.

McFadden's vision of discrete choice analysis has three essential features, which I will describe in turn. These are:

(a) Econometric analysis of behavior should be interpretable as describing the behavior of a population of heterogeneous decision makers, each of whom chooses the best available alternative.
(b) Econometric analysis should enable the researcher to predict choice behavior in counterfactual settings. In particular, it should enable the researcher to predict population behavior if new alternatives were to become available or existing ones were to become unavailable. To achieve this, alternatives and decision makers should be characterized in terms of their attributes.
(c) Econometric analysis should recognize that empirical researchers possesses incomplete data on the attributes of the decision makers that compose the population and the alternatives available to them.

Consistency with Utility Theory

McFadden assumed that each member of a study population faces a finite choice set and selects an action that maximizes personal welfare. I will suppose here that all members of the population face the same choice set, denoted C, which is a finite subset of a universe A of potential alternatives. The assumption of a common choice set simplifies exposition and is maintained in much of the literature, but it is not critical to what follows.

Let person j have a utility function $u_j(\cdot)$ that assigns a utility value to each alternative in A. Suppose that this person is observed to choose some action $c \in C$. Then the standard revealed preference argument holds that person j ranks c highest among the feasible alternatives. Thus, $u_j(c) \geq u_j(d)$, all $d \in C$.

Assume that indifference between alternatives occurs with probability zero. Then the fraction of the population who choose c equals the fraction of the population for whom c is the utility maximizing action. Hence, the *choice probability* for alternative c is:

(4.1) $$P(y = c) = P\left[u(\cdot): u(c) \geq u(d), \text{ all } d \in C\right].$$

Equation (4.1) is a *random utility model* interpretation of observed choices.

Prediction Using Attributes of Alternatives and Decision Makers

Suppose that one could learn the population distribution of utility functions. Then a random utility model would not only describe observed population behavior but would enable prediction of behavior in counterfactual scenarios where members of the population face choice sets other than C. Suppose, for example, that all persons were to face choice set D. The counterfactual choice probability for each c ∈ D is:

(4.2) $\qquad P[y(D) = c] = P[u(\cdot): u(c) \geq u(d), \text{ all } d \in D]$.

However, learning the distribution of utility functions from choice data is no small problem. Observation of the study population only yields Equation (4.1), or the analogous equation conditioning on observed covariates of decision makers. Clearly, many distributions of utility functions can solve this equation.

McFadden reasoned that the researcher should bring to bear assumptions that restrict the distribution of utility functions. His central idea was to transform the hitherto qualitative distinctions among alternatives and decision makers into quantitative differences in their attributes. Thus, the second step in the development of discrete choice analysis was to assume that each alternative d can be characterized by a vector of attributes, say w_d, and that each decision maker j can be characterized by a vector of attributes, say x_j. Then the utility of alternative d to person j has the form:

(4.3) $\qquad u_j(d) = u(w_d, x_j)$,

where $u(\cdot, \cdot)$ maps the attributes of alternatives and decision makers into utility values. With knowledge of these attributes and the form of $u(\cdot, \cdot)$, a researcher can determine the utility of any alternative to any decision maker and, hence, can predict the decision maker's choice behavior.

Characterization of alternatives and decision makers as attribute vectors marked a sharp departure from prevailing economic practice. In classical consumer theory, goods and consumers are qualitatively distinct. There is no way to predict the demand for a new good. Nor is there any way to predict the behavior of new consumers.

Incomplete Data and Conditional Choice Probabilities

One more conceptual step was needed to yield a viable approach to discrete choice analysis. It is not realistic to think that an empirical researcher will have complete data on the attributes of alternatives and decision makers. Nor is it realistic to think that the researcher fully knows the form of the function $u(\cdot, \cdot)$ mapping attributes into utility values.

A viable approach emerges if the researcher has enough partial knowledge of u(·,·) and of the population distribution of unobserved attributes. McFadden assumed that u(·,·) has the linear form:

$$(4.4) \qquad u(w_d, x_j) = v(w_{do}, x_{jo})\beta + \varepsilon_{jd}.$$

Here v(·, ·) is a known vector-valued function of the components of w_d and x_j that the researcher can observe, labeled w_{do} and x_{jo}, while β is a commensurate parameter vector. The unobserved variables $\varepsilon_j \equiv (\varepsilon_{jd}, d \in C)$ express the contribution of unobserved attributes to utility.

With this setup, McFadden derived choice probabilities conditional on the observed attributes. Let $W_{Co} \equiv (w_{do}, d \in C)$. Consider the subpopulation of persons with observed covariates x_o. Assume that the researcher knows the distribution $P(\varepsilon \mid x_o, W_{Co})$, assumed to be continuous, up to the value of a parameter vector α. Let this parametrized distribution be denoted F_α. Then the random utility model implies that the choice probability for alternative c conditional on (x_o, W_{Co}) is:

$$(4.5) \qquad P(y = c \mid x_o, W_{Co}) = F_\alpha\big[\varepsilon : v(w_{co}, x_o)\beta + \varepsilon_c \geq v(w_{do}, x_o)\beta + \varepsilon_d, \text{ all } d \in C \mid x_o, W_{Co}\big].$$

These conditional choice probabilities provide the basis for inference on the parameters (β, α) using data on the choices and attributes of decision makers. Observation of the study population reveals the conditional choice probabilities on the left-hand side of Equation (4.5). Hence, the identification region for (β, α) is the set of parameter values that make (4.5) hold for all alternatives c and for all values of x_o in the support of $P(x_o)$. The parameters are point-identified if these equations have a unique solution. If no parameter value solves (4.5) for all values of c and x_o, the model does not correctly portray choice behavior.

Econometric research on random utility models has mainly invoked strong assumptions on the structure of preferences that yield point identification of choice probabilities and population distributions of utility functions. This has made revealed preference analysis a powerful tool for applied economics, but only if one is willing to maintain assumptions that can be difficult to motivate. Thus, the Law of Decreasing Credibility asserts itself.

Aiming to enhance the credibility of discrete choice analysis, Manski (2007c) developed an abstract framework for study of partial identification. I showed how this framework may be applied to an important planning problem in Manski (2014b). I summarize this work next. Barseghyan, Coughlin, Molinari, and Teitelbaum (2021) develop partial identification analysis of discrete choice in a different direction, studying settings where choice sets are not directly observed.

4.2 IDENTIFICATION OF INCOME-LEISURE PREFERENCES FOR EVALUATION OF INCOME TAX POLICY

Economists have long recognized that the relative merits of alternative income tax policies depend on the preferences of persons for income and leisure. Among the simplifying assumptions that Mirrlees (1971) made in his seminal study of optimal utilitarian income taxation, he stated (p. 176): "The State is supposed to have perfect information about the individuals in the economy, their utilities and, consequently, their actions." Mirrlees also recognized the difficulty of inference on population preferences. In the conclusion to his article he wrote (p. 207): "The examples discussed confirm, as one would expect, that the shape of the optimum earned-income tax schedule is rather sensitive to the distribution of skills within the population, and to the income-leisure preferences postulated. Neither is easy to estimate for real economies."

Income-leisure preferences play both positive and normative roles in analysis of tax policy. The positive role is that preferences yield labor supply and other decisions that determine tax revenue. The normative role is that social welfare aggregates personal preferences in utilitarian policy evaluation. Thus, choice of an optimal tax policy requires knowledge of preferences both to predict tax revenue and to compute the welfare achieved by alternative policies.

Manski (2014b) studied identification of income-leisure preferences using revealed preference analysis of labor supply. I reached this pessimistic conclusion (p. 146): "As I see it, we lack the knowledge of preferences necessary to credibly evaluate income tax policies." I summarize here.

4.2.1 Taxation and Labor Supply

To begin, it is important to understand that economic theory does not predict the direction or magnitude of the response of labor supply to income taxation. To the contrary, it shows that a worker may rationally respond in disparate ways. As tax rates increase, a person may decide to work less, work more, or not change labor supply at all. The silence of theory on labor supply has long been appreciated; see Robbins (1930).

Modern labor economics envisions labor supply as a complex sequence of schooling, occupation, and work effort decisions made under uncertainty over the life course, perhaps with only bounded rationality. However, we need only consider a simple static scenario to see that a person may respond rationally to income taxes in disparate ways.

Suppose that a person with a predetermined wage and no unearned income allocates each day between paid work and the various nonpaid activities that economists have traditionally called leisure. Let a proportional income tax reduce his wage by the prevailing tax rate, yielding his net wage. Assume that the person allocates time to maximize utility, which is an increasing function of net income and leisure.

Different utility functions imply different relationships between the tax rate and labor supply. The labor supply implied by utility functions in the Constant-Elasticity-of-Substitution (CES) family increases or decreases with the tax rate depending on the elasticity of substitution. Other utility functions imply that labor supply is *backward-bending*. That is, hours worked may initially increase as net wage rises from zero but, above some threshold, decrease as net wage rises further. Still other utility functions yield more complex non-monotone relationships between net wage and labor supply. A review article by Stern (1986) describes a broad spectrum of possibilities.

Given that theory does not predict how income taxation affects labor supply, prediction requires empirical analysis. Robbins (1930) emphasized this, writing (p. 129), "we are left with the conclusion ... that any attempt to predict the effect of a change in the terms on which income is earned must proceed by inductive investigation of elasticities." Economists have performed a huge number of empirical studies of labor supply. I summarized the literature in Manski (2014b), referencing multiple review articles.

Reading the literature concerned with uncompensated (Marshallian) elasticities of labor supply, I was struck to find that while authors may differ on the magnitude of elasticities, they have largely agreed on the sign. The consensus has been that increasing tax rates usually reduces work effort. Keane (2011) stated the directionality of the effect without reservation, writing (p. 963), "the use of labor income taxation to raise revenue causes people to work less." Considering the effect of a rise in a proportional tax, Meghir and Phillips (2010) wrote (p. 207), "in most cases this will lead to less work, but when the income effect dominates the substitution effect at high hours of work it may increase effort." Here and elsewhere, researchers sometimes recognize the theoretical possibility that effort may increase with tax rates, but they typically view this as an empirical rarity rather than a regularity. This view has been accepted in official government forecasts of the response of labor supply to income taxation. See Congressional Budget Office (2007). Curiously, the opposite consensus prevailed early in the twentieth century. Gilbert and Pfouts (1958) cite assertions by Pigou and Knight in the 1920s that increasing tax rates increases work effort.

Examining the models of labor supply used in empirical research, I became concerned that the prevailing consensus on the sign of uncompensated elasticities may be an artifact of model specification rather than an expression of reality. Models of labor supply differ across studies, but they have generally shared two key restrictive assumptions. First, they suppose that labor supply varies monotonically with net wages. Thus, model specifications do not generally permit backward-bending labor supply functions or other non-monotone relationships. Second, models suppose that the response of labor supply to net wage is homogeneous within broad demographic groups. With occasional exceptions, researchers specify hours-of-work equations that permit hours to vary additively across group members but that assume homogeneous treatment response. That is, they assume that all group members would adjust hours worked in the same way in response to a conjectural change in net wage.

The literature contains some precedent for my concern that empirical findings on labor supply may be artifacts of model specification. Concluding his detailed comparison of alternative labor supply functions, Stern (1986) wrote (p. 173): "Our general conclusion must be in favour of diversity of functions and great caution in drawing policy conclusions on results based on a particular form." Stern and other writers such as Blundell and MaCurdy (1999) have called attention to the potential detrimental consequences of restrictive functional-form assumptions.

The reality may be that persons have heterogeneous income-leisure preferences and, consequently, heterogeneous labor-supply functions. Some may increase work time with net wage, others may decrease work time, and still others may exhibit a non-monotone relationship. Concerned with this possibility, Manski (2014b) examined afresh the problem of identification of income-leisure preferences. I studied identification when data on time allocation under status quo tax policies are interpreted through the lens of standard theory. To illuminate elemental issues, I found it productive to study the classical static model in which persons with separable preferences for private and public goods must allocate one unit of time to work and leisure.

I considered the use of revealed preference analysis to predict labor supply and tax revenue under a proposed policy that would alter persons' status quo tax schedules. My objective was to shed light on how maintained assumptions affect the conclusions that one may draw about counterfactual labor supply and tax revenue. As in my other research on identification, I found it illuminating to begin with weak assumptions and then to characterize the identifying power of stronger assumptions. In what follows, I first summarize a basic revealed preference analysis of the Samuelson type. I then describe my analysis adding assumptions about the structure of preferences.

4.2.2 Basic Revealed Preference Analysis

I first assumed only that persons prefer to have more income and leisure. Basic revealed preference analysis of the type pioneered by Samuelson (1938) shows that observation of a person's time allocation under a status quo tax policy may bound his allocation under a proposed policy or may have no implications, depending on the tax schedules and the person's status quo time allocation. Basic analysis assuming only that more-is-better generically does not predict the sign of labor-supply response to change in the tax schedule. I call this a "basic" analysis of revealed preference because it maintains no assumptions about preferences except that individual utility is an increasing function of net income and leisure. In short, more is better.

In the absence of assumptions that restrict the population distribution of preferences, predicting population labor supply under a proposed tax policy simply requires aggregation of individual predictions. Hence, it suffices to focus on one person. Suppose that a person labeled j is endowed with wage w_j, unearned income z_j, and one unit of time. The person must allocate his time endowment between leisure and work. If he allocates a fraction $L \in [0, 1]$ to leisure and $1 - L$ to work, he receives gross income $w_j(1 - L) + z_j$.

The status quo tax policy, denoted S, subtracts the work-dependent tax revenue $R_{jS}(L)$ from gross income, leaving j with net income:

(4.6) $$Y_{jS}(L) \equiv w_j(1-L) + z_j - R_{jS}(L).$$

Taxes may take positive or negative values. The $R_{jS}(\cdot)$ notation allows the status quo tax schedule to be specific to person j. The schedule that j faces depends on the current tax policy of the jurisdiction where he resides. Within a tax jurisdiction, the tax levied may depend on unearned income and on personal attributes that determine eligibility for exemptions and deductions.

Person j chooses a value of L from a set $\Lambda_j \subset [0, 1]$ of feasible leisure alternatives. Most analysis of labor supply supposes that $\Lambda_j = [0, 1]$. However, it may be more realistic to suppose that only a few allocations are feasible. For example, $\Lambda_j = \{0, \frac{1}{2}, 1\}$ means that the feasible options are full-time work (L = 0), half-time work (L = ½), and no work (L = 1).

Preferences are expressed in person j's utility function $U_j(\cdot,\cdot)$, whose arguments are (net income, leisure). Utility is strictly increasing in both arguments. Let $L_{jS} \in \Lambda_j$ denote the amount of leisure that j chooses under tax schedule $R_{jS}(\cdot)$. Utility maximization implies these inequalities:

(4.7) $\quad U_j\left[Y_{jS}(L_{jS}), L_{jS}\right] \geq U_j\left[Y_{jS}(L), L\right]$, all $L \in \Lambda_j$.

Using $U_j(\cdot, \cdot)$ to express preferences suppresses the possible dependence of preferences on the public goods produced with tax revenue under policy S. This is innocuous if preferences are separable in private and public goods.

Predicting Labor Supply under a Proposed Tax Schedule

Suppose that one observes the wage, unearned income, and other tax-relevant attributes of person j. One also observes the leisure L_{jS} chosen by j under tax schedule $R_{jS}(\cdot)$. Empirical microeconomic research on labor supply typically assumes observability of most of these quantities, the data source being surveys such as the Panel Study of Income Dynamics or the National Longitudinal Survey of Youth. An exception is the usual absence of wage data for persons who do not work at all. I abstract from this well-known difficulty of empirical research.

Let $R_{jT}(\cdot)$ denote the tax schedule if j were to face a proposed tax policy T. What can one predict about time allocation under $R_{jT}(\cdot)$? The answer depends on the value of L_{jS} and on the budget sets $\{[Y_{jS}(L), L], L \in \Lambda_j\}$ and $\{[Y_{jT}(L), L], L \in \Lambda_j\}$ that j faces under the status quo and proposed tax schedules. I developed a general analysis of the identification problem, which is somewhat complex. I give here a simple instructive special case, which modestly extends the original revealed preference argument of Samuelson (1938).

Consider the tax schedules in Figure 4.1. Policy S has a two-rate progressive schedule and T has a proportional one, the latter crossing the former from above when leisure equals L_j^*. Person j has no unearned income. Suppose that $L_{jS} \in [0, L_j^*]$, and consider any feasible $L > L_j^*$. The (income, leisure) pair $[Y_{jT}(L_{jS}), L_{jS}]$ is feasible under policy

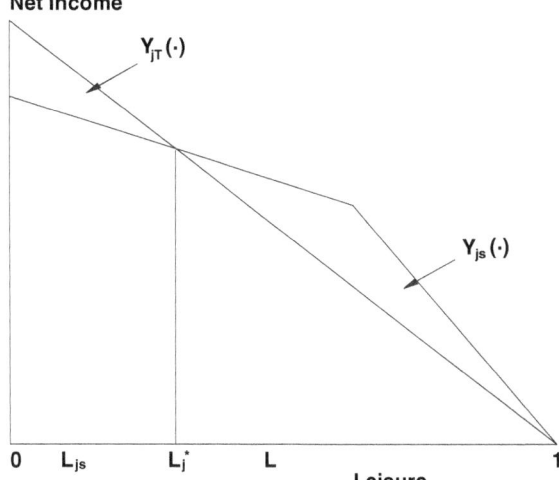

FIGURE 4.1 Net Income with Progressive and Proportional Tax Schedules

T. Since more income is better than less, this pair is strictly preferred to the pair $[Y_{jS}(L_{jS}), L_{jS}]$ chosen under S. Pair $[Y_{jS}(L), L]$ is feasible under policy S. Since more income is preferred to less, this pair is strictly preferred to $[Y_{jT}(L), L]$. The observation that j chose $[Y_{jS}(L_{jS}), L_{jS}]$ reveals that j weakly prefers this pair to $[Y_{jS}(L), L]$. Combining these preference inequalities implies that he strictly prefers $[Y_{jT}(L_{jS}), L_{jS}]$ to $[Y_{jT}(L), L]$. Thus, if person j were to face the proposed tax schedule, he would not choose any $L > L_j^*$. The analysis in Manski (2014b) proved that this exhausts the predictive power of basic revealed preference analysis.

I have written that the above derivation modestly extends Samuelson (1938). Samuelson considered use of data on the commodity bundle chosen under a status quo linear budget set to predict the bundle that would be chosen under a counterfactual linear budget set. Figure 4.1 differs only in that the budget set produced by policy S is not linear. Linearity of either budget set is immaterial. Samuelson's argument holds whenever the status quo and counterfactual budget sets cross one another.

4.2.3 Restrictions on the Preference Distribution

A huge distance separates basic revealed preference analysis from the prevailing practice of empirical analysis of labor supply. As noted earlier, the models used in empirical studies usually suppose that labor supply responds monotonically to variation in net wage. Moreover, it is common to assume that time allocation differs across persons only via a person-specific additive constant.

Manski (2014b) explored the identifying power of various assumptions restricting the distribution of preferences across persons. I supposed that one observes the time allocation of each person in a population whose members may have heterogeneous preferences, wages, and face various status quo tax schedules. I found it analytically helpful to suppose that persons choose among a finite set of feasible (income, leisure) values rather than the continuum often assumed in the literature. I used the discrete choice framework of Manski (2007c) to characterize preferences and to predict aggregate labor supply and tax revenue when assumptions restrict the distribution of preferences.

I studied the identifying power of two classes of assumptions. The first assumes exogenous variation in choice sets, in the formal sense that groups of persons who face different choice sets are assumed to have the same distribution of preferences. For example, one may assume that groups of persons who have different wages or who face different tax schedules have the same preference distribution. Exogenous variation makes the choice set an instrumental variable. The second class of assumptions restricted the shape of the distribution of preferences. For example, one may assume that all persons have preferences in the CES family, with possibly heterogeneous parameters.

These assumptions have identifying power, generically yielding partial rather than point identification of the preference distribution. Computation of the identification region is challenging in general, but it is tractable in some cases. I found it revealing to perform computational experiments that show the identifying power of alternative assumptions on the preference distribution.

Manski (2014b) reported illustrative computational experiments. Considering a hypothetical setting with choice data on labor supply observed under a status quo progressive tax schedule, the task was to predict the tax revenue per capita that would materialize under a proposed proportional schedule. I numerically found the predictive power of a sequence of increasingly strong assumptions: (1) More is better; (2) additionally, persons in specified wage groups have the same distribution of preferences; (3) additionally, preferences have the CES form; and (4) additionally, all CES utility functions in the specified wage groups have the same elasticity of substitution. The findings showed how the identified bound on tax revenue per capita narrows as one adds assumptions.

Identification of Choice Behavior and Personal Welfare   107

In the experiments performed, the bound assuming only (1) was [$593, $18969], assuming (1) and (2) was [$3744, $14149], and assuming (1) through (3) was [$6883, $10444]. Adding assumption (4) yielded an empty identification region for the preference distribution. Hence, the assumption of homogeneous elasticity of substitution was refuted.

4.2.4 Implications for Utilitarian Policy Evaluation

A familiar exercise in the study of optimal income taxation poses a utilitarian social welfare function and ranks tax policies by the welfare they achieve. Performing this ranking requires knowledge of income-leisure preferences both to predict tax revenues and to compute the welfare achieved by alternative policies. The analysis summarized above reached highly cautionary findings about present knowledge of income-leisure preferences, carrying implications for evaluation of tax policy. Partial knowledge of preferences implies that one can only partially predict tax revenue and one can only partially evaluate the utilitarian welfare of policies.

I concluded that we lack the knowledge of preferences necessary to credibly rank policies. Studying a simple static problem of time allocation showed that basic revealed preference analysis has little power to predict labor supply under proposed policies. Importantly, it does not predict whether increasing tax rates reduces or increases work effort. Restrictions on the population distribution of labor-leisure preferences have identifying power, but I found that credible versions of these assumptions yield fairly wide bounds on tax revenue in computational experiments. Thus, credible choice of tax policy is a problem of planning under ambiguity.

4.3 REVEALED PREFERENCE ANALYSIS OF CHOICES MAXIMIZING EXPECTED UTILITY

My discussion of revealed preference analysis has thus far supposed that members of the population have complete knowledge of their choice environments. Complete knowledge is a maintained assumption of the classical consumer demand problem studied by Samuelson. McFadden's development of discrete choice analysis does not necessarily assume complete knowledge. However, applications of the approach when persons act with partial knowledge must come to grips with a severe complication.

Economists have commonly assumed that persons form probabilistic expectations for unknown quantities and that they maximize expected utility. Given this assumption, revealed preference analysis combines choice data with assumptions to learn both the subjective probability distributions that express expectations and the utility functions that embody preferences. This is a much harder task than learning preferences alone.

4.3.1 Basic Analysis

The formal structure of basic revealed preference analysis as initiated by Samuelson remains unchanged if individuals maximize expected utility. Ranking actions by expected-utility yields a complete preference ordering, so the logic still holds. What differs is that this logic now yields partial identification of expected utilities, not of subjective probability distributions and utility functions separately. In general, many combinations of subjective distributions and utilities may generate the same expected utilities. Hence, the identification problem is more pronounced than earlier.

4.3.2 Random Expected-Utility Models

As with basic revealed preference analysis, the formal structure of random utility models remains unchanged if individuals maximize expected utility. Again, what differs is that the logic of identification applies to expected utilities, not to subjective probability distributions and utility functions separately.

Let S be the set of feasible states of nature. For $s \in S$, let $u_j(c, s)$ be the utility of action c to person j in state of nature s. Assume that person j places a subjective probability distribution on S, say π_j, and chooses an action that maximizes expected utility. If j faces choice set C and chooses action c, the standard revealed preference argument implies that $\int u_j(c, s) d\pi_j \geq \int u_j(d, s) d\pi_j$, all $d \in C$.

Suppose that indifference between alternatives occurs with probability zero across the population. Then the fraction of persons who choose alternative c is the fraction who have preferences and expectations such that c maximizes expected utility. Hence, the conditional choice probability for c is:

$$(4.8) \quad P(y = c \mid x_o, W_{Co}) = P\big[u(\cdot, \cdot), \pi : \int u(c, s) d\pi \geq \int u(d, s) d\pi, \text{ all } d \in C \mid x_o, W_{Co}\big].$$

Equation (4.8) gives a random expected-utility model interpretation of choice behavior.

Identification of Choice Behavior and Personal Welfare 109

The complication relative to settings with complete knowledge is clear. The earlier task was to learn the population distribution of utility functions. The problem now is to learn the joint distribution of utility functions and subjective probability distributions. The identification problem in the earlier context was difficult enough. It is all the more difficult now.

Rational Expectations Assumptions

Point identification of random expected-utility models plainly requires strong maintained assumptions. A common practice has been to assume that decision makers have specific expectations and to suppose that these expectations are objectively correct, aka *rational expectations*.

Imposition of expectations assumptions reduces the task of empirical research to learning preferences alone, but at a high cost in credibility. Researchers performing econometric analysis of choice data often have enormous difficulty defending the expectations assumptions they maintain. They consequently have difficulty justifying the findings they report.

Even if the common assumption of rational expectations were plausible, this assumption by itself does not pin down the specific expectations that persons hold. The assumption only asserts that persons hold objectively correct expectations conditional on the information they possess. A researcher must still ask what information persons possess and what constitutes objectively correct expectations conditional on this information. The standard practice has been for a researcher to pose a point-identified model of the economy, to assert that this model is correct, and also to assert knowledge of the information on which persons condition their expectations.

How Do Youth Infer Their Returns to Schooling?

To illustrate the implausibility of rational expectations assumptions, Manski (1993) considered the situation of youth in high school or college who contemplate whether to continue their schooling, join the labor force, or engage in other activities. Labor economists have commonly assumed that youth have rational expectations for the returns to further schooling and that they use these expectations to choose between schooling and other options. They have performed many empirical studies of the returns to schooling.

Reading this large literature reveals that researchers vary greatly in their specific assumptions and findings. Youth confront the same inferential problems as do labor economists studying the returns to schooling. If economists have not been able to reach consensus on the returns to schooling, is it plausible that youth have rational expectations? I think not.

I particularly stressed that youth and labor economists alike must contend with the unobservability of counterfactual outcomes. Much as economists attempt to learn the returns to schooling from data on schooling choices and outcomes, youth may attempt to learn through observation of the outcomes experienced by family, friends, and others who have made their own past schooling decisions. However, youth cannot observe the outcomes that these people would have experienced had they made other decisions. The implications for decision making depend fundamentally on the assumptions that youth maintain about counterfactual outcomes and how they cope with their own uncertainties.

4.4 ANALYSIS OF SUBJECTIVE DATA

The prevalence of revealed preference analysis in economic study of choice behavior and personal welfare stems to a considerable extent from a longstanding reluctance to collect and analyze subjective data. Economists have been skeptical of subjective statements that persons offer regarding their expectations, the choices they would make in hypothetical settings, or the welfare they would experience if they were to choose alternative actions. Students have been taught that a good economist believes what people do, not what they say.

It may be prudent to be skeptical of subjective statements, but there clearly is good reason to be skeptical of the strong assumptions that economists have commonly used to interpret choice data though revealed preference analysis. Empirical research reliant on assumptions that lack foundation is not more credible than research using informative, even if imperfect, subjective data. Gradually recognizing this, economists have lessened their historical inhibition against analysis of subjective data, generating a growing body of subjective data that can help to identify choice behavior and personal welfare. I call attention here to data measuring probabilistic expectations and eliciting potential behavior in hypothetical choice scenarios.

4.4.1 Measuring Probabilistic Expectations

Since about 1990, economists have generated a substantial body of empirical evidence on the probabilistic expectations of many populations. Collection and analysis of these data has been performed mainly by microeconomists and has consequentially been motivated primarily by a desire to inform microeconomic research. Macroeconomists have become engaged in the enterprise more recently. The prevalent practice has been to measure expectations on a 0–100 percent chance scale.

In an early review article (Manski, 2004a), I described the emergence of this field of empirical study and summarized a range of initial microeconomic applications. More recent review articles by Hurd (2009), Armantier et al. (2013), Delavande (2014), Schotter and Trevino (2014), and Manski (2018b) have respectively described research measuring expectations of older persons, inflation, populations in developing countries, subjects making decisions under uncertainty in lab experiments, and macroeconomic expectations. The *Handbook of Economic Expectations* (Bachman et al. 2023) brings together a wide range of contributions.

Researchers who employ random expected-utility models to predict choice behavior can use expectations data to relax assumptions about expectations. Consider, for example, the situation of labor economists studying schooling behavior. Researchers who observe only the choices that youth make confront a severe identification problem as they seek to infer both preferences and beliefs from data on observed choices. Observation of youths' expectations of the returns to schooling mitigates this problem. Elicitation of entire subjective distributions of life-cycle earnings may be impractical, but a researcher may use whatever expectations data as are available to lessen the dependence of inference on assumptions about expectations.

Having expectations data, a researcher need not assume that persons have rational or other specified expectations. It is enough to assume that elicited expectations describe persons' perceptions of their environments reasonably well. There is by now extensive empirical evidence that survey respondents are willing and able to report expectations in probabilistic form. Analysis of probabilistic expectations has become part of normal economic science.

Using Expectations and Choice Data to Estimate Random Expected-Utility Models

Research using probabilistic expectations data in econometric analysis of choice behavior has steadily accumulated over time. Early on, Nyarko and Schotter (2002) used a proper scoring rule to elicit expectations of opponent behavior from experimental subjects playing a two-person game and used the expectations to inform their analysis of decision making by subjects. An experimental literature performing research of this type has developed subsequently. See the review article of Schotter and Trevino (2014).

A large literature has developed using survey data on expectations in econometric choice analysis. Hurd, Smith, and Zissimopoulos (2004) investigated how the subjective survival probabilities elicited from respondents to the Health and Retirement Survey (HRS) affect the times when they choose to retire and to begin collecting Social Security benefits. Lochner (2007) combined data on arrest expectations and crime commission in the National Longitudinal Study of Youth to estimate a random utility model of criminal behavior. Van der Klaauw and Wolpin (2008) used HRS data on survival, retirement, and bequest expectations to help estimate a stochastic dynamic model of savings and retirement behavior. Delavande (2008) surveyed young women regarding their contraceptive choices and elicited expectations for the effectiveness and side effects of alternative methods. She combined expectations and choice data to estimate a random utility model of contraception behavior.

More recently, van der Klaauw (2012) used data on student expectations regarding future occupations to estimate a dynamic model of decisions to have careers in teaching. Zafar (2013) and Wiswall and Zafar (2015) surveyed college students regarding their choice of major, elicited expectations for the monetary and non-monetary returns to alternative majors, and combined the expectations and choice date to estimate random utility models of choice of major. Giustinelli (2016) surveyed teenagers completing middle school and their parents regarding choice among alternative types of high school and their expectations for successful performance in each type of school and their outcomes thereafter. She used these data to estimate random utility models of choice of high school, recognizing that families may use varying internal household decision processes.

4.4.2 Measuring Imprecise Probabilities

When considering expectations for uncertain events, economists have generally assumed that persons hold precise subjective probabilities. Yet some have long been concerned that this may not be the case, especially when available information is limited. Thus, persons may make decisions under ambiguity.

A simple way to formalize the idea is to suppose that a person holds a set of subjective distributions for an unknown event, not a single distribution, thus yielding lower and upper probabilities for events. Such a person may then be said to have imprecise probabilities (Walley, 1991). Psychologists have occasionally elicited imprecise probabilities in experimental settings (e.g., Wallsten, Forsyth, and Budescu, 1983; Budescu and Wallsten, 1987). However, very little has been known about the precision of the probabilistic expectations people hold in real life. The prevalence and nature of imprecision may vary across people and contexts. Hence, there has been a need to perform empirical research studying broad populations in contexts of substantive importance.

With this in mind, Manski and Molinari (2010) performed a pilot study in which respondents were asked to answer a sequence of questions about an uncertain event of interest. The elicitation procedure starts from the conventional precise percent-chance format, which requires respondents to report precise percent chances as numbers between 0 and 100, and then used two probing questions to learn more about the nature of respondents' expectations. The first probe asked whether the reported probability was intended to be an exact number or was rounded/approximated. When the response is rounded/approximated, a second probe permitted the respondent to give an exact precise probability or an imprecise probability, stated as a range.

Following up on this pilot, Giustinelli, Manski, and Molinari (2022) performed a full-scale study applying the same question format to study expectations of dementia and related choices connected to long-term care (LTC), matters of important personal consequence. Specifically, we elicited expectations of developing late-onset dementia and LTC decisions – purchasing LTC insurance or entering a nursing home – among over 1600 dementia-free respondents in the Health and Retirement Study.

We found that nearly half of respondents held imprecise probabilities of developing late-onset dementia. Similar fractions expressed imprecision regarding purchase of LTC insurance and entering a nursing home. Across LTC and dementia outcomes, over 60 percent of respondents expressed imprecision at least once. Respondents with imprecise probabilities varied in the extent of their imprecision. The distribution of interval widths featured a median of 20 points and a dispersion of 70 points as measured by the difference between the 9th decile (80 percent) and 1st decile (10 percent).

4.4.3 Elicitation of Potential Behavior in Hypothetical Choice Scenarios

Whereas economists have mainly used random utility models to interpret actual choice behavior, a common practice in market research and psychology, and an occasional one in economics, has been to pose choice scenarios and ask respondents to state what actions they would choose if they were to face these scenarios. See Ben Akiva, McFadden, and Train (2019) for a comprehensive review.

It has been usual to analyze stated hypothetical choices as if they were actual choices. Suppose that this assumption is credible and that individuals state what their choices would be in several choice scenarios. Then the data may be used, individual by individual, to perform Samuelsonian revealed preference analysis with observation of several choice settings, as discussed in Section 4.1.1. The data may also be used to estimate random utility models, now with richer data than was presumed available in Section 4.1.2. Thus, stated preference analysis has substantial promise to mitigate the severe identification problem encountered with revealed preference analysis.

The caveat, of course, is that it may not be credible to analyze stated choices as if they were actual ones. Multiple issues may arise. Focusing on one of them, Manski (1999) cautioned that stated choices may differ from actual ones if researchers provide respondents with different information than they would have when facing actual choice problems. The norm has been to pose *incomplete scenarios*, ones in which respondents are given only a subset of the information they would have in actual choice settings. When scenarios are incomplete, stated choices are point predictions of uncertain actual choices.

Given this, I proposed elicitation of choice probabilities rather than deterministic stated choices and I showed how the elicited choice probabilities may be used to estimate random utility models. This idea has subsequently been applied by Blass, Lach, and Manski (2010) and Delavande and Manski (2015). The former article analyzed consumer willingness to pay for alternative electricity options with differing prices and reliability of supply. The latter specified hypothetical election scenarios, elicited subjective probabilities that respondents would choose to vote in these scenarios, and used the expectations data to estimate a random utility of the decision to vote.

These studies have demonstrated that persons are willing and able to state choice probabilities in hypothetical choice scenarios, and they have illustrated how the data may be used to perform discrete choice analysis. Considerable further study will be required to determine the potential contribution of the idea to empirical research on choice behavior and personal welfare.

PART II

ANALYSES OF PLANNING PROBLEMS

5

Diversified Treatment under Ambiguity

Chapters 5 through 9 present the main features of many of my analyses of planning problems to date. Chapters 5 through 7 consider microplanning settings where a planner can treat persons differentially and where treatment affects only the person treated. I focus on clinical treatment of noninfectious disease. In Chapter 8, differential treatment remains feasible but social interactions connect outcomes across the population, the context being vaccination against infectious disease. Chapter 9 considers a fully macroplanning problem, this being choice of a global climate policy that affects the entire world population.

Here in Chapter 5, I discuss my work on diversified treatment under ambiguity. I initiated research on this theme in Manski (2007a), expanded it considerably in Manski (2009), and have carried it further in Manski (2015c), Cassidy and Manski (2019), and elsewhere.

To see the basic idea, observe that when it is feasible to treat persons differentially, a planner may make a *singleton* allocation, assigning all observationally identical persons to the same treatment. Or the planner may choose a *fractional* allocation, randomly assigning positive fractions of these persons to different treatments. Fractional allocations cope with ambiguity through diversification.

Suppose that there are two feasible treatments, labelled A and B. Diversification enables a decision maker to balance two types of potential error. A Type A error occur when treatment A is chosen but is actually inferior to B, and a Type B error occurs when B is chosen but is inferior to A. The singleton allocation assigning everyone to treatment A entirely avoids type B errors but may yield Type A errors, and vice versa for singleton assignment to treatment B. Fractional allocations make both types of errors but reduce their potential magnitudes. Treatment diversification is useful because it enables a planner to avoid gross errors that would occur if all persons were inadvertently given the inferior treatment.

Treatment diversification is analogous to financial diversification, a familiar recommendation for portfolio allocation under uncertainty. A financial portfolio is diversified if an investor allocates positive fractions of wealth to different investments. Diversification enables an investor facing uncertain asset returns to limit the potential negative consequences of placing "all eggs in one basket."

The finance literature on portfolio allocation shows that an investor seeking to maximize subjective expected utility chooses to diversify if the probability distribution of returns has sufficient spread and if the investor is sufficiently risk averse, utility being a sufficiently concave function of the return to the investment. Treatment diversification by a planner can be studied in the same manner.

I have taken a different approach, studying treatment allocation using the minimax regret criterion. The central result is that when there are two undominated treatments, a planner using this criterion always chooses to diversify. The specific fraction of persons assigned to each treatment depends on the available knowledge of treatment response.

5.1 TREATING X-POX

Before presenting the formal analysis, I give a simple illustration that originally appeared in Manski (2007a, Chapter 11). The illustration describes a dire scenario. Suppose that a new disease called x-pox is sweeping a community. Imagine that the disease is impossible to avoid. If untreated, ill persons always die. Thus, the entire community will die in the absence of effective treatment.

Suppose that researchers propose two treatments, A and B. The researchers know that one treatment is effective, but they do not know which one. They know that administering both treatments in combination is fatal. Thus, a person will survive if and only if she is administered the effective treatment alone. There is no time to experiment to learn which treatment is effective. Everyone must be treated right away.

Suppose that a public health agency must decide how to treat the community. Assume that the agency wants to maximize the survival rate of the population. It can select one treatment and administer it to everyone. Then the entire population will either live or die. Or it can give one treatment to some fraction of the community and the other treatment to the remaining fraction. Then the survival rate will be one of the two chosen fractions. If half the population receives each treatment, the survival rate is certain to be 50 percent.

What should the agency do? It could give everyone the same treatment and hope to make the right choice, recognizing the possibility that the outcome may be calamitous. Or it could give half the population each treatment, ensuring that half the community lives and half dies.

One can argue reasonably for either policy. The principles of decision theory discussed in Chapter 1 can be used to motivate either course of action. There are two states of nature. Treatment A is effective in one state and B is effective in the other. Hence, all treatment allocations are undominated. Allocating a higher fraction of patients to A improves welfare if A is the effective treatment and allocating a higher fraction to B improves welfare if B is the effective one. Hence, there exists no allocation that yields higher welfare in both states of nature.

The planner might use any of the three decision criteria discussed in Chapter 1 – maximization of subjective expected welfare, maximin, and minimax regret – to choose a treatment allocation. It will be shown in Section 5.2 that a planner who places subjective probabilities on the two states of nature and evaluates a treatment allocation by its subjective expected welfare would assign everyone to the treatment with the higher subjective probability of being effective. In contrast, the maximin and the minimax regret criteria both prescribe that the planner should assign half the population to each treatment. Ex post, a planner who maximizes the expected survival rate finds that either everyone lives, or everyone dies. One who maximizes the minimum survival rate or minimizes maximum regret definitely achieves a survival rate of ½.

Although the maximin and minimax regret criteria deliver the same treatment allocation in this case, the two criteria are not the same in general. They typically yield different choices. For example, let us amend the description of the x-pox problem by adding a third state of nature in which neither treatment is effective. It can be shown that adding this third state does not affect the choices made by a planner who maximizes expected welfare or minimizes maximum regret. However, all treatment allocations now solve the maximin problem. The reason is that there now exists a state of nature in which everyone dies, regardless of treatment.

One might ask what happens if the planner wants to maximize some increasing transformation of the population survival rate, rather than the survival rate per se. Researchers in finance often suppose that reducing the return on a portfolio by one percent subtracts more from an investor's welfare than raising the return by one percent adds to welfare. Similarly, in the x-pox example, reducing the survival rate of the population by one percent may subtract more from social welfare than raising the survival rate by one percent adds to welfare.

Manski (2009) showed that changing the social welfare function in this manner affects the three decision criteria differentially. The maximin allocation is unaffected. The MMR allocation may change, but it remains diversified. The expected welfare allocation may be unaffected or may become diversified, depending on the specifics of the welfare transformation and the subjective probabilities that the planner places on the states of nature. I will explain these findings in Section 5.2.4.

5.2 UTILITARIAN ALLOCATION TO TWO TREATMENTS

I now present the analysis that yields the findings regarding treatment of x-pox. I consider a planner who chooses a treatment for each member j of a population J of observationally identical persons. Persons who are observationally identical need not respond uniformly to treatment. Being observationally identical means only that persons share the same observed covariates. I likewise consider such groups of individuals in Chapter 6. Chapter 7 will generalize the analysis to discuss research on personalized treatments, where a planner may systematically vary treatment of persons with different observed covariates.

Suppose that the planner's objective is to maximize utilitarian social welfare, adding up personal welfare outcomes across the population. Equivalently, the planner wants to maximize the mean personal welfare in the population. For example, a clinician or public health agency may want to maximize the survival rate or the mean life span of patients who suffer from a life-threatening disease.

Let person j have a response function $y_j(\cdot)$ mapping treatments t into outcomes $y_j(t)$. Let $P[y(\cdot)]$ denote the population distribution of treatment response. It eases analysis to suppose that the population is large, with $P(j) = 0$ for all $j \in J$. Then, when treatment assignment is fractional, the realized fractions of persons who randomly receive different treatments have the same distribution of treatment response.

The task is to allocate the population to treatments A and B. An allocation $\delta \in [0, 1]$ randomly assigns a fraction δ of the population to

Diversified Treatment under Ambiguity 121

treatment B and the remaining $1-\delta$ to treatment A. Let $u_j(t) \equiv u_j[y(t), t]$ be the welfare of person j when this person receives treatment t and realizes outcome $y_j(t)$. Assuming that welfare is cardinal and interpersonally comparable, let $\alpha \equiv E[u(A)]$ and $\beta \equiv E[u(B)]$ be mean personal welfare if all members of the population receive treatment A or B. Then mean welfare with allocation δ is:

(5.1) $$w(\delta) = \alpha(1-\delta) + \beta\delta = \alpha + (\beta - \alpha)\delta.$$

Choosing $\delta = 1$ is optimal if $\beta \geq \alpha$ and $\delta = 0$ if $\beta \leq \alpha$. The problem of treatment choice under uncertainty arises when the planner has partial knowledge of the population distribution of welfare, rendering (α, β) partially known. The planner may have partial knowledge due to identification problems commonly faced in empirical research that seeks to predict treatment response. Many such problems were described in Chapter 3.

Let S index the feasible states of nature. Let the planner know that (α, β) lies in a bounded set $[(\alpha_s, \beta_s), s \in S]$. Let $\alpha_L \equiv \min_{s \in S} \alpha_s$, $\beta_L \equiv \min_{s \in S} \beta_s$, $\alpha_U \equiv \max_{s \in S} \alpha_s$, and $\beta_U \equiv \max_{s \in S} \beta_s$. Then the planner faces ambiguity if $\alpha_s > \beta_s$ for some values of s and $\alpha_s < \beta_s$ for other values.

The x-pox illustration is a special case. In that setting, $y_j(t)$ takes the value 0 or 1 and $u_j(t) = y_j(t)$. There are two states of nature. In state s_1, $[u_j(A) = 1, u_j(B) = 0$, all $j \in J]$. In state s_2, $[u_j(A) = 0, u_j(B) = 1$, all $j \in J]$. Hence, there are two feasible values of (α, β), being $(1, 0)$ and $(0, 1)$.

I assume below that the planner faces ambiguity. I consider the three decision criteria introduced in Chapter 1.

5.2.1 Bayesian Planning

A Bayesian planner places a subjective distribution π on S and solves:

(5.2) $$\max_{\delta \in [0, 1]} E_\pi(\alpha) + \lfloor E_\pi(\beta) - E_\pi(\alpha) \rfloor \delta,$$

where $E_\pi(\alpha) = \int \alpha_s d\pi$ and $E_\pi(\beta) = \int \beta_s d\pi$. The planner chooses $\delta = 0$ if $E_\pi(\beta) < E_\pi(\alpha)$ and $\delta = 1$ if $E_\pi(\beta) > E_\pi(\alpha)$. He is indifferent among all δ if $E_\pi(\beta) = E_\pi(\alpha)$. Thus, a Bayesian planner makes a singleton choice if $E_\pi(\beta) \neq E_\pi(\alpha)$.

In the x-pox setting, $E_\pi(\alpha) = \pi(s_1)$ and $E_\pi(\beta) = \pi(s_2) = 1 - \pi(s_1)$. Hence, the planner chooses $\delta = 0$ if $\pi(s_1) > \frac{1}{2}$, $\delta = 1$ if $\pi(s_1) < \frac{1}{2}$, and is indifferent among all δ if $\pi(s_1) = \frac{1}{2}$.

5.2.2 Maximin Planning

A maximin planner solves:

$$(5.3) \quad \max_{\delta \in [0,\,1]} \min_{s \in S} \alpha_s + (\beta_s - \alpha_s)\delta.$$

If (α_L, β_L) is feasible, the decision is $\delta = 0$ if $\beta_L < \alpha_L$, $\delta = 1$ if $\beta_L > \alpha_L$, and all δ if $\beta_L = \alpha_L$. Thus, a maximin planner makes a singleton choice if (α_L, β_L) is feasible and $\beta_L \neq \alpha_L$.

In the x-pox setting, (α_L, β_L) is not feasible, the only feasible states being $(1, 0)$ and $(0, 1)$. The feasible values of $\alpha_s + (\beta_s - \alpha_s)\delta$ are $1 - \delta$ and δ. Hence, the maximin choice is $\delta = \frac{1}{2}$, yielding the certain survival rate $\frac{1}{2}$.

5.2.3 Minimax Regret Planning

The regret of allocation δ in state of nature s is the difference between the maximum achievable welfare and the welfare achieved with allocation δ. Maximum welfare in state of nature s is $\max(\alpha_s, \beta_s)$. The minimax regret criterion is:

$$(5.4) \quad \min_{\delta \in [0,\,1]} \max_{s \in S} \max(\alpha_s, \beta_s) - [\alpha_s + (\beta_s - \alpha_s)\delta].$$

Manski (2007a, Chapter 11) derived the MMR treatment allocation. Let $S(A) \equiv \{s \in S : \alpha_s > \beta_s\}$ and $S(B) \equiv \{s \in S : \beta_s > \alpha_s\}$. Let $M(A) \equiv \max_{s \in S(A)}(\alpha_s - \beta_s)$ and $M(B) \equiv \max_{s \in S(B)}(\beta_s - \alpha_s)$. It can be shown that the MMR allocation to treatment B is the fraction $\delta_{MMR} = M(B) / [M(A) + M(B)]$. This is always an interior fraction in treatment under ambiguity, as $M(A) > 0$ and $M(B) > 0$. If (α_L, β_U) and (α_U, β_L) are feasible, the expression for the MMR treatment reduces to $\delta_{MMR} = (\beta_U - \alpha_L) / [(\alpha_U - \beta_L) + (\beta_U - \alpha_L)]$.

In the x-pox setting, (α_L, β_U) and (α_U, β_L) are feasible, being $(0, 1)$ and $(1, 0)$. The MMR treatment is $\delta_{MMR} = (1 - 0) / [(1 - 0) + (1 - 0)] = \frac{1}{2}$.

Choosing Sentences for Convicted Juvenile Offenders

To illustrate planning under ambiguity in a realistic setting rather than the hypothetical x-pox scenario, consider judicial sentencing for a population of convicted juvenile offenders. I will use the findings reported in Manski and Nagin (1998), which were discussed in Chapter 3.

In this case, the planner is the state of Utah and the population are males under age sixteen who are convicted of an offence. Let treatment A be the status quo policy, this being a decentralized system where judges have discretion to choose between residential confinement and a sentence that does not involve confinement. Let treatment B be an innovation mandating confinement for all convicted offenders. Let the outcome of interest be the binary measure of recidivism considered by Manski and Nagin. Thus, y(t) = 1 if an offender who receives treatment t is not convicted of another crime in the two-year period following sentencing and y(t) = 0 if the offender is convicted of a subsequent crime. Let u(t) = y(t). Then $\alpha = P[y(A) = 1]$ and $\beta = P[y(B) = 1]$.

Analyzing data on outcomes under the status quo policy, Manski and Nagin (1998) found that $\alpha = 0.61$. In the absence of knowledge of how judges choose sentences or how juveniles respond to their sentences, the data reveal only that $\beta \in [0.03, 0.92]$. Hence, the innovation may be much better or worse than the status quo. Manski and Nagin argued that this "worst-case" bound on β is germane to policy making because criminologists have found it difficult to learn how sentencing affects recidivism. Researchers have long debated the counterfactual outcomes that offenders would experience if they were to receive other sentences.

Consider policy choice when the state of Utah knows that $\alpha = 0.61$ and $\beta \in [0.03, 0.92]$. If the state makes a Bayesian decision, it adopts mandatory confinement if $E_\pi(\beta) > 0.61$ and leaves the status quo of judicial discretion in place if $E_\pi(\beta) < 0.61$. If the state applies the maximin criterion, it leaves the status quo in place because $\beta_L = 0.03 < 0.61$. If the state uses the MMR criterion, it randomly sentences to confinement $(\beta_U - \alpha)/(\beta_U - \beta_L) = (0.92 - 0.61)/(0.92 - 0.03) = 0.35$ of the offenders and leaves judicial discretion in place for the remaining fraction 0.65.

5.2.4 Welfare Increasing in Mean Personal Welfare

It is of interest to generalize the above analysis by considering social welfare functions that may increase nonlinearly with mean personal welfare. Thus, now let:

(5.5) $$w(\delta) = f\big[\alpha + (\beta - \alpha)\delta\big],$$

where f(·) is strictly increasing.

The Bayes decision is generically singleton if f(·) is convex, but it may be fractional if f(·) has concave segments. In finance, this is the well-known finding that an investor whose utility is convex in income does not diversify, but one whose utility is concave in income may diversify.

The shape of f(·) does not affect the maximin decision. The reason is that the maximin criterion only uses ordinal, not cardinal properties of the welfare function.

Manski (2009) showed that the MMR allocation is fractional whenever f(·) is continuous and the planner faces ambiguity. If f(·) = log(·) and {(α_L, β_U), (α_U, β_L)} are feasible, the MMR allocation is $\delta_{MMR} = [\alpha_U(\beta_U - \alpha_L)] / [\alpha_U(\beta_U - \alpha_L) + \beta_U(\alpha_U - \beta_L)]$.

5.3 DIVERSIFICATION AND EQUAL TREATMENT OF EQUALS

Proposing that an investor may want to choose a diversified portfolio is uncontroversial. It is similarly uncontroversial to suggest that a firm diversify when making production decisions. For example, it is common to recommend that a farmer diversify when planting crops. In this setting, the treatments are alternative crops, the population comprises a set of plots of land, and the farmer may be uncertain about crop yields or prices.

I have, however, found it controversial to propose diversification of treatments to humans. Presenting the idea in seminars and lectures, I have frequently received comments that, if persons are observationally identical, all persons should receive the same treatment. The concern is that treatment diversification violates the ethical principle calling for *equal treatment of equals*.

Utilitarian planning does not address this ethical concern. Equal treatment of equals is a deontological rather than consequentialist consideration. It supposes that actions have intrinsic value, apart from their consequences. I explain here, drawing on Manski (2009, 2013c).

5.3.1 Ex Ante and Ex Post Equal Treatment

Diversification is consistent with the equal-treatment principle in the ex ante sense that all members of the population have the same probability of receiving a particular treatment. It violates the principle in the ex post sense that different persons ultimately receive different treatments. Thus, equal treatment holds ex ante but not ex post.

The x-pox scenario illustrates the difference between ex ante and ex post equal treatment. Administering treatment A or B to the entire community provides equal treatment in both senses. Moreover, it equalizes realized outcomes, as the entire population either survives or dies. Administering each treatment to half the community treats everyone equally ex ante, every person having a 50 percent chance of receiving each treatment. However, it does not treat people equally ex post. Nor do it equalize outcomes, as half the community lives and half dies.

Democratic societies ordinarily adhere to the ex post sense of equal treatment. Americans who have the same income, deductions, and exemptions are required to pay the same federal income tax. The Equal Protection clause in the 14th Amendment to the U.S. Constitution is held to mean that all persons in a jurisdiction are subject to the same laws, not that all persons have the same chance of being subject to different laws.

Nevertheless, some important policies yield equal treatment ex ante but not ex post. American examples include random tax audits, drug testing and airport screening, random calls for jury service, and the Green Card and Vietnam draft lotteries. These policies have not been prompted by the desire to cope with uncertainty that motivates treatment diversification. Yet they do indicate some willingness of society to accept policies that provide ex ante equal but ex post unequal treatment.

Democratic societies come closer to treatment diversification as suggested here when they perform randomized experiments. Randomized experiments are undertaken explicitly to learn about treatment response. Combining ex ante equal treatment with ex post unequal treatment is precisely what makes randomized experiments informative. Modern medical ethics permits randomization only under conditions of *clinical equipoise*; that is, when partial knowledge of treatment response prevents a determination that one treatment is superior to another. The current practice of randomized experiments differs from treatment diversification mainly in that democracies do not ordinarily compel participation in experiments. Concern with compulsion has been particularly strong in medical trials, which advertise for volunteers and go to lengths to obtain informed consent from experimental subjects.

5.3.2 Planning Combining Consequentialism and Deontological Ethics

Suppose that a society is concerned with the ex post sense of equal treatment, but also wants to consider policies that diversify treatment. How might it proceed?

Philosophers often take the position that deontological considerations should supersede consequentialist ones. This suggests a lexicographic decision process in which one first restricts attention to actions deemed deontologically acceptable and only then considers the consequences of these actions. If one considers ex post unequal treatment to be unacceptable, diversification of treatment is off the table.

In contrast, economists typically think it permissible to make trade-offs, weighing the pros and cons of actions. Working from this perspective, Manski (2009) suggested amending the utilitarian welfare function of Section 5.2 by adding a term that expresses societal concern with ex post equal treatment.

The idea is to let the welfare function have this form:

(5.6) $$w(\delta) = \alpha + (\beta - \alpha)\delta - \gamma \cdot 1[0 < \delta < 1],$$

where $\gamma > 0$. Thus, one subtracts something from welfare when the allocation is fractional. Such a welfare function embodies both consequentialist and deontological considerations. I showed that expressing concern with ex post equal treatment in this manner does not affect the minimax regret treatment allocation if γ is not too large. However, the criterion assigns everyone to the same treatment if the magnitude of γ exceeds a threshold.

5.4 ADAPTIVE DIVERSIFICATION

I have thus far considered a one-time choice, in which a planner allocates treatments to one population of persons. Now consider a planner who makes treatment decisions in a sequence of periods, facing a new population each period. Assume that each successive population has the same distribution of treatment response. Then the planner may observe the outcomes of early decisions and use this evidence to inform treatment later. Diversification is advantageous for learning treatment response because it generates randomized experiments. As evidence accumulates, the planner can revise the fraction of persons assigned to each treatment in accord with the available knowledge. I have called this *adaptive diversification*.

It has long been appreciated that variation in policy promotes learning. More than a century ago, the American Progressive movement called attention to the fact that federalism enables the states to experiment with new policy ideas (Roosevelt, 1912). Twenty years later, Supreme Court Justice Louis Brandeis, in his dissent to the 1932 case *New York State Ice Co. v. Liebmann* (285 U.S. 311), added what has become a famous remark on this theme, commonly paraphrased as the observation that the states are the *laboratories of democracy*. What is new in the concept of adaptive diversification is recognition that policy variation at a point in time yields the benefit of diversification in reducing gross errors, which occurs even in the absence of learning over time.

Adaptive diversification can be achieved by a Bayesian planner who updates his prior subjective distribution on treatment response after observing the outcomes of each successive population. Manski (2009) suggested that a planner who does not want to specify a subjective distribution on treatment response might use the *adaptive minimax regret* (AMR) criterion. In each period, this criterion applies the static MMR criterion using the information available at the time. It is adaptive because successive populations may receive different allocations as knowledge of treatment response increases over time.

The AMR criterion is normatively appealing because it treats each population as well as possible, in the MMR sense, given the available knowledge. It does not ask persons in one period to sacrifice for the benefit of future persons. Nevertheless, the diversification of treatment performed for the benefit of the current population enables learning about treatment response.

The fractional allocations produced by the AMR criterion are randomized experiments, so it is natural to ask how application of AMR differs from conventional trials. There are important differences in the fraction and composition of the population randomized into treatment. The AMR criterion randomizes treatment of all observationally similar persons. In contrast, the treatment groups in trials are typically small fractions of a population. Moreover, trials draw subjects from pools of persons who volunteer to participate and who meet specific conditions. Hence, they reveal the distribution of treatment response within certain sub-populations, not within the full population.

Implementation of adaptive diversification may be possible in centralized health-care systems where there exists a planning entity who chooses treatments for a broad patient population. Examples are the Military Health System in the United States, the National Health Service in the United Kingdom, and some private health maintenance organizations.

5.4.1 Adaptive Treatment of a Life-Threatening Disease

To illustrate the AMR criterion, Manski (2009) considered a hypothetical medical treatment-choice problem where the outcome of interest unfolds over multiple periods. As empirical evidence accumulates, the AMR treatment allocation changes accordingly.

When treating a life-threatening disease, the outcome of interest may be the number of years that a patient survives within some time horizon. Let the horizon be five years and let the outcome of interest be the number of years that a patient lives during the five years following receipt of treatment. This outcome gradually becomes observable as time passes. At the time of treatment, years of survival can take any of the values [0, 1, 2, 3, 4, 5]. A year later, one can observe whether a patient is still alive and hence can determine whether years survived equals zero or at least one year. And so on until year five, when the outcome is fully observable.

Table 5.1 presents hypothetical data on annual death rates following receipt of a status quo treatment or an innovation, labelled A and B. The entries show that 20 (10) percent of the patients who receive the status quo (innovation) die in the first year after treatment. In each of the subsequent years, the death rates are 5 and 2 percent respectively. Overall, the entries imply that the mean numbers of years lived after treatment are 3.5 years with the status quo treatment and 4.3 years with the innovation.

I supposed that the death rates under the status quo treatment are known at the outset from historical experience. However, the planner has no initial knowledge of death rates with the innovation. That is, he does not initially know whether the innovation will be disastrous, with all patients dying in the first year following treatment, or entirely successful, with all patients living five years or more. Then the initial bound on mean number of years lived with the innovation is [0, 5]. Applying the analysis in Section 5.2, the AMR criterion initially allocates 0.70 of patients to the status quo and 0.30 to the innovation.

In year 1 the planner observes that, of the patients in cohort 0 assigned to the innovation, 10 percent died in the first year following treatment. This enables him to deduce that the fraction who live at least one year is 0.90. The planner uses this information to tighten the bound on mean years lived to [0.90, 4.50]. In each subsequent year the planner observes another annual death rate, tightens the bound on mean years lived with the innovation, and recomputes the treatment allocation accordingly. The result is that the fractions of patients allocated to the innovation in years (1, 2, 3, 4) are (0.28, 0.35, 0.50, 0.98). In year 5 the planner is certain that the innovation is better than the status quo, and so allocates all patients to the innovation.

The final two columns of Table 5.1 give the maximum regret and mean years lived of each cohort, both computed using the AMR treatment allocation. Maximum regret decreases to zero as information accumulates. Mean years lived initially declines slightly but increases thereafter.

TABLE 5.1 *Adaptive Diversification Treating a Life-Threatening Disease*

Cohort or year (n or k)	Death rate in year k		Bound on mean years lived with innovation, cohort n	AMR allocation, cohort n	Maximum regret of AMR allocation, cohort n	Mean years lived, cohort n
	Status quo	Innovation				
0			[0, 5]	0.30	1.05	3.74
1	0.20	0.10	[0.90, 4.50]	0.28	0.72	3.72
2	0.05	0.02	[1.78, 4.42]	0.35	0.60	3.78
3	0.05	0.02	[2.64, 4.36]	0.50	0.43	3.90
4	0.05	0.02	[3.48, 4.32]	0.98	0.02	4.28
5	0.05	0.02	[4.30, 4.30]	1	0	4.30

5.4.2 Adaptive Diversification of Regulatory Approval

In Manski (2015c), I proposed application of the adaptive diversification idea to regulatory approval. Modern societies legislate numerous requirements for regulatory approval of private activities. In the United States, pharmaceutical firms wanting to market new drugs require approval of the Food and Drug Administration, firms wanting to extract natural resources require approval of the Environmental Protection Agency, firms wanting to merge may require approval of the Federal Trade Commission or the Department of Justice, and entities wanting tax exempt status require approval of the Internal Revenue Service. Individuals require the approval of state governments to drive, vote, carry a concealed weapon, or marry. Firms and individuals wanting to use land for various purposes must comply with local zoning ordinances and obtain building permits.

How should society evaluate regulatory approval processes? The legal system makes this the task of judicial review, a process that begins when a legal person (an individual or firm) questions a specific agency action. In the United States, the Administrative Procedure Act (APA) provides the statutory foundation for judicial review of federal regulation, establishing a system for review of specific regulatory actions.

As I see it, society should evaluate regulatory approval more broadly than through scrutiny of specific agency actions. Scrutiny of specific actions may miss considerations that become evident when one views approval processes holistically. Among these is that society may want to randomize approval decisions. An action to randomly grant or deny approval to a given applicant may appear "arbitrary, capricious, [or] an abuse of discretion" under the APA when it is considered in isolation, but it may be justifiable as part of a well-motivated regulatory strategy.

In particular, adaptive diversification may be appealing when regulatory agencies make approval decisions under uncertainty. For example, the Food and Drug Administration may be unsure whether it should approve New Drug Applications, the Federal Trade Commission may be unsure whether it should approve merger proposals, or a local planning commission may be unsure whether it should approve applications to build new structures. In these and other settings, it may be socially desirable for an agency to diversify, randomly granting approval to some applicants and denying it to others who are observationally similar. At a point in time, diversification enables an agency facing uncertainty to limit potential errors. Over time, diversification generates randomized experiments that enable an agency to learn and improve its decision making.

6

Treatment with Data from Statistically Imprecise Trials

A central objective of empirical research performing randomized trials is to inform treatment choice. Identification problems combine with the necessity of inference from sample data to limit the informativeness of studies. Unfortunately, researchers analyzing trial data have commonly used concepts of statistical inference whose foundations are distant from treatment choice. It has been particularly common to use hypothesis tests to compare treatments.

Beginning in Manski (2004b) and continuing through Manski (2005b, 2007a, 2007b, 2019b, 2019c, 2021b, 2023) and Manski and Tetenov (2016, 2019, 2021, 2023), I have recommended use of the Wald (1950) development of statistical decision theory to design trials and analyze the data. This chapter describes basic ideas and presents illustrative findings. To keep the exposition simple and framed in a familiar setting, I focus on medical treatment with evidence from classical randomized clinical trials. This means that there are no problems of internal or external validity, hence no identification problems. The only difficulty is statistical imprecision due to finite sample size.

Randomized trials have long enjoyed a favored status in medical research, often being called the "gold standard" for collection of data on treatment response. The influential Cochrane system for grading the quality of evidence ordinarily reserves its highest rating for evidence from trials (Higgins and Green, 2011, Section 12.2.1). The drug approval process of the U.S. Food and Drug Administration (FDA) ordinarily considers only trial evidence when making decisions on drug approval.

I first review and critique the prevailing use of hypothesis tests to compare treatments. I then describe my application of statistical decision theory.

6.1 USING HYPOTHESIS TESTS TO COMPARE TREATMENTS

A longstanding practice in medical research has been to use trial data to test a specified null hypothesis against an alternative and to use the result of the test to compare treatments. A common procedure when comparing two treatments in a trial is to view one as the status quo and the other as an innovation. The usual null hypothesis is that mean response with the innovation and the status quo are the same. If the null hypothesis is not rejected, it is recommended that the status quo treatment continue to be used in clinical practice. If the null is rejected, with the innovation performing sufficiently better than the status quo in the sample, it is recommended that the innovation become the treatment of choice. This type of test is institutionalized in the FDA drug approval process, with the distinction that the recommendation is whether or not to approve the drug for marketing.

The convention has been to perform a test that fixes the probability of rejecting the null hypothesis when it is correct, the probability of a Type I error. Then sample size determines the probability of rejecting the alternative hypothesis when it is correct, the probability of a Type II error. The power of a test is defined as one minus the probability of a Type II error. The convention has been to choose a sample size that yields specified power at some value of the effect size deemed clinically important. International Conference on Harmonisation (1999) provided guidance for the design and conduct of trials evaluating pharmaceuticals, stating (p. 1923):

> Conventionally the probability of type I error is set at 5% or less or as dictated by any adjustments made necessary for multiplicity considerations; the precise choice may be influenced by the prior plausibility of the hypothesis under test and the desired impact of the results. The probability of type II error is conventionally set at 10% to 20%.

Trials with samples too small to achieve these error probabilities are called "underpowered" and are criticized as scientifically useless and medically unethical (e.g., Halpern, Karlawish, and Berlin, 2002).

Manski and Tetenov (2016) gave several reasons why hypothesis testing may yield unsatisfactory results for medical decisions and other forms of treatment choice. These are:

1. *Use of Conventional Asymmetric Error Probabilities*: It has been standard to fix the probability of Type I error at 5 percent and that of Type II error at 10–20 percent. The theory of hypothesis testing gives no rationale for use of these error probabilities. It gives no

reason why a clinician concerned with patient welfare should find it reasonable to make treatment choices that have a substantially greater probability of Type II than Type I error.
2. *Inattention to Magnitudes of Losses to Welfare When Errors Occur*: A clinician should care about more than the probabilities of Type I and II error. A clinician should care as well about the magnitudes of the losses to patient welfare that arise when errors occur. A given error probability should be less acceptable when the welfare difference between treatments is larger. The theory of hypothesis testing does not recognize this.
3. *Limitation to Settings with Two Treatments*: A clinician often chooses among several treatments. Some clinical trials compare more than two treatments. Yet the standard theory of hypothesis testing only contemplates choice between two treatments. Statisticians have struggled to extend the theory to deal sensibly with comparisons of multiple treatments.

Further critique has been presented in the *American Statistical Association Statement on Statistical Significance and P-Values* (Wasserstein and Lazar, 2016). Two principles of the Statement are:

Scientific conclusions and business or policy decisions should not be based only on whether a *p*-value passes a specific threshold.
A *p*-value, or statistical significance, does not measure the size of an effect or the importance of a result.

Moreover, it has become increasingly common to express concern that evaluation of empirical research by the results of hypothesis tests generates publication bias and diminishes the reproducibility of findings, a phenomenon called "p-hacking." See Ioannidis (2005) and Wasserstein and Lazar (2016).

6.2 USING STATISTICAL DECISION THEORY TO COMPARE TREATMENTS

In this section, I describe general principles of statistical decision theory, expanding the discussion initiated in Chapter 1 and opening consideration of application to trial data. The sections that follow deepen the focus on analysis and design of trials.

Wald (1950) considered the general problem of using sample data to make decisions. He posed the task as choice of a *statistical decision function* (SDF), which maps potentially available data into a choice among the feasible actions. Wald's seminal book is abstract, making it a difficult read. Ferguson (1967), Berger (1985), and Parmigiani and Inoue (2009) provide comprehensive expositions.

Wald recommended ex ante evaluation of statistical decision functions as *procedures* applied as the sampling process is engaged repeatedly to draw independent data samples. The idea of a procedure transforms the original problem of induction from a single sample into the deductive problem of assessing the probabilistic performance of a statistical decision function across realizations of the sampling process. Thus, the theory is frequentist.

Wald proposed that the decision maker evaluate an SDF by the mean welfare it yields across realizations of the sampling process. His presentation differed semantically from the one that I use to describe treatment choice in that he defined loss to be the negative of welfare and took the objective to be minimization of loss rather than maximization of welfare. He used the term *risk* to denote mean loss across realizations of the sampling process.

To choose among the feasible actions, a decision maker first eliminates dominated SDFs, which Wald termed *inadmissible*. One then uses some criterion to choose an admissible statistical decision function. Statistical decision theorists recognized from the outset that there is no optimal way to choose an admissible decision function. There at most are reasonable ways. Ferguson (1967) nicely wrote (p. 28):

It is a natural reaction to search for a "best" decision rule, a rule that has the smallest risk no matter what the true state of nature. Unfortunately, situations in which a best decision rule exists are rare and uninteresting. For each fixed state of nature there may be a best action for the statistician to take. However, this best action will differ, in general, for different states of nature, so that no one action can be presumed best overall.

He went on to write (p. 29): "A *reasonable* rule is one that is better than just guessing."

6.2.1 Bayes Decisions

What are reasonable ways to choose an admissible SDF? The Bayesian approach is particularly well known. DeGroot (1970) provides a classic treatise on the subject. Bayesian decision making is compelling when one feels able to place a credible subjective prior distribution on the state space. However, Bayesians have long struggled to provide guidance on specification of priors and the matter continues to be controversial. See, for example, the spectrum of views regarding Bayesian analysis of medical trials expressed by the authors and discussants of Spiegelhalter, Freedman, and Parmar (1994). The controversy suggests that inability to express a credible prior is common in actual decision settings. Perhaps as a result, Bayesian analysis is well known but seldom used in medical research.

When one finds it difficult to assert a credible subjective distribution, Bayesian statisticians who believe it essential to use a probability distribution to express uncertainty may suggest use of some default distribution, variously called a "reference" or "conventional," or "objective" prior distribution; see Berger (2006). However, there is no consensus on what distribution should play this role. The choice matters for decision making.

It has been common to think of the Bayesian process of transforming a prior into a posterior distribution as antithetical to frequentist statistics, but Wald provided a clear frequentist perspective on Bayes decisions. He showed that, when some regularity conditions hold, minimization of Bayes risk, a frequentist decision criterion, yields the same decisions as would occur if one performs Bayesian inference, combining the prior distribution with the data to form a posterior subjective distribution, and then uses the posterior distribution to choose an action. See the discussion in Berger (1985), Section 4.4.1.

6.2.2 Maximin and Minimax Regret Decisions

In the absence of a subjective distribution on the state space, a reasonable way to act is to use a decision criterion that achieves uniformly satisfactory results, whatever the true state of nature may be. The two most common formalizations of this idea are embodied in the maximin and minimax regret criteria. The maximin criterion considers only the worst outcome that an action may yield. MMR considers the worst outcome relative to the best achievable in each state of nature. Savage (1951) distinguished the two sharply, writing that the former is "ultrapessimistic" while the latter is not.

MMR decisions have been shown to behave more reasonably than maximin ones in common contexts of treatment choice with trial data. When outcomes take a bounded range of values, the MMR rule is well approximated by the *empirical success* (ES) rule, which chooses the treatment with the highest observed average outcome in the trial. The ES rule provides a simple and plausible way to use the results of a trial. The performance of the ES rule from the perspective of maximum regret was initiated by Manski (2004b). Schlag (2006) and Stoye (2009) showed that this rule either exactly or approximately minimizes maximum regret in settings with two treatments when sample size is moderate.

In contrast, the maximin rule sometimes ignores the trial data, whatever they may be. When Savage (1951) stated that the minimax criterion is "ultrapessimistic," he went on to write (p. 63): "it can lead to the absurd conclusion in some cases that no amount of relevant experimentation should deter the actor from behaving as though he were in complete ignorance." Savage did not flesh out this statement, but it is easy to show that this occurs with trial data. Manski (2004b) provided a simple example that I will present in Section 6.3.

As mentioned in Chapter 1, the conceptual appeal of using maximum regret to measure performance is that maximum regret quantifies how lack of knowledge of the true state of nature diminishes the quality of decisions. The term "maximum regret" is shorthand for the maximum sub-optimality of a decision criterion across the feasible states of nature. An SDF with small maximum regret is uniformly near optimal across all states. Maximum regret is determined jointly by the identification problem faced and by the statistical imprecision of sample data. When the true state of nature is point identified, maximum regret purely measures statistical imprecision. Traditional measures of statistical imprecision such as confidence sets and standard errors play no role in the Wald theory.

Maximum regret is well-defined in general settings with multiple treatments and when persons have heterogeneous observable covariates that may be used to differentiate treatment. The concept is especially transparent when there are two treatments, and the members of the population are observationally identical.

Suppose there are two feasible treatments, say A and B. In a state of nature where A is better, regret is the product of the probability across repeated samples that an SDF commits a Type A error (choosing B) and the magnitude of the loss relative to the optimum that occurs when choosing B. In a state where B is better, regret is the probability of a Type B error (choosing A) times the magnitude of the loss relative to the optimum when choosing A.

Recall the critique in Section 6.1 of the use of hypothesis testing to choose a treatment. I called attention to the asymmetric treatment of Type I and Type II error probabilities and the inattention to magnitudes of losses when errors occur. Evaluating treatment rules by regret overcomes both problems. Regret considers both error probabilities symmetrically and it measures the magnitudes of the losses that errors produce.

6.3 TREATMENT CHOICE WITH TRIAL DATA

I now formalize treatment choice as a statistical decision problem. In this setting, an SDF uses the data to choose an allocation of persons to treatments. Using terminology introduced in Manski (2004b), I call an SDF a *statistical treatment rule* (STR). The mean performance of an STR across repeated samples is its *expected welfare*. I consider utilitarian treatment in a simple setting with two treatments and a population of observationally identical persons. The presentation in this section draws on Manski (2007a, Chapter 12).

The basic setup is the same as in Chapter 5. A planner must assign treatment A or B to each member of population J. Each person $j \in J$ has a response function mapping treatments $t \in T$ into personal welfare outcomes $u_j(t) \in R$. The population distribution of treatment response is P. The members of the population may respond heterogeneously to treatment, but they are observationally identical to the planner.

For any $\delta \in [0, 1]$, the planner can allocate a fraction δ of patients to treatment B and $1 - \delta$ to A. The planner wants to choose δ to maximize the utilitarian welfare function:

$$(6.1) \quad w(\delta, P) = E[u(A)] \cdot (1-\delta) + E[u(B)] \cdot \delta = \alpha(1-\delta) + \beta\delta$$
$$= \alpha + (\beta - \alpha)\delta,$$

where $\alpha \equiv E[u(A)]$ and $\beta \equiv E[u(B)]$ are mean personal welfare if everyone were to receive treatment A or B respectively. The quantity $\beta - \alpha$ is the average treatment effect (ATE) in the population. It is optimal to set $\delta = 1$ if the ATE is positive and $\delta = 0$ if the ATE is negative. The problem of interest is treatment choice when incomplete knowledge of P implies that the sign of the ATE is unknown.

The new feature relative to Chapter 5 is that sample data on treatment outcomes are available. Let Q be the sampling distribution and let Ψ be the sample space. An STR is a function $\delta(\cdot): \Psi \to [0, 1]$ that maps sample data into a treatment allocation. The welfare realized with δ and data ψ is the random variable:

$$(6.2) \quad w(\delta, P, \psi) = \alpha + (\beta - \alpha) \cdot \delta(\psi).$$

The state space $[(P_s, Q_s), s \in S]$ is the set of (P, Q) pairs that the planner deems possible. In any state s, expected welfare across samples is:

(6.3) $\quad w(\delta, P_s, Q_s) = \alpha_s + (\beta_s - \alpha_s) \cdot E_s[\delta(\psi)].$

Here $E_s[\delta(\psi)] \equiv \int_\psi \delta(\psi) dQ_s(\psi)$ is the expected allocation of patients to treatment B, across samples.

Rule δ is admissible if there exists no rule δ' such that $w(\delta', P_s, Q_s) \geq w(\delta, P_s, Q_s)$ for all $s \in S$ and $w(\delta', P_s, Q_s) > w(\delta, P_s, Q_s)$ for some s. The Bayes, maximin, and MMR rules are respectively as follows:

(6.4) $\quad \max_{\delta} \int_S \{\alpha_s + (\beta_s - \alpha_s) \cdot E_s[\delta(\psi)]\} d\pi(s),$

(6.5) $\quad \max_{\delta} \min_{s \in S} \alpha_s + (\beta_s - \alpha_s) \cdot E_s[\delta(\psi)],$

(6.6) $\quad \min_{\delta} \max_{s \in S} \left[\max(\alpha_s, \beta_s) - \{\alpha_s + (\beta_s - \alpha_s) \cdot E_s[\delta(\psi)]\} \right].$

6.3.1 Choice between a Status Quo Treatment and an Innovation When Outcomes Are Binary

I now illustrate in perhaps the simplest non-trivial setting. Let the welfare outcomes u be binary, taking the value zero if treatment fails and one if it succeeds. Let A be a status quo treatment and B be an innovation. Suppose that the planner knows from experience the success probability $\alpha \equiv P[u(A) = 1]$ of the status quo treatment. However, the planner does not know the success probability $\beta \equiv P[u(B) = 1]$ of the innovation. The planner wants to choose treatments to maximize the success probability.

Let a trial be performed to learn about outcomes under the innovation, with N subjects randomly drawn from the population and assigned to treatment B. The observed trial outcomes are that n subjects experience outcome u = 1 and N − n realize u = 0. In this setting, N indexes the sampling process. The number n of experimental successes is a sufficient statistic for the data, with n being distributed binomial $B[\beta, N]$.

The feasible STRs are functions $\delta(\cdot) : [0, ..., N] \to [0, 1]$ that map the number of experimental successes into a treatment allocation. The expected welfare of rule δ in state s is:

(6.7) $\quad w(\delta, P_s, N) = \alpha_s + (\beta_s - \alpha_s) \cdot E_s[\delta(n)].$

The expected treatment allocation across samples is:

(6.8) $\quad E_s[\delta(n)] = \sum_{i=0}^{N} \delta(i) \cdot f(n = i; \beta_s, N),$

where $f(n = i; \beta_s, N) \equiv N![i!(N-i)!]^{-1}\beta_s^i(1-\beta_s)^{N-i}$ is the Binomial probability of i successes. The only unknown determinant of expected welfare is β_s.

It is reasonable in this setting to conjecture that admissible treatment rules should be ones in which the fraction of the population allocated to treatment B increases with n. It turns out that the admissible treatment rules are a subclass of these rules. A theorem of Karlin and Rubin (1956) shows that the admissible rules are the *monotone treatment rules*. Monotone rules assign all persons to the status quo if the experimental success rate is below some threshold and all to the innovation if the success rate is above the threshold. That is, δ is admissible if and only if:

(6.9a) $\quad\quad\quad\quad\quad\quad \delta(n) = 0$ for $n < n_0$,

(6.9b) $\quad\quad\quad\quad\quad\quad \delta(n) = \lambda$ for $n = n_0$,

(6.9c) $\quad\quad\quad\quad\quad\quad \delta(n) = 1$ for $n > n_0$,

for some $0 \leq n_0 \leq N$ and $0 \leq \lambda \leq 1$.

Observe that STRs satisfying (6.9) are singleton except in threshold cases where $n = n_0$. Thus, diversification is generically inadmissible in this setting, where the true state of nature is point-identified, and uncertainty stems purely from statistical imprecision. This finding contrasts sharply with that of Chapter 5, where uncertainty stemmed purely from partial identification. In that setting, all allocations were undominated when the sign of the ATE is unknown.

The Karlin–Rubin finding that the admissible STRs are the monotone rules rests not only on the point-identification yielded by classical trials but also on the assumption that the objective is to maximize mean personal welfare. Curious about the role played by the latter condition, Manski and Tetenov (2007) studied admissibility when the objective is to maximize a concave and strictly monotone function of the rate of treatment success, a setting discussed previously in Section 5.2.4. We showed that this generalization of the welfare function is consequential. Now admissible treatment rules need not be monotone in the Karlin–Rubin sense; in fact, monotone rules may be inadmissible. However, a weaker notion of monotonicity remains relevant. Define a *fractional monotone* rule to be one in which the fraction of the population assigned to the innovation weakly increases with the experimental success rate. We showed that the class of fractional monotone rules is *complete*. That is, given any rule which is not fractional monotone, there exists a fractional monotone rule that performs at least as well in all feasible states of nature and better in some state of nature.

In some mathematical senses, the collection of monotone treatment rules is a "small" subset of the space of all feasible treatment rules. Nevertheless, it still contains a broad range of rules. These include:

Data-Invariant Rules: These are the rules $\delta(\cdot) = 0$ and $\delta(\cdot) = 1$, which assign all persons to treatment A or B respectively, whatever n may be.

Empirical Success Rule: An optimal treatment rule allocates all persons to treatment A if $\beta < \alpha$ and all to B if $\beta > \alpha$. The ES rule emulates the optimal rule by replacing β with its sample analog, the empirical success rate n/N.

Bayes Rules: The form of the Bayes rule depends on the prior subjective distribution placed on β. Consider the class of Beta priors, which form the conjugate family for a Binomial likelihood. Let $(\beta_s, s \in S) = (0, 1)$ and let the prior be Beta with parameters (c, d). Then the posterior mean for β is $(c + n)/(c + d + N)$. The resulting Bayes rule is:

(6.10a) $\quad\quad\quad \delta(n) = 0 \text{ for } (c+n)/(c+d+N) < \alpha,$

(6.10b) $\quad \delta(n) = \lambda \text{ for } (c+n)/(c+d+N) = \alpha, \text{ where } 0 \leq \lambda \leq 1,$

(6.10c) $\quad\quad\quad \delta(n) = 1 \text{ for } (c+n)/(c+d+N) > \alpha.$

Maximin Rule: Minimum expected welfare for rule δ is:

(6.11) $\quad\quad\quad \min_{s \in S} w(\delta, P_s, N) = \alpha + \min_{s \in S}(\beta_s - \alpha) E_s[\delta(n)].$

$E_s[\delta(n)] > 0$ for all $\beta_s > 0$ and for all rules except $\delta(\cdot) = 0$. It follows that, when S contains states with $\beta_s < \alpha$, the maximin rule is $\delta(\cdot) = 0$. Hence, the maximin rule ignores the trial data on treatment response, whatever they may turn out to be. This illustrates the Savage (1951) statement that using the maximin rule can induce one to entirely ignore available sample data.

Minimax Regret Rule: The regret of rule δ in state s is:

(6.12)
$$\begin{aligned} &\max(\alpha, \beta_s) - \{\alpha + (\beta_s - \alpha) \cdot E_s[\delta(n)]\} \\ &= (\beta_s - \alpha)\{1 - E_s[\delta(n)]\} \cdot 1[\beta_s \geq \alpha] \\ &\quad + (\alpha - \beta_s) E_s[\delta(n)] \cdot 1[\alpha \geq \beta_s]. \end{aligned}$$

Thus, regret is the mean welfare loss when a member of the population is assigned the inferior treatment, multiplied by the expected fraction of the population assigned this treatment. The minimax regret rule does not have an analytical solution, but it can be determined numerically. Computation shows that, when all values of β are feasible, the minimax regret rule is well approximated by the ES rule.

6.4 SETTING SAMPLE SIZE TO ENABLE NEAR-OPTIMAL TREATMENT CHOICE

From the perspective of treatment choice, an ideal objective for the design of trials would be to collect data that enable subsequent implementation of an optimal treatment rule in the population of interest. Optimality is not achievable with finite sample size. However, near-optimal rules – ones with small maximum regret – exist when classical trials are large enough.

Manski and Tetenov (2016) investigated trial design that enables near-optimal treatment choices. We showed that, given any $\varepsilon > 0$, ε-*optimal* rules exist when trials have large enough sample size. An ε-optimal rule has expected welfare, across repeated samples, within ε of the welfare of the best treatment in every state of nature. Equivalently, it has maximum regret no larger than ε.

We considered trials that draw predetermined numbers of subjects at random within groups stratified by covariates and treatments. We reported exact results for cases of two treatments and binary outcomes. We gave sufficient conditions on sample sizes that ensure existence of ε-optimal treatment rules when there are multiple treatments and outcomes are bounded. These conditions were obtained by application of large deviations inequalities to evaluate the performance of the ES rule.

Choosing sample size to enable existence of ε-optimal treatment rules requires specification of a value for ε. The selected ε determines how much deviation from optimality a decision maker is willing to tolerate when making treatment choices. In medical contexts, the value of ε should be specified by clinical researchers concerned with patient care rather than by some universal convention. We suggested that clinical researchers may find it congenial to let ε equal the *minimum clinically important difference* in the average treatment effect comparing alternative treatments.

Medical research has long distinguished between the statistical and clinical significance of treatment effects. While the idea of clinical significance has been interpreted in various ways, many writers call an average treatment effect clinically significant if its magnitude is greater than a specified value deemed minimally consequential in clinical practice. International Conference on Harmonisation (1999) put it this way

(p. 1923): "The treatment difference to be detected may be based on a judgment concerning the minimal effect which has clinical relevance in the management of patients."

Our broad conclusion, which has subsequently been corroborated in Manski and Tetenov (2019, 2021), was that sample sizes determined by clinically relevant near-optimality criteria are much smaller than ones determined by conventional statistical power calculations. A variety of factors contribute to this conclusion. One is that the near-optimality perspective considers Type I and Type II errors symmetrically. In contrast, power calculations are usually performed with the probability of a Type I error set at 0.05 and that of a Type II error set at 0.10 to 0.2. Another factor is that the near-optimality perspective evaluates products of effect sizes and error probabilities. It tolerates larger error probabilities if the two treatments are nearly equivalent from a patient welfare perspective than if one treatment is substantially better for patients.

Reduction of sample size relative to prevailing norms can be beneficial in multiple ways. It lowers the cost of executing trials and the time needed to recruit adequate numbers of subjects. Reduction of sample size per treatment arm makes it feasible to perform trials that increase the number of treatment arms and, hence, yield information about more treatment options.

6.5 TREATMENT WITH PRIMARY AND SECONDARY OUTCOMES

It has been common in medical research to study multiple patient outcomes, with one designated as the primary outcome and the others as secondary outcomes. When the latter are harmful, they are called side effects or adverse events. The prevailing approach to trial design has been to focus entirely on the primary outcome of a treatment. The statistical power calculations used to choose sample size commonly consider only the primary outcome. It is also common to perform hypothesis tests only to evaluate the primary outcome, relegating consideration of secondary outcomes to qualitative discussion. These practices may be reasonable when the primary outcome is the dominant determinant of patient welfare or, put another way, when there is little variation in secondary outcomes across treatments. They are not reasonable otherwise.

When the secondary effects of treatments vary markedly across treatments, a utilitarian planner should consider how the primary and secondary outcomes jointly determine patient welfare. Manski and Tetenov

(2019) showed how to accomplish this using maximum regret to assess the empirical success rule. We developed and applied a refined version of the work in Manski and Tetenov (2016), which studied settings in which there is only a primary outcome.

In Manski and Tetenov (2019), we considered trials that compare aggressive treatment of patients with surveillance. Patient care abounds with instances of this clinical decision problem. Internists choose between prescription of pharmaceuticals and surveillance when treating patients at risk of heart disease or diabetes. Oncologists choose between surveillance and aggressive treatments such as surgery or chemotherapy when treating cancer patients at risk of metastasis. Aggressive treatment may be appealing to the extent that it better prevents disease onset or reduces the severity of illness. Surveillance may be attractive to the extent that it avoids side effects that may occur with aggressive treatment. An important aspect of choice between surveillance and aggressive treatment is that the latter may have harmful side effects.

6.5.1 Reconsidering Choice of Sample Size in the MSLT-II Trial

To provide a realistic case study illustrating general issues, we reconsidered a prominent trial comparing *nodal observation* and *lymph node dissection (lymphadenectomy)* when treating patients with early-stage cutaneous melanoma at risk of metastasis. Nodal observation is surveillance of lymph nodes by ultrasound scan, a procedure that has negligible side effects. Lymph node dissection is a surgical procedure in which the lymph nodes in the relevant regional basin are removed. Dissection is an aggressive treatment. A particularly concerning side effect is chronic swelling in the region of lymph node removal, a condition called lymphedema, which may reduce patient quality of life substantially (Cheville et al., 2010). Choice between nodal observation and lymph node dissection is a decision commonly faced in early treatment of melanoma, breast cancer, and other localized cancers. We focused on melanoma because there has long been controversy about the merits of dissection relative to observation in this context. See Faries (2018).

The Multicenter Selective Lymphadenectomy Trial II (MSLT-II) compared dissection and observation for melanoma patients who had recently undergone sentinel lymph-node biopsy and who had obtained a positive finding of malignancy. The investigators defined the primary outcome to be melanoma-specific survival for three years following the date of randomization. Findings were reported in Faries et al. (2017).

Our concern was the choice of sample size in the trial. We approached this question presuming that treatment choice will be made with the empirical success rule. We assumed a simple patient welfare function that transparently expresses patient concern with both survival, the primary outcome, and lymphedema, a possible secondary outcome. We let personal welfare with nodal observation equal 1 if a patient survives for three years and equal 0 otherwise. Welfare with dissection depends on whether a patient experiences lymphedema. When a patient does not experience lymphedema, we let welfare with dissection equal 1 if the patient survives for three years and equals 0 otherwise. When a patient experiences lymphedema, we supposed that welfare is lowered by a specified constant h, whose value expresses the harm associated with lymphedema. Thus, a patient who experiences lymphedema has welfare $1 - h$ if he survives and $-h$ if he does not survive.

When making the treatment decision, a clinician ordinarily does not know whether a given patient will survive and/or experience lymphedema. To cope with uncertainty about treatment response, a utilitarian clinician would maximize mean personal welfare in the relevant patient population.

To formalize the clinical decision problem, let nodal observation be treatment A. Let $y(A)$ denote the primary outcome with treatment A. Thus, $y(A) = 1$ if a patient survives with observation, and let $y(A) = 0$ if the patient does not survive. Mean welfare with observation is the survival probability $P[y(A) = 1]$.

Let lymph node dissection be treatment B. Let $y(B) = 1$ if a patient survives with dissection and $y(B) = 0$ otherwise. Let $v(B)$ denote the secondary outcome with treatment B. Thus, $v(B) = 1$ if a patient experiences lymphedema and $v(B) = 0$ otherwise. Mean welfare with dissection is the difference between the survival probability and h times the probability of lymphedema; that is, $P[y(B) = 1] - h \cdot P[v(B) = 1]$.

The optimal treatment is the one yielding the higher mean patient welfare. Thus, observation is optimal if $P[y(A) = 1] \geq P[y(B) = 1] - h \cdot P[v(B) = 1]$. In this setting, a state of nature is a set of values for the four probabilities $P[y(A) = 1]$, $P[y(B) = 1]$, $P[v(B) = 1 \mid y(B) = 0]$, and $P[v(B) = 1 \mid y(B) = 1]$. Trial data enables estimation of these probabilities of survival and lymphedema. Sample size determines statistical precision. For any positive constant ε, a sample of size N per treatment arm enables ε-optimal treatment if N is sufficiently large. We explained how to compute sample sizes that enable ε-optimal treatment for any values of h and ε, assuming use of the ES rule. We suggested how to choose ε, using what the MSLT-II trial investigators specified to be the minimum clinically important difference between treatments.

Using a statistical power calculation, the MSLT-II investigators assigned 971 patients to dissection and 968 to observation. Our reconsideration of the trial concluded that assigning 244 patients to each option would yield findings that enable adequately near-optimal treatment choice. Thus, a much smaller sample size would have sufficed to inform clinical practice.

6.6 COVID-19 TREATMENT WITH DATA FROM AN IMPRECISE TRIAL

Manski and Tetenov (2021) applied the near-optimality (maximum regret) perspective to an early trial assessing a proposed drug treatment for Covid-19. We critiqued the investigators' use of hypothesis testing to evaluate the trial findings. I first summarize the trial and how the authors reported their findings.

Summary of the Trial and the Reported Findings: At the beginning of the Covid-19 pandemic, Cao et al. (2020) reported on a randomized trial in China comparing standard-care treatment of severe cases of Covid-19 with standard-care combined with the drug pair lopinavir–ritonavir. The trial assigned 99 hospitalized adult patients to the lopinavir–ritonavir group and 100 to the standard-care only group. The pre-declared primary outcome measured time to clinical improvement. A secondary outcome was mortality within 28 days.

The authors summarized the primary finding as follows (p. 1): "In a modified intention-to-treat analysis, lopinavir–ritonavir led to a median time to clinical improvement that was shorter by 1 day than that observed with standard care (hazard ratio, 1.39; 95% CI, 1.00 to 1.91)." Regarding mortality, 19 of the 99 patients assigned to lopinavir–ritonavir died within 28 days and 25 of the 100 receiving only standard care died. The authors characterized this finding as follows (p. 1): "Mortality at 28 days was similar in the lopinavir–ritonavir group and the standard-care group (19.2% vs. 25.0%; difference, –5.8 percentage points; 95% CI, –17.3 to 5.7)." They reported raw findings on side effects, but they performed no statistical analysis. They concluded (p. 1): "In hospitalized adult patients with severe Covid-19, no benefit was observed with lopinavir–ritonavir treatment beyond standard care." ∎

A clinician might reasonably view the estimated reductions in median time to clinical improvement and in mortality to be suggestive, albeit not definitive, evidence that treatment with lopinavir–ritonavir was beneficial relative to standard care alone. Yet the study authors concluded (p. 1): "no benefit was observed with lopinavir–ritonavir treatment beyond standard care." This conclusion was reached because estimated treatment effects were not statistically significant, having confidence intervals that cover zero.

Requiring statistical significance to recommend a treatment innovation shows deference to standard care, placing the burden of proof on the innovation. A clinician might perhaps argue that it is reasonable to place the burden on an innovation when standard care is known to yield good patient outcomes. However, this argument lacked credibility in the Covid-19 setting. In early 2020, standard care for this new disease evolved rapidly in the face of great uncertainty. At the time, there did not yet exist a standard treatment yielding notably good patient outcomes.

How should clinicians act with imprecise evidence such as in the Cao et al. study? We compared decision making using hypothesis testing and the ES rule. We supposed that the patient outcome of primary clinical concern is 28-day mortality rather than time to clinical improvement. We posed a state space that encompasses all possible values of patient mortality; that is, mortality with either treatment option could take any value in the [0, 1] interval.

Calculating maximum regret for treatment choice based on hypothesis testing, we found it to equal 0.071 with the Cao et al. sample size. Specifically, maximum regret occurs in the state where the new treatment has mortality rate 0.548 and standard care has rate 0.661. In this state, the error probability is 0.624 and regret is $(0.661 - 0.548) \times 0.624 = 0.071$.

We found that the ES rule is about 6 times nearer to optimality than the test-based decision criterion. In a trial with 100 patients in each arm, similar to Cao et al., the ES rule achieves near-optimality of 0.012. Maximum regret occurs in the state where standard care and the new treatment have mortality rates of 0.527 and 0.473. In this state, standard care is erroneously prescribed with probability 0.226. The empirical success rule is symmetric, so the same maximum regret occurs when standard care has mortality rate 0.473 and the new treatment has rate 0.527. Then the new treatment is erroneously prescribed with probability 0.226. In both states, regret in the state with maximum regret is $(0.527 - 0.473) \times 0.226 = 0.012$. Thus, use of the empirical success rule yields a dramatic improvement in near-optimality relative to hypothesis testing.

6.7 MANAGING UNCERTAINTY IN FDA DRUG APPROVAL

At the beginning of this chapter I noted that the FDA uses hypothesis tests to evaluate new drugs. To close, I critique the present FDA drug approval process and suggest modifications. I draw on the discussion in Manski (2019b), Chapter 7.

6.7.1 The FDA Approval Process

The FDA process begins with laboratory and animal testing of new compounds. Those that seem promising then go through three phases of trials, in which the new drug is compared with an accepted treatment or placebo. Phase 1 trials aim to determine the basic pharmacological action of the drug and the safety of different doses. Phase 2 trials, which usually take about two years and are performed with several hundred patients who are ill with a specific disease, give preliminary evidence on the efficacy and short-term side effects of the drug. Phase 3 trials, which usually take about three years and are performed with several hundred to several thousand patients ill with the disease, give more substantial evidence on efficacy and side effects. After Phase 3, the firm files a New Drug Application and the FDA either approves or disapproves the drug. See U.S. Food and Drug Administration (2017).

FDA evaluation of new drugs occurs with partial knowledge of treatment response. Type I errors occur when new drugs that are inferior to accepted treatments are approved because they appear superior when evaluated using the available information. Type II errors occur when new drugs that are superior to accepted treatments are disapproved because they appear inferior when evaluated using the available information.

Type II errors commonly are permanent. The FDA provides no public documentation of rejected New Drug Applications. After a drug is disapproved, use ceases and no further data on treatment response are produced. Some Type I errors eventually are corrected after drug approval through the FDA's post-market surveillance program, which analyzes data on outcomes experienced when the drug is used in clinical practice; see U.S. Food and Drug Administration (2020). However, the post-market surveillance program only aims to detect adverse side effects of approved drugs, not to assess their effectiveness in treating the conditions for which they are intended. The data available for post-market surveillance is limited by the fact that FDA cannot compel a firm to perform new trials after a drug has been approved. The main instrument of post-market surveillance is the Adverse Event Reporting System, which encourages patients and physicians to submit reports of adverse side effects related to drug administration.

The FDA limits the frequency of statistical errors by requiring that trial sizes suffice to perform hypothesis tests with specified power. The dominant source of errors is wishful extrapolation. The approval process essentially assumes that treatment response in the relevant patient population will be similar to response in the study population. It assumes that response in clinical practice will be similar to response with double-blinded treatment assignment. It assumes that drug effectiveness measured by unmeasured outcomes of interest will be similar to effectiveness measured by measured surrogate outcomes. These assumptions may be unsubstantiated, but they have become enshrined by long use.

6.7.2 FDA Rejection of Formal Decision Analysis

In 2012, Congress responded to continuing controversy about the drug approval process by requiring the FDA to implement a "structured risk-benefit assessment framework." The Food and Drug Administration Safety and Innovation Act of 2012 (Public Law 112–144) amended Section 505(d) of the Federal Food Drug and Cosmetic Act by requiring the FDA to: "implement a structured risk-benefit assessment framework in the new drug approval process to facilitate the balanced consideration of benefits and risks, a consistent and systematic approach to the discussion and regulatory decision-making, and the communication of the benefits and risks of new drugs." I think it reasonable to interpret this language as requiring the FDA to approach drug approval as a formal problem of decision under uncertainty. The FDA, however, has rejected the use of formal decision analysis in drug approval.

Following enactment of the 2012 legislation, the FDA published a plan intended to fulfill the Congressional requirement (U.S. Food and Drug Administration, 2013). The agency responded skeptically to unnamed critics of the prevailing approval process who have recommended that the FDA use formal decision analysis. The agency stated (p. 1):

In the past, some FDA stakeholders have indicated that there is room for improvement in the clarity and transparency of FDA's benefit-risk assessment in human drug review. When FDA approves a new product, the agency publishes the various relevant documents, such as discipline reviews (e.g. clinical, non-clinical, clinical pharmacology, biostatistics, and chemistry) and decision memoranda, on its website. While FDA takes great care to clearly explain the reasoning behind a regulatory decision in these documents, the clinical analysis may not always be readily understood by a broad audience who may wish to understand FDA's thinking. In addition, some have argued that drug regulatory decisions should be based on more formalized and quantitative approaches to benefit-risk assessment, including the assignment of weights to benefit and risk considerations. Others, however, are skeptical of fully quantitative approaches, and consider such attempts to be a highly subjective exercise that would add little clarity to regulatory decision making.

The agency then defended its preferred approach to drug approval. The agency rejected quantitative/formal decision analysis and argued for continuation of the "structured qualitative" approach that it has used in the past. The agency stated in part (p. 4):

In the last few years, as other disciplines such as decision science and health economics have been applied to drug regulatory decision-making, there has been much discussion among regulators, industry, and other stakeholders regarding "qualitative" versus "quantitative" approaches to benefit-risk assessment. The term "quantitative benefit-risk assessment" can have various meanings depending on who is asked. Some hold the view that a quantitative benefit-risk assessment encompasses approaches that seek to quantify benefits and risks, as well as the weight that is placed on each of the components such that the entire benefit-risk assessment is quantitative. This approach is typical of quantitative decision modeling. It usually requires assigning numerical weights to benefit and risk considerations in a process involving numerous judgments that are at best debatable and at worst arbitrary. The subjective judgments and assumptions that would inevitably be embodied in such quantitative decision modeling would be much less transparent, if not obscured, to those who wish to understand a regulator's thinking ...

These concerns have led FDA to the conclusion that the best presentation of benefit-risk considerations involves focusing on the individual benefits and risks, their frequency, and weighing them appropriately. FDA believes that this can be accomplished by a qualitative descriptive approach for structuring the benefit-risk assessment that satisfies the principles outlined earlier in this section, while acknowledging that quantification of certain components of the benefit-risk assessment is an important part of the process to support decision-making.

The FDA rejection of formal decision analysis in drug approval is similar to the Institute of Medicine (2011) rejection of decision analysis in the development of clinical practice guidelines. In Chapter 1, I quoted the Institute of Medicine (IOM) statement that "Clinical practice guidelines are statements that include recommendations intended to optimize patient care." Yet the IOM report did not formalize what it may mean to "optimize patient care." It discussed decision analysis only briefly and expressed skepticism, stating (p. 171): "A frontier of evidence-based medicine is decision analytic modeling in health care alternatives' assessment.... Although the field is currently fraught with controversy, the committee acknowledges it as exciting and potentially promising, however, decided the state of the art is not ready for direct comment." The report did not explain the basis for this assessment.

6.7.3 Adaptive Partial Drug Approval

I have argued against the FDA rejection of formal decision analysis. In Manski (2019b) and elsewhere, I have observed that adaptive diversification of drug treatment after FDA approval of new drugs could reduce the impact of Type I errors in drug approval, diversifying treatment choice and producing new post-market information on treatment response. However, adaptive diversification after drug approval would not reduce Type II errors. Healthcare providers can only choose among the drugs that are approved by the FDA.

I have suggested that two policy changes could reduce the incidence and impact of Type II errors. First, the federal government could amend the Food, Drug, and Cosmetics Act to enable specified healthcare providers to treat their patients with drugs that have not received FDA approval. In return for exemption from the FDA approval process, these providers could be required to apply appropriate diversification of treatment and to report findings on treatment response.

Second, the FDA could replace its present approval process with one of adaptive partial drug approval. The permitted use of a new drug now has a sharp discontinuity at the date of the FDA approval decision. Beforehand, a typically tiny fraction of the patient population receives the new drug in trials. Afterwards, use of the drug is unconstrained if approval is granted and zero if approval is not granted. An adaptive approval process would eliminate this discontinuity and instead permit use of a new drug to vary smoothly as evidence accumulates.

7

Personalized Treatment

Chapters 5 and 6 concerned individualistic treatment of a population whose members are observationally identical to the planner. I now consider individualistic treatment when persons differ in observable covariates. Observation of covariates may enable a planner to differentially treat persons in a systematic rather than random manner. Systematic variation in treatment with observed covariates is a common planning practice, with several terms used to describe it. It may be called *screening* or *profiling*, or *personalized* or *precision* treatment. Arrow (1973b) called it *statistical discrimination*.

Consider a clinician choosing medical treatments for a population of patients. The clinician may observe a patient's demographic attributes, medical history, and the results of screening or diagnostic tests. He may choose treatment as a function of these covariates. Or consider a judge choosing sentences for a population of convicted offenders. The judge may observe an offender's criminal record, demeanor in court, and other attributes. Subject to sentencing guidelines, the judge may consider these covariates when choosing sentences.

The planning problem has a simple solution when the planner is utilitarian, has sufficient knowledge of treatment response to make optimization feasible, and does not face an institutional or budget constraint that limits how treatments can vary across the population. Then it is optimal to separate members of the population by their covariates and to optimize in each subpopulation separately. The planning problem is generally more complex beyond this domain.

I have mainly studied a tractable setting of utilitarian planning under uncertainty, where the uncertainty stems from partial knowledge of the probabilistic risk of occurrence for a personal binary outcome that affects treatment outcomes. A leading case is clinical treatment of patients when a clinician has incomplete knowledge of the personal risk of illness. I discuss this case throughout the chapter. I also discuss non-utilitarian decision making in the criminal justice system, where the uncertainty stems from partial knowledge of criminal behavior.

Section 7.1 examines the idealized setting where optimal utilitarian planning is feasible. I quantify the value of covariate information in improving achievable social welfare. Conditioning treatment choice on more refined covariate information cannot lower social welfare in this setting. It increases welfare if covariate refinement has predictive power that affects treatment choice. I also discuss nonutilitarian arguments to disregard certain covariate information when making clinical and criminal justice decisions.

The remainder of the chapter considers planning when uncertainty about treatment response makes optimization infeasible. Section 7.2 distinguishes settings where the planning problem does or does not decompose into a set of separable covariate-specific problems. The former situations are easier to study than the latter. Section 7.3 considers the common medical problem of choice between surveillance and aggressive treatment of patients, with partial knowledge of personalized risk of illness. Section 7.4 extends the analysis to sequential choice of whether to acquire costly covariate information as a prelude to treatment choice. I focus on medical choice to perform a diagnostic test before making the treatment decision.

7.1 OPTIMAL TREATMENT WITH PERSONALIZED RISK

Medical economists studying patient care have viewed a clinician as a utilitarian planner who treats each person in a population of patients. The clinician observes certain covariates for each patient, who has some risk of illness. The objective is to maximize mean personal welfare. Maximizing personal welfare is suggested by the Hippocratic Oath, part of which states: "Into whatsoever houses I enter, I will enter to help the sick."

Let care be individualistic, meaning that the care received by one patient may affect that person but does not affect other members of the population. This assumption is generally realistic when considering non-infectious diseases. Chapter 8 will discuss research on vaccination against infectious disease, a context where the assumption is not realistic.

A common problem in clinical decision making is that treatments must be chosen with incomplete knowledge of their outcomes. Medical economists have typically assumed that the clinician has rational expectations. That is, the clinician knows the probability distribution of personal welfare outcomes that will occur if a patient with specified observed covariates is given a specified treatment. This assumption does not assert that the clinician can predict patient outcomes with certainty. It means that the clinician makes accurate probabilistic predictions conditional on observed patient covariates.

If a clinician has rational expectations, the problem of optimizing utilitarian patient care has a simple solution: patients should be divided into groups having the same observed covariates and all patients in a group should be given the care that yields the highest within-group mean patient welfare. Patients with the same observed covariates should be treated uniformly.

Analysis shows that achievable utilitarian welfare across the population weakly increases as more patient covariates are observed. Observing more covariates enables a clinician to refine the probabilistic predictions of treatment outcomes on which decisions are based. Refining these predictions is beneficial if doing so affects optimal treatment choices. This important result has been discussed in the literature on medical economics in Phelps and Mushlin (1988), Basu and Meltzer (2007), Manski (2013a), and elsewhere. Manski, Mullahy, and Venkataramani (2023) provide proof in the simple instructive setting of choice between two treatments. I summarize this analysis here.

7.1.1 Optimal Choice between Two Treatments

Suppose that a clinician must choose between treatments A and B. The choice is made without knowing each patient's illness outcome, which is $y = 1$ if the patient is ill and $y = 0$ if not. The clinician observes patient covariates (x, z). I use separate notation to denote covariates x and z because I will compare two situations. In one, the clinician predicts illness conditional only on x. In the other, the prediction conditions on (x, z). The analysis does not require any specific interpretations of x and z. They may be any observable variables that predict illness; for example, age, sex, race, health history, and findings in medical examinations.

Having rational expectations, the clinician knows a patient's probability of illness conditional on these covariates. Thus, the clinician knows $p_x = P(y = 1 | x)$ and $p_{xz} = P(y = 1 | x, z)$. Consider patients who have the same value of x but who vary in their values of z. Suppose that z takes values in a finite set Z and that each value of z occurs for a positive fraction of patients; thus, $P(z | x) > 0$ for all $z \in Z$. Suppose that p_{xz} varies with z. Thus, z has some predictive power for illness, conditional on x.

Patient outcomes with each treatment depend on whether a patient has the disease. Patients may be heterogeneous, so treatment response may differ across patients. Let $u_x(y, t)$ denote the mean personal welfare that patients with covariates x would experience with treatment t, should the illness outcome be y. To simplify analysis, Manski, Mullahy, and Venkataramani (2023) assumed that this mean welfare does not vary across patients with different values of z. We assumed that the clinician knows $u_x(y, t)$ for each possible value of (x, t, y). However, the clinician does not know whether y equals 0 or 1 for each patient.

With rational expectations and knowledge of $u_x(y, t)$, the clinician can compute mean patient welfare conditional on observed covariates, but unconditional on illness outcomes. The computation may be performed in two ways, using the illness probabilities p_x or p_{xz}. Let the objective be to maximize mean patient welfare among patients with covariates x. Assume that no institutional or budget constraint limits how treatments can vary across these patients. Depending on whether the clinician uses p_x or p_{xz} to predict illness, the treatment-choice criterion is:

(7.1a) choose A if $p_x \cdot u_x(1, A) + (1 - p_x) \cdot u_x(0, A) \geq p_x \cdot u_x(1, B) + (1 - p_x) \cdot u_x(0, B),$

(7.1b) choose B if $p_x \cdot u_x(1, A) + (1 - p_x) \cdot u_x(0, A) \leq p_x \cdot u_x(1, B) + (1 - p_x) \cdot u_x(0, B),$

or

(7.2a) choose treatment A if $p_{xz} \cdot u_x(1, A) + (1 - p_{xz}) \cdot u_x(0, A) \geq p_{xz} \cdot u_x(1, B) + (1 - p_{xz}) \cdot u_x(0, B),$

(7.2b) choose treatment B if $p_{xz} \cdot u_x(1, A) + (1 - p_{xz}) \cdot u_x(0, A) \leq p_{xz} \cdot u_x(1, B) + (1 - p_{xz}) \cdot u_x(0, B).$

7.1.2 The Value of Covariate Information

Criterion (7.2) yields weakly greater mean personal welfare than (7.1). To see this, observe that with criterion (7.1), the maximized value of mean welfare for patients with covariates x is:

(7.3) $$\max\left[p_x \cdot u_x(1, A) + (1-p_x) \cdot u_x(0, A), p_x \cdot u_x(1, B) + (1-p_x) \cdot u_x(0, B)\right].$$

With criterion (7.2), the maximized mean welfare for patients with covariates (x, z) is:

(7.4) $$\max\left[p_{xz} \cdot u_x(1, A) + (1-p_{xz}) \cdot u_x(0, A), p_{xz} \cdot u_x(1, B) + (1-p_{xz}) \cdot u_x(0, B)\right].$$

In this case, the maximized value of mean welfare for patients with covariates x is the mean of (7.4) with respect to the distribution of z conditional on x; that is,

(7.5) $$E_{z|x}\left\{\max\left[p_{xz} \cdot u_x(1, A) + (1-p_{xz}) \cdot u_x(0, A), p_{xz} \cdot u_x(1, B) + (1-p_{xz}) \cdot u_x(0, B)\right]\right\}.$$

The magnitude of (7.5) weakly exceeds that of (7.3), implying that criterion (7.2) performs at least as well as (7.1). In particular,

(7.6) $$\begin{aligned} & E_{z|x}\left\{\max\left[p_{xz} \cdot u_x(1, A) + (1-p_{xz}) \cdot u_x(0, A), p_{xz} \cdot u_x(1, B) + (1-p_{xz}) \cdot u_x(0, B)\right]\right\} \\ & \geq \max\left\{E_{z|x}(p_{xz}) \cdot u_x(1, A) + \left[1 - E_{z|x}(p_{xz})\right] \cdot u_x(0, A), E_{z|x}(p_{xz}) \cdot u_x(1, B) + \left[1 - E_{z|x}(p_{xz})\right] \cdot u_x(0, B)\right\} \\ & = \max\left[p_x \cdot u_x(1, A) + (1-p_x) \cdot u_x(0, A), p_x \cdot u_x(1, B) + (1-p_x) \cdot u_x(0, B)\right]. \end{aligned}$$

The inequality in (7.6) is strict if and only if there exist some values of z for which criterion (7.2) yields a different treatment than criterion (7.1). Thus, for conditioning on z to be useful in patient care, it is not enough that z have predictive power for illness. The predictive power must be strong enough to affect treatment decisions.

The above derivation provides a simple proof that a utilitarian clinician should use all observed covariates to predict illness. However, it does not reveal the extent to which criterion (7.2) outperforms criterion (7.1). We can do this through direct comparison of the criteria.

Without loss of generality, let treatment A be optimal in (7.1). Let A be optimal in (7.2) for all $z \in Z_A$ and let Z_B be the complement of Z_A. That is, inequality (7.2a) holds for $z \in Z_A$, some non-empty proper subset of Z. It does not hold for $z \in Z_B$, also a non-empty proper subset of Z. Criterion (7.2) yields better outcomes than (7.1) for persons with $z \in Z_B$

and the same outcomes as (7.1) for persons with $z \in Z_A$. Using criterion (7.2), social welfare within the subpopulation with covariates x exceeds that obtained using criterion (7.1) by the amount:

$$(7.7) \quad \begin{aligned} P(z \in Z_B \mid x) \cdot E\{&[p_{xz} \cdot u_x(1, B) + (1 - p_{xz}) \cdot u_x(0, B)] \\ &- [p_{xz} \cdot u_x(1, A) + (1 - p_{xz}) \cdot u_x(0, A)] \mid x, \ z \in Z_B\}. \end{aligned}$$

The bracketed difference $[p_{xz} \cdot u_x(1, B) + (1 - p_{xz}) \cdot u_x(0, B)]$ $-[p_{xz} \cdot u_x(1, A) + (1 - p_{xz}) \cdot u_x(0, A)]$ is positive for all $z \in Z_B$. Hence, (7.7) is positive. Moreover, (7.7) quantifies the extent to which criterion (7.2) outperforms (7.1). The magnitude of (7.7) is the product of two factors. One is the fraction $P(z \in Z_B \mid x)$ of patients for whom treatment B yields strictly larger personal welfare than treatment A. The other is the mean gain in welfare that criterion (7.2) yields for the subset Z_B of patients.

7.1.3 Surveillance or Aggressive Treatment

An important class of choice between two treatments occurs when a clinician decides between surveillance and aggressive treatment of patients at risk of disease. Prominent cases include the choice between surveillance and drug treatment for patients at risk of heart disease or diabetes. Chapter 6 discussed the choice between surveillance and nodal dissection for patients diagnosed with melanoma.

As discussed in Chapter 6, the clinical decision requires resolution of a tension between benefits and costs. Aggressive treatment may be more beneficial to the extent that it reduces the risk of disease development or the severity of disease that does develop. It may be more harmful to the extent that it generates health side effects and financial costs beyond those associated with surveillance.

Manski (2018a, 2019b) showed that analysis is simple when aggressive treatment affects disease in one of two polar ways. In one polar case, aggressive treatment prevents the occurrence of disease. In the other, it does not affect the occurrence of disease, but it reduces the severity of disease when it occurs. In both cases, aggressive treatment is the better option if the probability of illness exceeds a computable threshold that varies with patient covariates. Surveillance is the better option otherwise.

I consider here the polar case where aggressive treatment does not affect the occurrence of disease but reduces its severity. Let t = A denote surveillance and t = B denote aggressive treatment. The clinician must choose between A and B without knowing the illness outcome. Maximization of mean personal welfare yields the optimal treatment rule (7.2).

The optimal treatment depends on the magnitude of the illness probability p_{xz} relative to the z-invariant threshold value that equalizes the mean patient welfare of the two treatments:

$$(7.8) \qquad p_X^* = \frac{u_x(0, A) - u_x(0, B)}{\left[u_x(0, A) - u_x(0, B)\right] + \left[u_x(1, B) - u_x(1, A)\right]}.$$

It typically is reasonable to suppose that surveillance yields higher mean welfare when a patient does not have the disease and that aggressive treatment is better when a patient does have the disease. That is, $u_x(0, A) > u_x(0, B)$, and $u_x(1, B) > u_x(1, A)$. Then $0 < p_X^* < 1$. Treatment A is optimal if $p_{xz} \leq p_X^*$ and B is optimal if $p_{xz} \geq p_X^*$.

The threshold probability (7.8) has a simple interpretation. When a patient is not ill ($y = 0$), surveillance ($t = A$) is the better treatment. Then a clinician who chooses aggressive treatment ($t = B$) makes a Type A error and incurs regret $u_x(0, A) - u_x(0, B)$. When a patient is ill ($y = 1$), aggressive treatment ($t = B$) is better. Then a clinician who chooses surveillance ($t = A$) makes a Type B error and incurs regret $u_x(1, B) - u_x(1, A)$. Hence, the threshold probability is the regret from a Type A error divided by the sum of the regrets from Type A and Type B errors.

A further simplification, considered in Manski (2023), occurs when aggressive treatment neutralizes disease in the sense that $u_x(0, B) = u_x(1, B)$, now called u_{xB} for short. For example, aggressive treatment might be surgery to remove a localized tumor that may ($y = 1$) or may not ($y = 0$) be malignant. Suppose that surgery always eliminates cancer when present. Then surgery neutralizes the disease. Being invasive and costly, performance of surgery has a negative side effect on welfare that is the same regardless of whether cancer is present. If aggressive treatment neutralizes disease, (7.8) reduces to $p_X^* = [u_x(A, 0) - u_{xB}]/[u_x(A, 0) - u_x(A, 1)]$.

7.1.4 Finding a Defendant Guilty or Not Guilty of a Crime

The choice between surveillance and aggressive treatment has an analog in judicial decision making, but there has been a striking contrast in the norms for judicial and clinical decision making. As discussed above, when clinicians are uncertain about the health and treatment response of a patient, they view the patient as a member of a subpopulation with the same observed covariates. They make care decisions using available knowledge about the health status and treatment response of this population. Medical research uses data on illness outcomes and patient covariates to estimate the probability with which patients having specified covariates develop a disease of concern.

Quantitative research in criminology operates in much the same way as medical research. Criminologists use data on criminal behavior to estimate the probability with which persons having specified observed covariates commit crimes. Yet research on criminal risk prediction is not used in judicial decision making in the manner that medical research is used in clinical decision making. Legal systems ordinarily do not permit an individual to be convicted of a crime based on a frequentist justification that persons with similar observed covariates often commit this crime. To convict a defendant, a judge or jury must conclude that this person committed a specific crime, meeting legal definitions of causation and intent. It does not suffice to reason that persons like him often commit similar crimes.

Judges and juries are permitted to use probabilistic reasoning when they are uncertain whether defendants meet legal criteria for guilt. This is evident in legal use of terms such as "probable cause" and "balance of probabilities." However, legal systems apply these terms in the Bayesian sense of a subjective probability of occurrence of an individual event, not in the frequentist sense of the prevalence of an event in a population. See Kaplan (1967).

Manski (2020d) suggested that, emulating the clinical use of research assessing frequentist risk of illness, legal systems could permit judges and juries to bring to bear research that assesses rates of crime commission. I did not go so far as to argue outright that legal systems should permit judicial decisions to be made using frequentist information on rates of crime commission. I only raised the possibility, having in mind that the prevailing subjective assessment of uncertainty in legal systems can itself be problematic. Judges and juries may vary in the accuracy of their subjective judgments. Hence, I thought it warranted to consider frequentist assessment as a potentially more objective and uniform way to cope with uncertainty.

I focused on the decision of a judge to find a criminal defendant guilty. I considered a judge rather than a jury because a judge is a single decision maker, thus a planner, whereas a jury is a group whose decision may reflect social interactions. The judicial decision problem is analogous to clinical choice between surveillance and aggressive treatment. Now the choice is to find a defendant guilty or not guilty of a crime. The defendant is analogous to the patient. A guilty decision is analogous to aggressive treatment, whereas a not-guilty one is analogous to surveillance. Uncertainty about whether a defendant committed the crime is analogous to uncertainty about whether a patient is ill.

The assumption of individualistic treatment response made when considering patient care now means that the judicial decision made for one defendant does not affect judicial decision making or crime commission elsewhere. It may or may not be reasonable to assume that judicial decisions have only individualistic implications. Kaplow (2011) emphasized that convictions may deter future crime, making judicial decisions similar to medical treatment of infectious disease. This warrants consideration, but I leave it aside here.

Optimal Conviction Decisions with Frequentist Risk Assessment

Judicial and clinical decision making differ in that the judicial welfare function is not ordinarily utilitarian. The usual presumption is that social welfare in the presence of criminality differs from the sum of the personal welfares of the population, whose members include criminals. Nevertheless, the judicial choice problem has the same formal structure as clinical choice when aggressive treatment does not affect the occurrence of disease but reduces its severity. It is typically reasonable to assume that a guilty judgment yields higher social welfare than a not-guilty one if the defendant committed the crime, but lower welfare if he did not. This is analogous to the assumption made earlier that aggressive treatment yields higher welfare than surveillance if a patient is ill, but lower welfare if the patient is healthy.

With these analogies to medical treatment, repetition of the analysis of Section 7.1.3 shows that finding a defendant guilty is the better choice if the probability of crime commission exceeds a computable defendant-specific threshold. A finding of not guilty is better otherwise.

Legal Precedents

Analysis of optimal judicial decision making in the above manner has some precedent in legal scholarship. Kaplan (1967) advocated a threshold probability for conviction. However, he was adamant that probability should be conceptualized in subjective rather than frequentist terms. See also Burtis, Gelbach, and Kobayashi (2018).

The prevailing legal criterion for dealing with uncertainty when deciding whether to convict a criminal defendant is that the person should be guilty "beyond a reasonable doubt." The English jurist William

Blackstone (1769) gave a famous quantification, remarking that: "It is better that ten guilty persons escape than that one innocent suffer." Earlier, the English jurist Sir Matthew Hale (1736) wrote, "it is better five guilty persons should escape unpunished, than one innocent person should die." Centuries earlier, the medieval Sephardi philosopher Maimonides wrote, "It is better and more satisfactory to acquit a thousand guilty persons than to put a single innocent man to death"; see Chavell (1967).

These declarations suggest a welfare evaluation that the loss to society when convicting a defendant who did not commit a crime (a Type A error) is ten or five or a thousand times the loss when not convicting a defendant who did commit a crime (a Type B error). Applying them to the declarations of Blackstone, Hale, or Maimonides implies that the threshold probability for conviction should be 10/11 or 5/6 or 1000/1001.

Observe that each of these quantitative interpretations of "beyond a reasonable doubt" renders the threshold probability for conviction invariant across crime types and defendant attributes. Thus, each assumes that the losses to society associated with Type A and Type B errors do not vary across crimes or classes of defendants. With a few exceptions, the literature in criminal law does not motivate this invariance assumption. I think it highly plausible that society may want to evaluate the relative losses of Type A and B errors differently for different crime types. The evaluation might vary with the severity of the crime and with the nature of the sentences received by convicted defendants. It is also conceivable that society may want to evaluate losses from errors in a manner that varies with certain defendant covariates.

Among the few authors who have questioned the invariance assumption, Kaplan (1967) did so at length and persuasively. Epps (2015) observed that the quantifications asserted by Blackstone, Hale, and Maimonides were offered in a historical context where numerous crimes, including ones that are considered minor today, were punished exclusively by execution of the convicted person. Epps argued that these quantifications should not be used in the modern context, where capital punishment has become rare. Epps also suggested that criteria for conviction decisions should vary across crimes because (p. 1091), "the costs of false acquittals ... likely vary significantly among crimes."

7.1.5 Nonutilitarian Arguments to Exclude Race as a Covariate in Medical Risk Prediction

I return now to clinical decision making. Utilitarian medical treatment choice uses all available covariate information to maximize mean patient welfare. In this sense, it embeds a specific, clear idea that clinical decision making should be fair and just. It expresses the idea that clinicians should strive to do as well as possible for their patients, given what is known about them.

Utilitarian optimization does not imply that patients with different observed covariates should receive the same treatments or that they will experience the same health. Thus, it may yield treatment or health disparities across groups of patients. As shown above, cross-covariate disparities in treatment and health are well motivated from the utilitarian perspective if clinicians have rational expectations and act accordingly.

The above notwithstanding, a growing segment of the medical community in the United States have deemed treatment and health disparities undesirable from nonutilitarian perspectives on fairness and justice, particularly when the disparities are by race. Indeed, there has recently been an influential movement to remove race as a covariate in existing algorithms for medical risk prediction. Cerdeña et al. (2020), Vyas et al. (2020), and Briggs (2022) exemplify calls to cease the use of race as a covariate.

In some medical fields, leading institutions have formally recommended race-free risk prediction. A notable case is Delgado et al. (2021), which presented the recommendations of the National Kidney Foundation-American Society of Nephrology Task Force on Reassessing the Inclusion of Race in Diagnosing Kidney Disease. The Task Force considered the prevailing use of race as a predictor in computation of estimated glomerular filtration rate (eGFR), a measure of kidney function. It recommended removal of race as a determinant of eGFR. The recommendation has since been implemented in some major medical centers.

Manski (2022) questioned four assertions that have been advanced as arguments against the inclusion of race as a covariate in risk prediction. These assertions are:

(i) race is a social, not biological, concept.
(ii) race should not be considered if there is no established causal link between race and the illness.
(iii) using race may perpetuate or worsen racial health inequities.
(iv) many persons are offended by the use of race in risk assessment.

With the stated goal of making clinical decisions that would maximize utilitarian welfare, I concluded with this observation (p. 2113):

> If an alternative perspective is to have a compelling foundation, it should explain why society should find it acceptable to make risk assessments using other patient characteristics that clinicians observe, but not race. It should explain why the social benefit of omitting race from risk assessment is sufficiently large that it exceeds the harm to the quality of patient care.

I made this statement, with some frustration, because advocates of removing race from medical risk assessments have only argued verbally, without performing analysis or specifying an explicit social welfare function. Hence, it has been difficult to understand and assess the reasoning motivating their recommendation.

Manski, Mullahy, and Venkataramani (2023) elaborated on this theme. We observed that, from the utilitarian perspective, it does not matter whether race is a social concept, a biological one, or a combination of the two. It does not matter whether race "causes" illness or is only statistically associated with illness. As shown in Section 7.1.1, all that matters is whether use of race as a covariate (say z) when predicting risk of illness has predictive power that affects optimal treatment, when used in conjunction with other observed covariates (say x).

When considering the controversy regarding inclusion of race in clinical prediction and decision making, it is important to recognize that the two sides of the debate may not only differ in advocating different strategies for attaining the same goal. The core differences may also concern the attainment of different goals. Thus, the two sides of the debate may have different social welfare functions in mind.

The utilitarian objective of maximizing mean patient welfare is straightforward to define. The utilitarian prescription to improve decision making is to improve knowledge of patient illness probabilities. The utilitarian perspective implies that these solutions would be better for society than to discard information on race from clinical prediction.

It is less obvious how to conceptualize other objectives that have only been stated verbally, which include the achievement of equity and elimination of disparities in healthcare; see Sen (2002). Different parties may have different goals, reflecting different values. A clear articulation of goals is a necessary antecedent of productive discussion and policy making.

7.1.6 Assessing Benefits, Costs, and Disparate Racial Impacts of Confrontational Proactive Policing

To conclude my discussion of optimal treatment with personalized risk, I use the Manski and Nagin (2017) analysis of confrontational proactive policing to illustrate the potential for formal study of nonutilitarian planning in a setting where racial impacts have been a prominent societal concern.

As discussed in Section 7.1.4, judicial decision making is a normatively subtle planning problem. The subtlety is how society should value the social losses from errors of convicting defendants who have not committed crimes relative to errors of not convicting defendants who have committed crimes. When considering this matter, I viewed the observed defendant covariates abstractly.

It is apparent that modern democratic societies do not view all observable covariates neutrally in criminal justice contexts. Racial disparities in police searches, arrests, convictions, and sentencing have drawn particular concern. In Section 7.1.5, I called attention to the prevailing qualitative verbal consideration of racial disparities in patient care and emphasized the importance of specifying an explicit social welfare function to enable coherent planning. Discussion of racial disparities in criminal justice has been similarly qualitative and verbal. Specification of an explicit welfare function is similarly important.

With this in mind, Manski and Nagin (2017) focused on one core aspect of criminal justice, policing. Effective policing in a democratic society must balance the sometimes conflicting objectives of public safety and community trust. We used a model of optimal policing to explore how society might reasonably resolve the tension between these two objectives as well as evaluate disparate racial impacts. We did so by considering the social benefits and costs of confrontational types of proactive policing such as stop, question, and frisk (SQF). We discussed three features of the optimum that are particularly relevant to policy choices: (1) The cost of enforcement against the innocent, (2) the baseline level of crime rate without confrontational enforcement, and (3) differences across demographic groups in the optimal rate of enforcement.

Concern with racial disparities has motivated an empirical research literature on racial profiling by police in traffic stops for the purpose of identifying drug dealers and other offenders; see Knowles, Persico, and Todd (2001), Persico (2002), and Dominitz (2003). Being stopped as a suspected drug dealer on the pretext of a traffic violation and being the target of a confrontational police tactic such as SQF are noxious experiences, particularly when the subject of the treatment is innocent (Durlauf, 2006). In the United States, the targets of confrontational policing tactics have disproportionately been Blacks and other racial minorities. The literature on racial profiling has sought to determine the extent to which observed racial disparities in confrontational policing reflects racial discrimination rather than racial differences in crime rates. Related legal literature examines the constitutional constraints on policing practice, mostly as it relates to the 4th Amendment restrictions on "unreasonable searches and seizures" and the Equal Protection Clause (Harmon, 2012).

Our concern was not detection of discrimination or constitutionally prohibited use of confrontational policing tactics. Instead, we sought to shed light on the difficult planning problem that confrontational policing raises even in the absence of discrimination or other illegalities attending their use. We brought to bear a model of optimal policing adapted from earlier work of Manski (2005a, 2006). The adaptation was designed to explore the trade-off between the social benefits and costs of confrontational proactive policing tactics. I summarize the analysis below.

Model
Police serve diverse social functions – notably crime control, traffic safety, responding to emergencies, and helping persons in distress. We focused on the crime control function. We supposed that the objective of proactive policing policy is to optimize a social welfare function that recognizes the social costs and benefits of proactive policing. Here I describe a simple special case of the model that highlights key features of the optimal policy.

We must first define what we mean by "proactive policing." In general, the term connotes efforts by the police to actively prevent crime. Police may prevent crime by many means. One is by arresting persons who have already committed crimes. Their arrest may deter others from committing crimes. If incarceration is a consequence of the arrest, it may also prevent crime by incapacitation of offenders.

A second prevention mechanism involves police presence. A would-be robber of a liquor store will likely be deterred if a police car is idling outside. More generally, knowledge that police may be nearby may deter crime.

A third mechanism by which police may prevent crime is by interacting directly with citizens. Some forms of interaction are benign or even socially beneficial, for example communication with business owners about how they might better secure their property. Others, however, are confrontational and result in social costs. SQF is an example of such a policing tactic. Another is so-called "broken windows" policing, in which police crack down on disorder by dispersing lingering groups in public places or by arresting individuals or issuing summons for minor legal infractions. Broken windows policing is predicated on the theory that disorderly places are a breeding ground for more serious crime, particularly involving violence.

Manski and Nagin (2017) focused on forms of proactive policing that use confrontational tactics having social cost. Our model expressed a central tension: Increasing the intensity of a confrontational tactic yields more benefit in crime reduction but also a higher cost of intrusiveness. The planning problem is to choose a level of intensity that appropriately recognizes this benefit and cost.

The delicate issue of disparate racial impacts may arise if crime rates in the absence of confrontational tactics vary with race. Then a policy that strives to optimize social welfare may be implemented without racial animus yet nonetheless generate disparities in the intensity with which confrontational tactics are directed at innocent persons of different races.

To introduce the model, consider proactive policing aiming to deter a specific type of crime in a specific neighborhood. Let D_i denote demographic group i. Let x denote background characteristics such as the state of the economy that affect the crime rate of members of D_i in the absence of proactive policing. We abstracted from the reality that criminally involved individuals may commit multiple crimes of different types in different places. We instead assumed that individuals either commit a single crime per year or none in their neighborhoods.

Let $\rho(D_i, x)$ denote the fraction of persons in group D_i who would commit a crime in background setting x in the absence of proactive policing. We measured the intensity of proactivity directed at D_i by the probability that a member of D_i is the target of proactive enforcement activity. We denoted this probability by t_i and assumed it is equal across all members of D_i. We assumed for simplicity that if a would-be offender is the target of proactive enforcement, that crime is always foiled, and the individual is brought into custody. We assumed that crimes are not foiled in the absence of proactive enforcement.

We assumed that proactive policing deters crime. That is, the crime rate in group D_i decreases as the intensity t_i of proactive policing increases. Our general model did not assume a particular relationship between the crime rate and intensity of policing, but the simple special case considered here assumed that the proportion of group D_i who commit a crime declines linearly as t_i increases. Thus, assume that the crime rate in group D_i in setting x with proactive policing intensity t_i is $\rho(D_i, x)(1-t_i)$.

The social cost function that we assumed society seeks to minimize includes three components: (i) the cost of successful crimes, (ii) the cost of punishing apprehended offenders, and (iii) the cost of proactive enforcement directed at innocent persons. Under the assumption of linear deterrence, the specific form of the social cost function to be minimized for each group D_i is:

$$(7.9) \quad \begin{aligned} & a \cdot \rho(D_i, x) \cdot (1-t_i)^2 + b \cdot \rho(D_i, x) \cdot (1-t_i) \cdot t_i \\ & + c \cdot [1 - \rho(D_i, x) \cdot (1-t_i)] \cdot t_i. \end{aligned}$$

The terms of (7.9) express the three components of the social cost function when the policing intensity is t_i. The first term gives the cost of successful crime. The crime rate in group D_i under policing intensity t_i is $\rho(D_i, x) \cdot (1-t_i)$ and the fraction of crimes that are not foiled is $(1-t_i)$. Hence, $\rho(D_i, x) \cdot (1-t_i)^2$ is the rate of successful crimes. The constant $a > 0$ denotes the cost of each successful crime.

The second term gives the cost of apprehending offenders. The crime rate under policing intensity t_i is $\rho(D_i, x) \cdot (1-t_i)$ and the fraction of crimes that are foiled is t_i. Hence, $\rho(D_i, x) \cdot (1-t_i) t_i$ is the rate of foiled crimes. The constant $b > 0$ denotes the cost of apprehending and punishing the offender in each foiled crime.

The third term gives the cost of subjecting innocent persons to enforcement. The fraction of innocents in group D_i under policing intensity t_i is $1 - \rho(D_i, x) \cdot (1-t_i)$. The fraction of these persons who are the subject of proactive enforcement is t_i. Hence, $[1 - \rho(D_i, x) \cdot (1-t_i)] \cdot t_i$ is the rate at which innocents are the subject of enforcement. The constant $c > 0$ denotes the social cost of enforcement directed at innocent persons.

We showed how the optimal value of t_i depends on the values of the cost parameters (a, b, c). Suppose that $a - b + c > 0$, which we thought the most salient case in practice. This condition means that the combined social costs of a successful crime and of subjecting an innocent person to enforcement is larger than the cost of apprehending an offender. Then the optimal intensity equals zero for some parameter values (no proactive policing), equals one for other values (comprehensive proactive policing), and takes a value between zero and one otherwise. Specifically, the optimal intensity is:

$$(7.10) \quad t^*(D_i, x) = \frac{(2a-b) \cdot \rho(D_i, x) + c[\rho(D_i, x) - 1]}{2(a-b+c)\rho(D_i, x)}$$

if the expression on the right-hand side is between zero and one. Optimal intensity is zero if this expression is negative and is one if the expression exceeds one.

Three features of the optimum are particularly relevant to policy choice:

(i) The optimal intensity of enforcement decreases as c, the cost of enforcement borne by innocent persons increases. Hence, the more intrusive proactive policing is, the lower the optimal intensity of enforcement.
(ii) The optimal intensity of enforcement increases with the value of $\rho(D_i, x)$, the base crime rate with no proactive policing. Thus, a high level of proactive enforcement may be optimal in a high crime rate environment but not in a low crime rate environment.
(iii) The optimal intensity of proactive enforcement varies by group. For some groups with low base crime rates, it may be zero. For other groups with high base crimes, a high intensity may be optimal.

The discussion in Manski and Nagin (2017) expanded on these three features in the modern American context.

7.2 SEPARABILITY OF TREATMENT CHOICE BY COVARIATES UNDER UNCERTAINTY

I now leave behind the simple setting of optimal treatment choice and consider treatment under uncertainty. An important question is whether a planner using a Bayesian, maximin, or MMR criterion separates members of the population by their observed covariates and considers each subpopulation separately, as occurs with utilitarian optimization. Or must the planner approach the problem globally, jointly determining the treatment allocations for all subpopulations? The answer depends on the decision criterion and the structure of the state space. I explain here.

7.2.1 Treatment Allocation with Partial Identification of Mean Treatment Response

Manski (2009) extended the analysis discussed in Section 5.1 to consider treatment allocation when persons have observable covariates. Suppose that the planner observes covariates $x_j \in X$ for each person j, where the covariate space X is finite and $P(x = \xi) > 0$, $\xi \in X$. Assume that the planner knows the covariate distribution $P(x)$. The uncertainty is mean treatment response conditional on x. Assume that no institutional or budget constraint limits how treatment can vary across persons. Then the planner can choose any vector δ_ξ, $\xi \in X$ of treatment allocations.

Welfare with this vector of allocations is:

$$(7.11) \qquad w(\delta_\xi, \xi \in X) = \sum_{\xi \in X} P(x = \xi) \cdot \left[\alpha_\xi + (\beta_\xi - \alpha_\xi)\delta_\xi\right],$$

where $\alpha_\xi \equiv E[u(A) \mid x = \xi]$ and $\beta_\xi \equiv E[u(B) \mid x = \xi]$. The welfare function is additively separable in ξ. Hence, an optimal allocation vector separates the population into subpopulations of observationally identical persons, setting $\delta_\xi = 1$ when $\beta_\xi \geq \alpha_\xi$ and $\delta_\xi = 0$ when $\beta_\xi \leq \alpha_\xi$.

Now consider treatment choice under ambiguity. The state space S comprises all feasible values of (α_ξ, β_ξ), $\xi \in X$. I show below that the Bayes criterion is separable across covariates whatever S may be. However, the maximin and MMR criteria are separable only when S has special structure. In particular, the latter criteria are both separable when S has the Cartesian Product form $S = \Pi_{\xi \in X} S_\xi$, where S_ξ contains the feasible values of (α_ξ, β_ξ).

The state space has the Cartesian Product form when the planner has no information that relates the values of (α_ξ, β_ξ) across $\xi \in X$. It lacks this form otherwise. For example, X could be an ordered set and the planner may know that α_ξ or β_ξ is monotone in ξ. Then the covariate is a monotone instrumental variable, as discussed in Chapter 3.

Bayesian Planning

A Bayesian planner solves the problem:

$$(7.12) \qquad \max_{\delta_\xi \in [0, 1], \xi \in X} \sum_{\xi \in X} P(x = \xi) \cdot \left\{E_\pi(\alpha_\xi) + \left[E_\pi(\beta_\xi) - E_\pi(\alpha_\xi)\right] \cdot \delta_\xi\right\},$$

where $E_\pi(\alpha_\xi) = \int \alpha_{\xi s} d\pi$ and $E_\pi(\beta_\xi) = \int \beta_{\xi s} d\pi$ are the subjective means of α_ξ and β_ξ. The Bayesian objective function is separable in ξ, whatever S and π may be. The Bayes criterion assigns all persons with covariates ξ to treatment B if $E_\pi(\beta_\xi) \geq E_\pi(\alpha_\xi)$ and all such persons to treatment A if $E_\pi(\beta_\xi) \leq E_\pi(\alpha_\xi)$.

Maximin Planning

The maximin problem is:

$$(7.13) \qquad \max_{\delta_\xi \in [0, 1], \xi \in X} \min_{s \in S} \sum_{\xi \in X} P(x = \xi) \cdot \left[\alpha_{\xi s} + (\beta_{\xi s} - \alpha_{\xi s})\delta_\xi\right].$$

Minimization over S implies that this objective function generally is non-separable in ξ. Hence, determination of the maximin allocation generally requires joint choice of $(\delta_\xi, \xi \in X)$.

The maximin objective function is separable in ξ if S has the Cartesian Product form. Then, for each allocation vector $\delta_\xi \in [0, 1], \xi \in X$,

$$
\begin{aligned}
&\min_{s \in S} \sum_{\xi \in X} P(x = \xi) \cdot \left[\alpha_{\xi s} + (\beta_{\xi s} - \alpha_{\xi s})\delta_\xi\right] \\
&= \sum_{\xi \in X} P(x = \xi) \cdot \left[\min_{s \in S_\xi} \alpha_{\xi s} + (\beta_{\xi s} - \alpha_{\xi s})\delta_\xi\right].
\end{aligned}
\tag{7.14}
$$

Hence, maximin decision making conditional on ξ yields the global maximin treatment allocation.

Although equation (7.14) does not generally hold when S lacks the Cartesian Product form, the minimum of a sum is always greater than or equal to the sum of the minima of the components in the sum. Hence, the left-hand side of (7.14) is greater than or equal to the right-hand side for all $(\delta_\xi, \xi \in X)$, whatever S may be. This implies that the minimum welfare of the STR which solves the global maximin problem is greater than or equal to the sum of the ξ-specific maximin welfare values.

MMR Planning

The MMR problem is:

$$
\min_{\delta_\xi \in [0, 1], \xi \in X} \max_{s \in S} \sum_{\xi \in X} P(x = \xi) \cdot \Big\{\max\left(\alpha_{\xi s}, \beta_{\xi s}\right) - \left[\alpha_{\xi s} + (\beta_{\xi s} - \alpha_{\xi s})\delta_\xi\right]\Big\}.
\tag{7.15}
$$

Maximization over S implies that this objective function is generally non-separable in ξ. Hence, determination of the MMR allocation generally requires joint choice of $\delta_\xi, \xi \in X$.

The objective function is separable in ξ if S has the Cartesian Product form. Then, for each allocation vector $\delta_\xi \in [0, 1], \xi \in X$,

$$
\begin{aligned}
&\max_{s \in S} \sum_{\xi \in X} P(x = \xi) \cdot \Big\{\max\left(\alpha_{\xi s}, \beta_{\xi s}\right) - \left[\alpha_{\xi s} + (\beta_{\xi s} - \alpha_{\xi s})\delta_\xi\right]\Big\} \\
&= \sum_{\xi \in X} P(x = \xi) \cdot \Big\{\max_{s \in S_\xi} \left\{\max(\alpha_{\xi s}, \beta_{\xi s}) - \left[\alpha_{\xi s} + (\beta_{\xi s} - \alpha_{\xi s})\delta_\xi\right]\right\}\Big\}.
\end{aligned}
\tag{7.16}
$$

Hence, MMR decision making conditional on ξ yields the global MMR treatment allocation.

Although equation (7.16) does not generally hold when S lacks the Cartesian Product form, the maximum of a sum is always less than or equal to the sum of the maxima of the components in the sum. Hence, the left-hand side of (7.16) is less than or equal to the right-hand side for all $(\delta_\xi, \xi \in X)$, whatever S may be. This implies that the maximum regret of the STR which solves the global MMR problem is less than or equal to the sum of the ξ-specific MMR values.

7.2.2 Should a Planner Condition on All Observed Covariates?

A delicate and unresolved question arises when a planner knows more about treatment response conditional on coarse covariates than conditional on refined covariates. Should a planner condition treatment choice on refined covariates or only on coarse covariates? Reasonable use of covariate information may depend on the decision criterion and on the available knowledge.

An important instance of this question occurs in the setting of Section 3.2.3. I observed there that standard summaries of trial findings in medical journals partition subjects into coarse subgroups, typically into binary categories. Hence, short mean treatment response, conditioning on the coarse covariates, is point-identified when the findings pertain to a classical trial.

I summarized the work of Li, Litvin, and Manski (2023), who showed that reported summaries of trial findings only partially identify long mean response, conditioning on all observed covariates. We found that the summaries per so are often nearly uninformative regarding long mean response, but the summaries combined with bounded-variation assumptions may have substantial identifying power. The state space for long mean response does not have the Cartesian Product form, because short and long mean response are related by the Law of Iterated Expectations; see equation (3.14). Bounded-variation assumptions of the forms (3.17) and (3.18) imply further connections in mean long response across covariate values.

Planning in this setting is a complex subject that warrants future research. Here I will make only a cautionary remark about Bayesian planning. Even though reported summaries of trial findings yield much more knowledge of short treatment response than long response, we have seen that a Bayesian planner makes ξ-separable treatment choices, whatever S and π may be. This feature of Bayesian decision making has long been known. See, for example, Good (1967) and Kadane, Shervish, and Seidenfeld (2008).

The Bayesian prescription to condition on all observed covariates is logically coherent. The Bayesian paradigm views the planner's subjective distribution as a primitive concept. It compares subjective expected welfare when the planner does or does not condition on the available evidence. It makes no reference to the actual state of nature. The Bayesian does not evaluate the objective welfare achieved by maximization of subjective expected welfare.

Although Bayesian treatment choice is logically coherent, it may be nonsensical from the perspective of objective welfare maximization. Recall the statement of Berger (1985, p. 121) that I quoted in Chapter 1, "a Bayesian analysis may be 'rational' in the weak axiomatic sense, yet be terrible in a practical sense if an inappropriate prior distribution is used."

7.2.3 Treatment Allocation with Sample Data

Personalized treatment allocation with sample data is a complex subject. I will touch on it only briefly. The Bayesian, maximin, and MMR problems with sample data are:

$$(7.17) \quad \max_{\delta_\xi(\cdot),\, \xi \in X} \int_S \sum_{\xi \in X} \alpha_{\xi s} + (\beta_{\xi s} - \alpha_{\xi s}) \cdot E_{\xi s}\left[\delta(\psi)\right] d\pi,$$

$$(7.18) \quad \max_{\delta_\xi(\cdot),\, \xi \in X} \min_{s \in S} \sum_{\xi \in X} \alpha_{\xi s} + (\beta_{\xi s} - \alpha_{\xi s}) \cdot E_{\xi s}\left[\delta(\psi)\right],$$

$$(7.19) \quad \min_{\delta_\xi(\cdot),\, \xi \in X} \max_{s \in S} \left[\sum_{\xi \in X} \max(\alpha_{\xi s}, \beta_{\xi s}) - \sum \alpha_{\xi s} + (\beta_{\xi s} - \alpha_{\xi s}) \cdot E_{\xi s}\left[\delta(\psi)\right] \right].$$

The Bayesian objective function is again separable in ξ, whatever S and π may be. The maximin and MMR planning problems are again generally nonseparable in ξ. An argument paralleling that in Section 7.1.1 shows that these problems are separable if the state space has the Cartesian Product form. This now means not only that the planner has no information that relates the values of (α_ξ, β_ξ) across $\xi \in X$, but also that the sampling process yields data that are informative only in a covariate-specific manner. The sampling process has this structure when data on treatment outcomes are generated by a classical trial. With trial data, outcomes observed for subjects with a specified covariate value are uninformative about treatment response for subjects with other covariate values.

A few technical studies have been performed that analyze MMR planning with sample data in settings where the planning problem is not separable across covariates. Stoye (2012) studied MMR planning with data from a classical trial when bounded variation assumptions connect mean treatment response across persons with different covariates. Manski and Tetenov (2016) studied trial design to achieve global ε-optimality, without requiring that it be achieved within each covariate group. Kitagawa and Tetenov (2018) studied nonrandomized treatment allocation with sample data when institutional or budget constraints limit the feasible set of treatment rules in a manner that connects treatment across subpopulations. Manski (2021b, 2023) studied the maximum regret of STRs that use sample data to point estimate the true state of nature and then optimize as if the estimate is correct. These are subtle problems.

7.3 SURVEILLANCE OR AGGRESSIVE TREATMENT WITH PARTIAL KNOWLEDGE OF PERSONALIZED RISK

I now return to the choice between surveillance and aggressive treatment, in a simple but instructive setting where uncertainty stems from partial identification, examined in Manski (2018a). I supposed there that the state space has the Cartesian Product form, so planning is separable across covariates. Given separability, I can simplify the present discussion by considering patients with a specified covariate value (x, z) and by suppressing this value in the notation.

Suppose that a clinician knows that a patient's probability p of illness lies in some interval $[p_L, p_H]$. To simplify analysis and eliminate concern with the issue of equal treatment of equals, I assumed that only singleton treatment allocations are feasible. Thus, the clinician chooses between prescribing treatment A and B, fractional allocations being infeasible.

A clinician in this setting can optimize treatment if he knows that the patient's threshold probability p* given in (7.8) is not interior to the interval $[p_L, p_H]$. Treatment A is sure to be optimal if $p_H \leq p^*$ and B is sure to be optimal if $p^* \leq p_L$. The clinician cannot optimize if p* is interior to $[p_L, p_H]$. Then there exist feasible values of p that make only A optimal and other values that make only B optimal.

Bayesian planning places a subjective distribution on p and maximizes subjective expected welfare. The Bayesian decision is easy to characterize because mean personal welfare is linear in p. Let p_π denote the subjective mean that a Bayesian clinician holds for p. The clinician acts as if $p = p_\pi$. Thus, treatment A maximizes subjective expected welfare if $p_\pi \leq p^*$ and B if $p_\pi \geq p^*$.

The maximin criterion evaluates each treatment by the worst mean welfare that it may yield and chooses the treatment with the least-bad worst mean welfare. The worst feasible results under treatments A and B both occur when p equals its upper bound p_H. Then A and B yield mean welfare $p_H \cdot u(A, 1) + (1 - p_H) \cdot u(A, 0)$ and $p_H \cdot u(B, 1) + (1 - p_H) \cdot u(B, 0)$. Hence, the maximin choice is A if $p_H \leq p^*$ and B if $p_H \geq p^*$.

The MMR criterion evaluates each action by the worst reduction in mean welfare that it may yield relative to the highest mean welfare achievable. Maximum regret under treatment A occurs when p equals its upper bound p_H and equals the mean welfare difference:

$$(7.20) \quad \begin{aligned} & [p_H \cdot u(B, 1) + (1 - p_H) \cdot u(B, 0)] \\ & - [p_H \cdot u(A, 1) + (1 - p_H) \cdot u(A, 0)]. \end{aligned}$$

Maximum regret under B occurs when p equals its lower bound p_L and equals:

$$(7.21) \quad \begin{aligned} & [p_L \cdot u(A, 1) + (1 - p_L) \cdot U(A, 0)] \\ & - [p_L \cdot u(B, 1) + (1 - p_L) \cdot u(B, 0)]. \end{aligned}$$

Hence, A is an MMR choice if the magnitude in (7.20) is less than or equal to that in (7.21).

A more transparent representation of this finding emerges if we define p_M to be the midpoint of interval $[p_L, p_H]$. Rearrangement of terms in (7.20) and (7.21) shows that a clinician using the MMR criterion acts as follows:

$$(7.22a) \quad \begin{aligned} \text{Choose A if } & p_M \cdot u(A,1) + (1 - p_M) \cdot u(A,0) \geq p_M \cdot u(B, 1) \\ & + (1 - p_M) \cdot u(B, 0), \end{aligned}$$

$$(7.22b) \quad \begin{aligned} \text{Choose B if } & p_M \cdot u(B,1) + (1 - p_M) \cdot u(B,0) \geq p_M \cdot u(A, 1) \\ & + (1 - p_M) \cdot u(A, 0). \end{aligned}$$

Hence, the MMR choice is the same as a utilitarian clinician would make if he were to know that the probability of illness is $p = p_M$

7.4 DIAGNOSTIC TESTING AND TREATMENT

I have thus far supposed that the observable covariates of population members are predetermined. In some settings, a planner can invest in costly acquisition of covariate data prior to treatment choice. Then the planner faces a two-stage decision problem. The first stage is to determine whether to acquire costly covariate data. The second is to make the treatment choice.

Manski (2013a) studied this two-stage problem in the context of clinical care. Prior to treatment choice, clinicians may decide whether to order a costly diagnostic test whose result yields more accurate prediction of risk of illness. Cassidy and Manski (2019) built on this analysis to consider diagnosis and treatment of tuberculosis (TB). I summarize here, first presenting the two-stage optimization problem and then considering planning under ambiguity.

7.4.1 The Two-Stage Optimization Problem

Phelps and Mushlin (1988) studied the two-stage problem of optimizing testing and treatment under the assumption that the clinician has rational expectations. I use here the concepts and notation of Manski (2013a), which extended their analysis.

Consider a clinician who cares for a population of patients. The clinician initially observes patient covariates that may include medical history, demographic attributes, measures of health status, and patient statements expressing their preferences for care and outcomes. With this background, the clinician can choose a treatment immediately based on the observed covariates, or the clinician can order a test providing further evidence. In the latter case, the clinician chooses a treatment after observing the test result.

Let x denote the initially observed patient covariates and let t denote a treatment. There are two feasible treatments, A and B. In the context of TB, treatment B is prescription of antibiotics. Treatment A is surveillance without prescription of antibiotics.

Let d indicate whether the clinician orders the test, with d = 1 if she orders it and d = 0 otherwise. Let z denote the test result. Suppose that z can take two values: p, positive, indicating that the patient has the illness; or n, negative, indicating that the patient does not have illness. In practice, the test result is typically informative about the presence of illness but is not definitive.

The feasible actions, and the accompanying knowledge of patient covariates, may be expressed as a decision tree. The clinician first chooses d = 1 or d = 0 with knowledge of x. If d = 0, she chooses t = A or t = B with knowledge of x. If d = 1, she chooses t = A or t = B with knowledge of (x, z).

When the clinician makes the testing decision, patients with the same value of x are observationally identical, while those with different values are observationally distinct. Hence, the clinician can make systematically different testing decisions for patients with different values of x. The clinician also can randomly differentiate among patients with the same value of x, ordering testing for some fraction and not testing the remainder. This constitutes diversification in testing.

To formalize this, let $\delta(x)$ be the fraction of patients with covariates x who are tested and let $1 - \delta(x)$ be the fraction who are not tested. The clinician can choose $\delta(x)$ to be any fraction in the interval [0, 1].

When considering treatment, we need to distinguish three groups of patients. Those who are not tested have observed covariates x when treated. Those who are tested have observed covariates (x, z) when treated, with z equaling n or p. Among patients who are not tested, let $\delta_{T0}(x)$ be the fraction with covariates x who receive treatment B, and let $1 - \delta_{T0}(x)$ be the fraction who receive A. Among those who are tested, let $\delta_{T1}(x, z)$ be the fraction with covariates (x, z) who receive B, and let $1 - \delta_{T1}(x, z)$ be the fraction who receive A.

Optimization with Utilitarian Welfare

Phelps and Mushlin (1988) and Manski (2013a) assumed that the clinician maximizes utilitarian welfare. To derive transparent findings, Cassidy and Manski (2019) made the dependence of welfare on illness explicit. Let y = 1 if the patient is ill and y = 0 otherwise. The clinician does not know y when choosing (d, t). Given this, testing and treatment decisions depend on a patient's risk of illness rather than on realized illness outcomes.

Let $u_j(y, d, t)$ be the welfare of patient j with testing decision d and treatment decision t if the patient's illness outcome is y. This welfare measure may express not only health outcomes but also patient preferences and financial costs. Patients may respond heterogeneously to testing and treatment, so $u_j(y, d, t)$ may vary across patients.

Mean welfare across patients is determined by the fraction with each covariate value that the clinician assigns to each option for testing and treatment. Let x lie in a finite set X. For each $x \in X$, let P(x) denote the fraction of patients with value x. For each $z \in \{p, n\}$, let f(z | x) denote the fraction of the patients with covariate x who would have test result z if they were tested.

For each value of (d, t), let E[u(y, d, t) | x] be the mean welfare that results if all patients with covariate value x receive (d, t). Let E[u(y, d, t) | x, z] be the mean welfare that results if all those with covariate value x and test result z receive (d, t). It then follows from the Law of Iterated Expectations that:

(7.23a) $E\big[u(y, d, t) | x\big] = (1 - p_x) E\big[u(0, d, t) | x\big] + p_x E\big[u(1, d, t) | x\big],$

(7.23b) $\begin{aligned} E\big[u(y, d, t) | x, z\big] &= (1 - p_{xz}) E\big[u(0, d, t) | x, z\big] \\ &\quad + p_{xz} E\big[u(1, d, t) | x, z\big], \end{aligned}$

where $p_x = P(y = 1 | x)$ and $p_{xz} = P(y = 1 | x, z)$ as in Section 7.1.

In the medical literature on diagnostic testing, p_x is called the base rate or the prevalence of the illness for patients with covariates x. p_{xp} is called the positive predictive value of a test and $1 - p_{xn}$ is called the negative predictive value. In general, $p_{xp} > p_{xn}$. An ideal test that perfectly predicts disease would have $p_{xp} = 1$ and $p_{xn} = 0$. In practice, tests are imperfect predictors, so $1 > p_{xp} > p_{xn} > 0$.

Let $\delta = [\delta(x), \delta_{T0}(x), \delta_{T1}(x, z), x \in X, z \in \{p, n\}]$ denote a testing-treatment allocation. The mean welfare $w(\delta)$ that results if the clinician chooses δ is obtained by averaging the various mean welfare values $E[u(y, d, t) | x]$ and $E[u(y, d, t) | x, z]$ across the groups who receive them. That is,

(7.24)
$$w(\delta) = \sum_{x \in X} P(x) \Big[[1 - \delta(x)][1 - \delta_{T0}(x)] E[u(y, 0, A) | x]$$
$$+ [1 - \delta(x)] \delta_{T0}(x) E[u(y, 0, B) | x]$$
$$+ \sum_{z \in \{p, n\}} f(z | x) \{\delta(x)[1 - \delta_{T1}(x, z)] E[u(y, 1, A) | x, z]$$
$$+ \delta(x) \delta_{T1}(x, z) E[u(y, 1, B) | x, z]\} \Big].$$

An optimal testing and treatment allocation maximizes $w(\cdot)$. Manski (2013a) showed that an optimal allocation is:

(7.25a)
$$\delta(x) = 1 \text{ if } \sum_{z \in \{p, n\}} f(z | x) \big[\max\{E[u(y, 1, A) | x, z],$$
$$E[u(y, 1, B) | x, z]\} \big]$$
$$\geq \max\{E[u(y, 0, A) | x], E[u(y, 0, B) | x]\},$$
$$= 0 \text{ otherwise}.$$

(7.25b) $\delta_{T0}(x) = 1$ if $E[u(y, 0, B) | x] \geq E[u(y, 0, A) | x]$,
$= 0$ otherwise.

(7.25c) $\delta_{T1}(x, p) = 1$ if $E[u(y, 1, B) | x, p] \geq E[u(y, 1, A) | x, p]$,
$= 0$ otherwise.

(7.25d) $\delta_{T1}(x, n) = 1$ if $E[u(y, 1, B) | x, n] \geq E[u(y, 1, A) | x, n]$,
$= 0$ otherwise.

Each maximum is unique when the inequality is strict. All allocations yield the same welfare when the values are equal.

Choice of treatment without performing a diagnostic test is optimal when the inequality in (7.25a) does not hold. In the TB context, aggressive treatment without testing may be optimal if a patient's probability of having TB is high even following a negative test result. For example, given the poor predictive value of the standard smear microscopy test among HIV-positive patients with advanced levels of immunosuppression, a clinician may find it optimal to prescribe antibiotics to such patients even following a negative test result.

To simplify further computations, I henceforth use a more compact notation for $E[u(y, d, t) | x]$ and $E[u(y, d, t) | x, z]$, as follows:

(7.23a′) $\quad E[u(y, d, t) | x] = (1 - p_x)u_x(0, d, t) + p_x u_x(1, d, t),$

(7.23b′) $\quad E[u(y, d, t) | x, z] = (1 - p_{xz})u_{xz}(0, d, t) + p_{xz}u_{xz}(1, d, t).$

We can simplify further if we assume that knowledge of a test result does not directly affect patient welfare in a given illness state: formally, $u_{xz}(0, d, t) = u_x(0, d, t)$ and $u_{xz}(1, d, t) = u_x(1, d, t)$. With this assumption, knowledge of the test result affects decision making purely by changing risk assessment from p_x to p_{xz}, not for any other reason. With this notation and assumption, the treatment criteria in (7.25b)–(7.25d) are as follows:

(7.25b′)
treatment with no diagnostic test:
choose B if $(1 - p_x)u_x(0, 0, B) + p_x u_x(1, 0, B)$
$\geq (1 - p_x)u_x(0, 0, A) + p_x u_x(1, 0, A),$
choose A otherwise.

(7.25c′)
treatment with positive test result:
choose B if $(1 - p_{xp})u_x(0, 1, B) + p_{xp}u_x(1, 1, B)$
$\geq (1 - p_{xp})u_x(0, 1, A) + p_{xp}u_x(1, 1, A),$
choose A otherwise.

(7.25d′)
treatment with negative test result:
choose B if $(1 - p_{xn})u_x(0, 1, B) + p_{xn}u_x(1, 1, B)$
$\geq (1 - p_{xn})u_x(0, 1, A) + p_{xn}u_x(1, 1, A),$
choose A otherwise.

Threshold Risk Assessments

Treatment criteria (7.25b′)–(7.25d′) are analogous to those studied in Section 7.1.3. As discussed there, it is often credible to make various assumptions about patient welfare when comparing surveillance and aggressive treatment. In the present setting, these assumptions are typically credible:

(i) Health is better than illness: $u_x(0, d, t) > u_x(1, d, t)$, all (d, t).
(ii) Testing is costly/harmful: $u_x(y, 0, t) > u_x(y, 1, t)$, all (y, t).

(iii) Surveillance is better than aggressive treatment when healthy: $u_x(0, d, A) > u_x(0, d, B)$, all d.
(iv) Aggressive treatment is better than surveillance when ill: $u_x(1, d, B) > u_x(1, d, A)$, all d.

These assumptions are realistic in the TB context: (i) A patient is better off not having TB than having TB; (ii) although performance of a diagnostic test does not harm patients, it does incur financial costs; (iii) when a patient is healthy, there is no benefit from prescription of antibiotics but there are financial costs and possible harms to patients; (iv) when a patient is ill with TB, the health benefits of antibiotic treatment exceed the financial costs and harms.

Analysis akin to Section 7.1.3 shows that under assumptions (iii) and (iv), the treatment criteria in (7.25b′)–(7.25d′) yield simple solutions. Aggressive treatment is optimal if the risk of illness equals or exceeds a threshold that equalizes mean welfare under treatments A and B. Surveillance is better if illness risk is less than or equal to the threshold. Without testing, risk of illness is measured by p_x and the threshold yielded by criterion (7.25b′) is:

$$(7.26a) \quad p_{x0}^* \equiv \frac{u_x(0, 0, A) - u_x(0, 0, B)}{\left[u_x(0, 0, A) - u_x(0, 0, B)\right] + \left[u_x(1, 0, B) - u_x(1, 0, A)\right]}.$$

With testing, risk of illness is measured by p_{xp} or p_{xn} respectively. The threshold yielded by both the criteria in (7.25c′) and (7.25d′) is:

$$(7.26b) \quad p_{x1}^* \equiv \frac{u_x(0, 1, A) - u_x(0, 1, B)}{\left[u_x(0, 1, A) - u_x(0, 1, B)\right] + \left[u_x(1, 1, B) - u_x(1, 1, A)\right]}.$$

Under assumptions (iii) and (iv), both thresholds lie in the open interval (0, 1).

7.4.2 Testing and Treatment under Ambiguity

Optimization of testing and treatment for patients is feasible if one knows the mean welfare function $u_x(\cdot, \cdot, \cdot)$, the illness probabilities (p_x, p_{xn}, p_{xp}), and the probability $f(z \mid x)$ of test result z. A clinician with incomplete knowledge may not be able to optimize.

Cassidy and Manski (2019) observed that there are several reasons why these quantities are partially known in the context of TB. One is that when epidemiological studies estimate disease prevalence, they typically report illness probabilities only conditioning on a subset of the covariates that a clinician observes. For example, the World Health Organization reports TB prevalence by (country, HIV status, age, sex), but not by patient socioeconomic status or comorbidities. This means that a clinician faces ambiguity about p_x.

The same issue arises when the accuracy of diagnostic tests is studied. Research reports test accuracy only conditioning on a subset of clinician-observable covariates. Thus, studies do not reveal $f(z \mid x)$.

A further difficulty is partial knowledge of the welfare function. Knowledge of the effectiveness of antibiotic treatment in curing patients who have TB is incomplete. So is knowledge of the harms stemming from treatment errors. There is uncertainty as to what will happen to patients if they are treated for TB when they in fact have a different condition. There is uncertainty as to whether and when a patient will present for examination again, if they are not treated after a first visit.

Piecemeal MMR Decision Making

One may in principle study decision making regarding diagnostic testing and treatment when clinicians maximize subjective expected welfare or use the maximin or minimax regret criterion. Maximization of subjective expected welfare is a standard dynamic programming problem and thus is tractable. In my work with Cassidy on TB, we would have liked to characterize MMR planning, but this posed an analytic challenge beyond our capacity.

Instead, Cassidy and Manski (2019) proposed a simple, heuristically-motivated piecemeal MMR criterion. We considered each value of x and each of the four component decisions in isolation from one another. The component decisions are, (1) test or not test, (2) choose A or B without testing, (3) choose A or B with testing and a positive result, and (4) choose A and B with testing and a negative result.

Each component is a decision between two options, making piecemeal decision making simple to study. We argued that piecemeal decision making may be realistic if each component decision is performed by a different clinician. For example, a different clinician may be on duty for the follow-up consultation with a patient to make the treatment decision after the test result has been received. In such a setting, the clinician making the testing decision cannot control what the clinician making the subsequent treatment decision will do. Thus, a reasonable approach may be to model each decision separately.

We performed an analysis that extends the study of minimax regret decision making in Manski (2009), discussed in Chapter 5 and Section 7.2. The extension was especially simple because we supposed that $u_x(\cdot, \cdot, \cdot)$ is known; hence, the threshold risk assessment is known. Nevertheless, considerable scope for ambiguity remained through incomplete knowledge of (p_x, p_{xn}, p_{xp}) and $f(z\,|\,x)$. We regarded our work as only an exploratory beginning of research on an important medical planning problem that warrants considerable attention.

8

Vaccination with Unknown Indirect Effects

When analyzing planning problems in Chapters 5 through 7, I assumed that treatment response is individualistic. Vaccination against infectious disease is a realm in which social interactions in treatment response are a central concern. This chapter discusses my research on vaccination planning, reported in Manski (2010, 2017). I focus on the latter study.

8.1 BACKGROUND

Social interactions in treatment response make infectious disease a core concern of public health policy. Spread of infection creates a negative external effect. Preventive administration of vaccines, therapeutic administration of antimicrobial drugs, and separation of infected persons from the general population may reduce disease transmission. In a decentralized healthcare system, infected and at-risk persons may not adequately recognize the social implications of their actions. Hence, there may be a rationale for government to seek to influence treatment of infectious disease. Policies range from quarantines of infected persons to mandatory vaccination to subsidization of vaccines and drugs.

A prevalent difficulty is scarcity of evidence about how interventions affect illness. Randomized trials, which have been central to evaluation of treatments for noninfectious diseases, are less informative about treatment of infectious diseases. As discussed in Section 3.3, the usual argument for classical trials assumes individualistic treatment response. This assumption does not hold when treating infectious diseases.

A leading planning problem is choice of a vaccination policy. Vaccination of a particular person may benefit him directly by generating an immune response that reduces susceptibility to the disease. It may also reduce the infectiousness of this person and thereby inhibit transmission of the disease to others who are unvaccinated or are unsuccessfully vaccinated. Thus, vaccination may have both a direct preventive effect on the person vaccinated and an indirect preventive effect on other persons. The indirect effect is often called herd or community immunity. Fine (1993) and Fine, Eames, and Heymann (2011) discuss the history and use of this concept in epidemiology.

Ordinarily, a trial that randomly vaccinates a specified fraction of the population may enable evaluation of the direct effect of vaccination on illness but cannot reveal the indirect effect. The trial only reveals the illness outcomes that occur with the vaccination rate used in the trial. The outcomes that the population would experience with other vaccination rates remain counterfactual. Yet policy choice requires comparison of alternative vaccination rates.

Rare exceptions to the above statement occur in special cases where the population partitions into many isolated groups of persons. Then the members of each group may infect one another but not the members of other groups. In such cases, one can define treatment units to be groups rather than persons, randomly assign varying vaccination rates to different groups, and use the trial to learn about illness outcomes under alternative vaccination rates. Hudgens and Halloran (2008) developed methodology for analysis of trials performed in such settings. Loeb et al. (2010) reported a trial performed on isolated Hutterite communities in Canada. However, populations rarely partition in modern societies. I pointed out in Section 3.3 that trials have no identifying power in a fully connected society, where social interactions are global rather than local.

Attempting to cope with the dearth of evidence, researchers studying vaccination have used epidemiological models of disease transmission to forecast the outcomes that would occur with counterfactual policies. See, for example, Brito, Sheshinski, and Intriligator (1991), Becker and Starczak (1997), Ball and Lyne (2002), Scuffham and West (2002), Hill and Longini (2003), Patel, Longini, and Halloran (2005), Boulier, Datta, and Goldfarb (2007), Althouse, Bergstrom, and Bergstrom (2010), and Keeling and Shattock (2012). However, authors typically provide little information that would enable one to assess the accuracy of their assumptions about individual behavior, social interactions, and disease transmission. Hence, it is prudent to view their forecasts more as computational experiments than as accurate predictions of policy impacts.

With this background, Manski (2010, 2017) considered the decision problem of a health planner who observes the illness outcomes that occur in some status quo vaccination setting and who contemplates enactment of a new policy. The two studies differed in their specification of the status quo and the proposed policies. Manski (2010) considered a planner who can choose to vaccinate any fraction of a population, randomly choosing which persons are vaccinated. The available evidence is the rate of illness that occurs with the status quo vaccination rate. The planner ideally wants to choose the optimal vaccination rate. This is a theoretically interesting problem, but it is not necessarily realistic. Choosing a fractional vaccination rate may generate concern with equal treatment of equals, discussed in Chapter 5.

In Manski (2017), the status quo is a realistic setting where members of the population make decentralized vaccination choices and the planner contemplates whether to mandate vaccination of essentially the entire population. In the American federal system, the planner who decides whether to mandate vaccination typically is a state public health agency. States may mandate that specific populations be vaccinated against specific diseases. Immunization Action Coalition (2023) lists state mandates.

The indirect effect of vaccination is a prevalent consideration. For example, the state of Washington has listed it as a reason that may motivate universal vaccination of children and young adults, stating (Washington State Board of Health, 2006):

> Vaccinating the infant, child, or adolescent against this disease reduces the risk of person–to–person transmission. Having some proportion of the population vaccinated with the antigen helps to stem person to person transmission of the disease (i.e., herd immunity). Even community members who are not vaccinated (such as newborns and those with chronic illnesses) are offered some protection because the disease has less opportunity to spread within the community. Vaccinating children in school and/or childcare centers can increase the percentage of children in these groups who are immune and thus reduce the risk of outbreaks of the disease in these groups and in the community at large.

Mandatory vaccination has been a subject of considerable controversy, centered on the tension between personal freedom and public health. Vamos, McDermott, and Daley (2008) gave arguments for and against mandatory administration of the HPV vaccine to middle-school girls. Stewart (2009) and May and Silverman (2005) did likewise for mandatory vaccination of healthcare workers against influenza and children against multiple diseases. Reiss and Caplan (2020) discussed legal and ethical considerations regarding mandatory Covid-19 vaccination. These and other articles in the medical and public health literatures make clear that society has conflicting objectives when contemplating whether to mandate vaccination. They did not address how society might reconcile the conflicting objectives to choose a policy.

Whether a planner has the power to choose any vaccination rate or only to mandate universal vaccination, the welfare-economic practice of specifying a social welfare (or social cost) function and considering a planner who wants to optimize this function provides a useful normative framework for policy formation. The planner's objective presumably is to minimize the social cost of illness and vaccination. Vaccination is socially costly, as is illness. Vaccination is beneficial to the extent that it prevents illness. Mandatory vaccination improves population health relative to decentralized decision making. However, a mandate increases the cost of production and administration of the vaccine and reduces personal freedom. The specified social cost function quantifies how society evaluates these advantages and disadvantages of a mandate.

Researchers have previously studied choice of vaccination policy as a deterministic planning problem, supposing that the planner knows the outcomes that alternative policies would yield. Brito, Sheshinski, and Intriligator (1991) focused on the decision to mandate universal vaccination. These authors observed that decentralization Pareto dominates mandatory vaccination if the vaccine is perfectly effective, the social cost function is utilitarian, and decentralized decision makers have rational expectations. However, they cautioned that (p. 83): "If there is a probability that the vaccine will not be effective it is possible that the compulsory solution requiring that all individuals be vaccinated is no longer dominated by the market solution."

Further research on this subject ranges from Francis (1997) to Chen and Toxvaerd (2014). Vaccines typically are imperfectly effective in practice, the degree of effectiveness varying with the vaccine. Hence, even if one assumes utilitarian social cost and rational expectations, comparison of decentralization and mandatory vaccination is a relevant subject for welfare-economic analysis.

The focus of my research has been choice of vaccination policy when a planner (a) wants to minimize the social cost of illness and vaccination, (b) observes a study population whose vaccination rate has been chosen previously, and (c) does not know the magnitude of the indirect preventive effect of vaccination. In both of Manski (2010, 2017), I derived explicit conditions under which the planner can determine that a feasible policy option is dominated; that is, inferior whatever the indirect effect of vaccination may be. In both, I posed several criteria for choice among undominated alternatives – maximization of subjective expected welfare, minimax, and minimax-regret – and compared the policies they generate.

Constraining the planner to two alternatives in Manski (2017) simplified the planning problem relative to the setting in Manski (2010), where the planner could choose any vaccination rate. However, the presumption in the 2017 study that decentralized decision making is the status quo made the identification problem encountered there more complex, the reason being that persons may nonrandomly choose to be vaccinated in a decentralized system.

8.1.1 Differentiating Epidemic Suppression from Social Cost Minimization

Before proceeding, I find it important to distinguish the welfare economic objective of minimization of social cost from the epidemiological objective of suppressing epidemics. Epidemiologists have used susceptible-infectious-removed (SIR) and related models of disease transmission to study epidemics and to evaluate policies that seek to prevent their onset or stop them once begun. An epidemic is a dynamic concept, defined to occur when the infected fraction of the population increases with time relative to some baseline (Centers for Disease Control and Prevention, 2006). Studies of vaccination policy performed by epidemiologists use SIR and related dynamic models to frame their research.

Dynamic epidemiological modeling can help to evaluate vaccination policy, but such modeling has practical and conceptual drawbacks. A practical problem has been that the analytical and computational complexity of epidemiological models inhibits understanding of their mathematical properties and their realism. Researchers use models of disease transmission to forecast outcomes that would occur with various policies. Unfortunately, these forecasts rest on considerable incredible certitude. I will discuss this issue further in Chapter 10.

A conceptual drawback has been the prevailing focus of epidemiologists on the goal of suppressing epidemics rather than on the objective of minimizing the social cost of illness and vaccination. Epidemiologists commonly seek a policy that keeps the *effective reproduction rate*, a parameter governing the rate of disease transmission, below the rate at which a model forecasts that a new epidemic will begin or that an ongoing one will cease. An epidemic is forecast to cease when the fraction of the population who are immune, either through natural infection or vaccination, reaches the so-called *herd immunity threshold* (HIT). Definitions of the effective reproduction rate and the HIT vary with the epidemiological model studied. See Anderson and May (1991), Fine (1993), and Fine, Eames, and Heymann (2011). Epidemiological research does not show that keeping the effective reproduction rate below the HIT is necessary or sufficient to minimize social cost.

My research has abstracted from the dynamics of infectious disease and has studied minimization of social cost as a static planning problem. I have assumed that vaccination occurs at a specified point in time, rather than as a process performed gradually over time. I have assumed that society is concerned with social cost over a specified horizon following vaccination. I have studied choice of an aggregate vaccination rate rather than disaggregated choice of whom to vaccinate.

Studying vaccination as a static planning problem transparently expresses the core tension of a mandate decision: using a mandate to increase the vaccination rate reduces illness but raises the social cost of vaccination. Analysis of the static problem is much simpler than study of policy making with a dynamic model.

The trade-off is that abstracting from dynamics is an idealization. It disregards the possibility that the social cost of illness and vaccination may depend not only on the prevalence of illness and vaccination but also on the timing. For example, capacity constraints in hospitals might make the social cost of illness depend on the timing of severe cases, not just their totality. Heterogeneity in susceptibility and infectiousness may make policy effectiveness depend on the temporal sequence of vaccination of persons with different attributes. Analysis of a dynamic planning problem could shed light on these matters.

Given its static nature, my analysis applies most directly to endemic diseases. It applies as well to epidemic-prone diseases in which vaccination is performed ex ante with the objective of preventing onset of epidemics and in which social cost depends mainly on the prevalence of illness in the population rather than on the timing of new cases.

8.2 CHOICE BETWEEN DECENTRALIZATION AND A UNIVERSAL MANDATE WITH A REPRESENTATIVE AGENT

This section and the next present the analysis in Manski (2017), in two stages. This section considers a simple representative-agent setting in which members of a large population share identical cost of vaccination, cost of illness, probability of vaccine effectiveness, and probability of illness when unvaccinated or unsuccessfully vaccinated. The next section generalizes to vaccination of a heterogeneous population.

The representative-agent setting is an idealization, but it is instructive. It yields transparent findings showing when, despite lack of knowledge of the illness rate produced by mandatory vaccination, a planner can determine whether it is optimal to institute a mandate. When optimal policy is indeterminate, I compare the policies generated by alternative decision criteria.

Section 8.2.1 sets up the optimization problem that I assume the planner would like to solve. Section 8.2.2 studies policy choice when the planner does not know the indirect effect of vaccination.

8.2.1 The Optimization Problem

Suppose that the vaccine under consideration generates a protective immune response in a vaccinated person with probability $\lambda > 0$, preventing the person from becoming ill and from infecting others. Contrariwise, the vaccine confers no immunity with probability $1 - \lambda$. Then λ measures the direct effect of vaccination. If fraction v of the population are vaccinated, the *effective vaccination rate* is λv and the fraction $1 - \lambda v$ of the population are susceptible to the disease.

The indirect-response function $p(\cdot)$: $[0, 1] \to [0, 1]$ gives the probability that a susceptible person becomes ill when a specified fraction of the population are effectively vaccinated. If vaccination yields an indirect preventive effect, then $p(\cdot)$ is a decreasing function. When the effective vaccination rate is λv, the fraction of the population who become ill is $p(\lambda v) \cdot (1 - \lambda v)$.

The planner wants to minimize a social cost function with two additive components, the cost of illness and the cost of vaccination. Let $b > 0$ denote the cost per illness and let $c > 0$ denote the cost per vaccination, measured in commensurate units. The social cost of vaccination rate v is:

(8.1) $$C(v) \equiv bp(\lambda v) \cdot (1 - \lambda v) + cv.$$

The first term measures the social cost of illness and the second gives the social cost of vaccination.

Policy choice poses a constrained optimization problem in which the planner chooses between vaccinating the entire population (the mandate) and the vaccination rate, say v_d, generated by decentralized decision making in the absence of the mandate. Assuming that a mandate would vaccinate the entire population approximates reality. In practice, mandates do not require vaccination of immunocompromised persons. Some states grant religious exemptions to mandatory vaccination. A state may lack the legal power to mandate vaccination of nonresidents with whom residents may come into contact.

A mandate is consequential if and only if $v_d < 1$. Given social cost function (8.1), the optimal decision is:

$$(8.2) \quad \begin{array}{l} \text{mandate if} \\ \text{do not mandate if} \end{array} \quad \begin{array}{l} bp(\lambda)(1-\lambda) + c \leq bp(\lambda v_d)(1-\lambda v_d) + cv_d, \\ bp(\lambda)(1-\lambda) + c \geq bp(\lambda v_d)(1-\lambda v_d) + cv_d. \end{array}$$

This simple problem expresses the core tension of vaccination policy: the higher vaccination rate achieved by a mandate reduces illness relative to decentralized decision making, but it raises the cost of vaccination.

8.2.2 Policy Choice without Knowledge of the Indirect Effect of a Mandate

A planner can make an optimal decision if he has sufficient knowledge of the social costs of vaccination and illness, the direct and indirect effects of vaccination, and the vaccination rate that results from decentralized decision making. Given criterion (8.2), it suffices to know $[b, c, \lambda, p(\lambda), v_d, p(\lambda v_d)]$. The criterion is an inequality, so it is not necessary to know the precise values of these quantities. One only needs to know enough to determine which inequality holds. I assume that the planner knows $[b, c, \lambda, v_d, p(\lambda v_d)]$ but not $p(\lambda)$. Parameters b and c express society's evaluation of the social cost of illness and vaccination. An RCT can measure the immune responses that a vaccine generates in vaccinated subjects, which provides evidence on λ. The planner should be able to observe the decentralized vaccination rate v_d and illness rate $p(\lambda v_d)$ that occur when decentralization is the status quo policy.

The planner cannot observe $p(\lambda)$, which would be observable only after a mandate is enacted. What might a planner realistically know about $p(\lambda)$? A basic assumption of epidemiological analysis of infectious disease has been that raising the vaccination rate increases the indirect protective effect of vaccination. Hence, the indirect-response function $p(\cdot)$ is decreasing. When combined with available evidence, this assumption of monotone treatment response yields an upper bound on $p(\lambda)$. Knowing $p(\lambda v_d)$, a planner can deduce that $0 \leq p(\lambda) \leq p(\lambda v_d)$.

Beyond monotonicity, epidemiology yields no clearly credible assumption about the shape of $p(\cdot)$. Different models of disease transmission imply different shapes for the function. Researchers have chosen models to be analytically and computationally tractable, with only limited examination of the realism of their assumptions. Hence, a planner may not know much about the shape of p(·) beyond its monotonicity.

Optimization with Partial Knowledge

Knowledge of the upper bound on p(λ) may suffice to determine whether mandatory vaccination is optimal. A key parameter is $\gamma \equiv c/b$, the ratio of the social cost per vaccination to the social cost per illness. Rewriting (8.2), a mandate is optimal if:

(8.2′) $\quad p(\lambda)(1-\lambda) \leq p(\lambda v_d)(1-\lambda v_d) - \gamma(1-v_d)$

and is sub-optimal otherwise. The bound $0 \leq p(\lambda) \leq p(\lambda v_d)$ suffices to determine the optimality of a mandate if either of two conditions hold:

(8.3a) $p(\lambda v_d)(1-\lambda) \leq p(\lambda v_d)(1-\lambda v_d) - \gamma(1-v_d)$ ⇨ mandate is optimal,

(8.3b) $0 > p(\lambda v_d)(1-\lambda v_d) - \gamma(1-v_d)$ ⇨ mandate is not optimal.

The inequality on the left-hand side of (8.3a) implies that (8.2′) holds for all feasible values of p(λ); hence, a mandate must be optimal. The inequality on the left-hand side of (8.3b) implies that (8.2′) holds for no feasible value of p(λ); hence, a mandate cannot be optimal. If neither inequality holds, a mandate is optimal for some feasible values of p(λ) but not for others.

Conditions (8.3a) and (8.3b) show that a planner lacking knowledge of the indirect effect of vaccination may nonetheless be able to determine if a mandate is optimal. One or the other condition necessarily holds if λ = 1. In this case, p(λ)(1 − λ) = 0 for all values of p(λ). Hence, indeterminacy of the optimum can happen only if the vaccine has an imperfect direct effect.

To study indeterminate cases when λ < 1, it is instructive to rewrite (8.3) in the equivalent form:

(8.3a′) $\quad \gamma \leq \lambda p(\lambda v_d)$ ⇨ mandate is optimal,

(8.3b′) $\quad \gamma > p(\lambda v_d)[(1-\lambda v_d)/(1-v_d)]$ ⇨ mandate is not optimal.

Condition (8.3a′) considers the worst-case scenario in which increasing the vaccination rate from v_d to 1 has no indirect preventive effect. The inequality shows that, all else equal, a mandate is still optimal if the cost of vaccination relative to the cost of illness is sufficiently small.

Condition (8.3b′) considers the best-case scenario in which increasing the vaccination from v_d to 1 has the largest possible indirect effect. This inequality shows that, all else equal, a mandate cannot be optimal if γ is sufficiently large. The optimality of a mandate is indeterminate if:

(8.4) $\quad \lambda p(\lambda v_d) < \gamma \leq p(\lambda v_d)\left[(1-\lambda v_d)/(1-v_d)\right].$

Planning When the Optimal Policy Is Indeterminate

When the optimality of a mandate is indeterminate, a planner might use one of the decision criteria discussed throughout this book. The state space S indexes feasible values of $p(\lambda)$.

Consider minimization of subjective expected cost. Let π denote the subjective distribution placed on S. For $s \in S$, let $p_s(\lambda)$ denote the value of $p(\lambda)$ in state s. Let $f(\cdot): R \to R$ be a specified increasing function expressing the risk preference of the planner. Minimization of subjective expected cost means replacement of optimality criterion (8.2) with the criterion:

(8.5)
$$\begin{aligned}
\text{mandate if} \quad & \int_S f\left[p_s(\lambda)(1-\lambda)+\gamma\right]d\pi \\
& \leq f\left[p(\lambda v_d)(1-\lambda v_d)+\gamma v_d\right], \\
\text{do not mandate if} \quad & \int_S f\left[p_s(\lambda)(1-\lambda)+\gamma\right]d\pi \\
& \geq f\left[p(\lambda v_d)(1-\lambda v_d)+\gamma v_d\right].
\end{aligned}$$

Criterion (8.5) simplifies if $f(\cdot)$ is the identity function, in which case the planner is risk neutral. It reduces to:

(8.6)
$$\begin{aligned}
\text{mandate if} \quad & \left[\int_S p_s(\lambda)d\pi\right](1-\lambda)+\gamma \\
& \leq p(\lambda v_d)(1-\lambda v_d)+\gamma v_d, \\
\text{do not mandate if} \quad & \left[\int_S p_s(\lambda)d\pi\right](1-\lambda)+\gamma \\
& \geq p(\lambda v_d)(1-\lambda v_d)+\gamma v_d.
\end{aligned}$$

Thus, a risk-neutral planner acts as if $p(\lambda) = \int_S p_s(\lambda)d\pi$.

A planner who uses the minimax criterion and who assumes that $p(\cdot)$ is monotone acts as if $p(\lambda) = p(\lambda v_d)$. He thus replaces optimality criterion (8.2) with the criterion:

(8.7)
$$\begin{aligned}
\text{mandate if} \quad & p(\lambda v_d)(1-\lambda)+\gamma \leq p(\lambda v_d)(1-\lambda v_d)+\gamma v_d, \\
\text{do not mandate if} \quad & p(\lambda v_d)(1-\lambda)+\gamma \geq p(\lambda v_d)(1-\lambda v_d)+\gamma v_d.
\end{aligned}$$

This simplifies to:

(8.7′)
$$\begin{aligned}
\text{mandate if} \quad & \gamma \leq \lambda p(\lambda v_d), \\
\text{do not mandate if} \quad & \gamma \geq \lambda p(\lambda v_d).
\end{aligned}$$

Thus, the minimax criterion resolves indeterminacy in favor of no mandate.

Vaccination with Unknown Indirect Effects

To form the MMR criterion, let S_m and S_d respectively be the subsets of S in which a mandate yields strictly lower and higher social cost than decentralized decision making. For states in S_m, regret is zero if the planner mandates vaccination and takes the positive value $[p(\lambda v_d)(1-\lambda v_d)+\gamma v_d]-[p_s(\lambda)(1-\lambda)+\gamma]$ if he does not mandate. Analogously, for states in S_d, regret is zero if the planner does not mandate and takes the positive value $[p_s(\lambda)(1-\lambda)+\gamma]-[p(\lambda v_d)(1-\lambda v_d)+\gamma v_d]$ if he does mandate.

Maximum regret in each subset of states is:

(8.8a) $\quad R_m \equiv \max_{s \in S_m}\left[p(\lambda v_d)(1-\lambda v_d)+\gamma v_d\right]-\left[p_s(\lambda)(1-\lambda)+\gamma\right],$

(8.8b) $\quad R_d \equiv \max_{s \in S_d}\left[p_s(\lambda)(1-\lambda)+\gamma\right]-\left[p(\lambda v_d)(1-\lambda v_d)+\gamma v_d\right].$

The maximum regret of decisions to mandate and not mandate are R_m and R_d, respectively. Hence, the MMR decision is:

(8.9) $\quad$ mandate if $\quad R_m \leq R_d,$
$\quad\quad\quad$ do not mandate if $\quad R_m \geq R_d.$

To obtain an explicit solution, observe that the maximum in (8.8a) occurs in the best-case scenario for vaccination, where $p_s(\lambda) = 0$. The maximum in (8.8b) occurs in the worst-case scenario where $p_s(\lambda) = p(\lambda v_d)$. Hence,

(8.10a) $\quad R_m = p(\lambda v_d)(1-\lambda v_d)-\gamma(1-v_d),$

(8.10b) $\quad R_d = (1-v_d)\left[\gamma-\lambda p(\lambda v_d)\right].$

8.3 CHOICE BETWEEN DECENTRALIZATION AND A UNIVERSAL MANDATE IN A HETEROGENEOUS POPULATION

I now drop the idealization of a representative agent and consider the planning problem in a more realistic setting where persons may have heterogeneous costs of vaccination and illness as well as heterogeneous probabilities of vaccine effectiveness and illness. This setting is more complex because decentralized vaccination decisions may be nonrandom. Nevertheless, most of the findings of Section 8.2 extend in a straightforward manner.

To formalize a population with heterogeneous attributes, let J denote the set of persons constituting the population. Whereas I earlier assumed that $[\lambda, p(\cdot), b, c]$ are identical across persons, now each $j \in J$

has person-specific values $[\lambda_j, p_j(\cdot), b_j, c_j]$. The population distribution of attributes is $P[\lambda, p(\cdot), b, c]$.

The indirect-response function $p_j(\cdot)$: $[0, 1] \to [0, 1]$ gives the probability that person j, if susceptible to disease, becomes ill when a specified fraction of the population are effectively vaccinated. Whereas the effective vaccination rate previously was λv, the present analysis requires attention to the composition of the vaccinated subpopulation in the decentralized setting. Let $z_j = 1$ denote that person j is vaccinated and $z_j = 0$ otherwise. Then the vaccination rate with population vaccination configuration $(z_j, j \in J)$ is $E(z) \equiv \int z_j dP(j)$ and the effective rate is $E(\lambda z) \equiv \int \lambda_j z_j dP(j)$.

8.3.1 The Optimization Problem

As earlier, the planner wants to minimize a social cost function with two components, the social cost of illness and vaccination. Consider any vaccination configuration $(z_j, j \in J)$. For each j, the social cost of illness is b_j and vaccination is c_j. The probability that j becomes ill is $p_j[E(\lambda z)](1 - \lambda_j)$ if j is vaccinated and $p_j[E(\lambda z)]$ if unvaccinated. Hence, the full contribution of j to social cost is $b_j p_j[E(\lambda z)](1 - \lambda_j z_j) + c_j z_j$. Averaging the person-specific contributions to social cost across the population yields the aggregate social cost function:

$$(8.11) \quad C(z_j, j \in J) \equiv \int \{b_j p_j[E(\lambda z)](1 - \lambda_j z_j) + c_j z_j\} dP(j)$$
$$= E\{bp[E(\lambda z)](1 - \lambda z)\} + E(cz).$$

The planner chooses between vaccinating the entire population $(z_j = 1, j \in J)$ and the vaccination configuration $(z_{dj}, j \in J)$ obtained by decentralized decision making. The optimal decision is:

$$(8.12) \quad \begin{aligned} \text{mandate if} \quad & E\{bp[E(\lambda)](1-\lambda)\} + E(c) \\ & \leq E\{bp[E(\lambda z_d)](1 - \lambda z_d)\} + E(cz_d), \\ \text{do not mandate if} \quad & E\{bp[E(\lambda)](1-\lambda)\} + E(c) \\ & \geq E\{bp[E(\lambda z_d)](1 - \lambda z_d)\} + E(cz_d). \end{aligned}$$

Rewriting criterion (8.12), a mandate is optimal if and only if:

$$(8.12') \quad E[c(1 - z_d)] \leq E\{bp[E(\lambda z_d)](1 - \lambda z_d)\} - E\{bp[E(\lambda)](1 - \lambda)\}.$$

The left-hand side of (8.12′) expresses the disadvantage of a mandate relative to decentralization, namely the marginal social cost of vaccinating persons who choose not to be vaccinated in a decentralized regime.

Vaccination with Unknown Indirect Effects   193

The right-hand side expresses the advantage of a mandate, namely the improvement in public health relative to decentralized decision making.

8.3.2 Policy Choice without Knowledge of Indirect Effects, Redux

Optimization with Partial Knowledge
Assume that the planner observes the population in the status quo context of decentralization and learns $P[b, c, \lambda, z_d, p[E(\lambda z_d)]]$. The planner does not know the counterfactual illness rates that susceptible persons would incur under a mandate but, indirect effects being non-negative, he knows that $0 \leq p_j[E(\lambda)] \leq p_j[E(\lambda z_d)]$, $j \in J$. These bounds determine the optimality of a mandate if either of two conditions hold:

(8.13a) $$E\left[c(1 - z_d)\right] \leq E\{bp\left[E(\lambda z_d)\right]\lambda(1 - z_d)\} \Rightarrow \text{mandate is optimal,}$$

(8.13b) $$E\left[c(1 - z_d)\right] > E\{bp\left[E(\lambda z_d)\right](1 - \lambda z_d)\} \Rightarrow \text{mandate is not optimal.}$$

The inequality on the left-hand side of (8.13a) implies that inequality (8.12′) holds for all feasible values of $\{p_j[E(\lambda)], j \in J\}$; hence, a mandate must be optimal. The inequality on the left-hand side of (8.13b) implies that (8.12′) holds for no feasible value of $\{p_j[E(\lambda)], j \in J\}$; hence, a mandate cannot be optimal.

If neither inequality holds, a mandate is optimal for some feasible values of $\{p_j[E(\lambda)], j \in J\}$ but not for others. Hence, the optimality of a mandate is indeterminate if:

(8.14) $$E\{bp\left[E(\lambda z_d)\right]\lambda(1 - z_d)\} < E\left[c(1 - z_d)\right] \leq E\{bp\left[E(\lambda z_d)\right](1 - \lambda z_d)\}.$$

Planning When the Optimal Policy Is Indeterminate
Minimization of subjective expected cost with a heterogenous population is a straightforward generalization of the criterion with a representative agent. Let S denote the state space, now indexing feasible values of the unknown quantities $\{p_j[E(\lambda)], j \in J\}$. Let π denote the subjective distribution placed on S. Let $\{p_{sj}[E(\lambda)], j \in J\}$ denote the value of $\{p_j[E(\lambda)], j \in J\}$ in state s. Let $f(\cdot): R \to R$ be a specified increasing function expressing the risk preference of the planner. Then minimization of subjective expected cost means replacement of optimality criterion (8.12) with the computable criterion:

(8.15)
$$\text{mandate if } \int_S f\left[E\{bp_s[E(\lambda)](1-\lambda)\} + E(c)\right] d\pi$$
$$\leq f\left[E\{bp[E(\lambda z_d)](1-\lambda z_d)\} + E(cz_d)\right],$$
$$\text{do not mandate if } \int_S f\left[E\{bp_s[E(\lambda)](1-\lambda)\} + E(c)\right] d\pi$$
$$\geq f\left[E\{bp[E(\lambda z_d)](1-\lambda z_d)\} + E(cz_d)\right].$$

Although (8.15) is analogous to the earlier criterion (8.5) in abstraction, it is much more complex in practice. Whereas the representative-agent setting only required that one place a subjective distribution on the scalar unknown $p(\lambda)$, the planner now must place one on the collection of unknowns $\{p_j[E(\lambda)], j \in J\}$.

The minimax criterion with a heterogenous population is a straightforward generalization of the criterion with a representative agent. The planner acts as if he faces the worst-case scenario, in which $E(\lambda) = E(\lambda z_d)$. This done, he replaces optimality criterion (8.12) with the criterion:

(8.16)
$$\text{mandate if } E\{bp[E(\lambda z_d)](1-\lambda)\} + E(c)$$
$$\leq E\{bp[E(\lambda z_d)](1-\lambda z_d)\} + E(cz_d),$$
$$\text{do not mandate if } E\{bp[E(\lambda z_d)](1-\lambda)\} + E(c)$$
$$\geq E\{bp[E(\lambda z_d)](1-\lambda z_d)\} + E(cz_d).$$

Equivalently, a mandate is a minimax solution to the planning problem if and only if:

(8.16′)
$$E[c(1-z_d)] \leq E\{bp[E(\lambda z_d)]\lambda(1-z_d)\}.$$

As previously, the minimax criterion resolves indeterminacy in favor of no mandate.

To form the minimax regret criterion, again let S_m and S_d be the subsets of S in which a mandate yields strictly lower and higher social cost than decentralized decision making. For $s \in S_m$ regret is zero if the planner mandates vaccination and equals $E\{bp[E(\lambda z_d)](1-\lambda z_d)\} - E\{bp_s[E(\lambda)](1-\lambda)\} - E[c(1-z_d)]$ if he does not. Analogously, for $s \in S_d$, regret is zero if the planner does not mandate and equals $E\{bp_s[E(\lambda)](1-\lambda)\} - E\{bp[E(\lambda z_d)](1-\lambda z_d)\} + E[c(1-z_d)]$ if he does.

Maximum regret in each subset of states is:

(8.17a)
$$R_m \equiv \max_{s \in S_m} E\{bp[E(\lambda z_d)](1-\lambda z_d)\}$$
$$- E\{bp_s[E(\lambda)](1-\lambda)\} - E[c(1-z_d)],$$

(8.17b) $$R_d \equiv \max_{s \in S_d} E\{bp_s[E(\lambda)](1-\lambda)\} \\ -E\{bp[E(\lambda z_d)](1-\lambda z_d)\} + E[c(1-z_d)].$$

Mandating is a minimax regret decision if and only if $R_m \leq R_d$.

The maximum in (8.17a) occurs in the best-case scenario for vaccination, where $p_s[E(\lambda)] = 0$. The maximum in (8.17b) occurs in the worst-case scenario where $p_s[E(\lambda)] = p[E(\lambda z_d)]$. Hence,

(8.18a) $\quad R_m = E\{bp[E(\lambda z_d)](1-\lambda z_d)\} - E[c(1-z_d)],$

(8.18b) $\quad R_d = E[c(1-z_d)] - E\{bp[E(\lambda z_d)]\}\lambda(1-z_d)\}.$

8.4 DISCUSSION

In Manski (2017), I developed a welfare-economic framework for choice between decentralized and mandatory vaccination policies when the magnitude of the indirect effect of vaccination on illness is unknown. Study of the representative-agent setting yields simple findings. Analysis of policy choice when population members have heterogeneous attributes requires more abstract notation but also yields explicit findings.

Public health agencies may find most congenial the conclusion that observation of the decentralized regime sometimes suffices to determine optimal policy even without knowledge of the illness rate that would occur with a mandate. When optimal policy is indeterminate, I do not assert that agencies should use a specific decision criterion. What criterion a planner should use to cope with uncertainty is a matter to be decided by the planner.

9

Climate Planning with Uncertainty in Climate Modeling and Intergenerational Discounting

The microplanning settings analyzed in Chapters 5 through 7 exemplify one pole of the broad problem of social planning under uncertainty, where a planner can treat people differentially and where treatment only affects the person treated. The social interactions setting of Chapter 8 is intermediate, in that differential treatment remains feasible but outcomes across the population are connected. I now turn to a problem that exemplifies the pole of macroplanning under uncertainty, choice of a global climate policy that affects the entire world population.

My research on climate planning is embodied in two studies co-authored with Stephen DeCanio and Alan Sanstad. This chapter summarizes the analysis of DeCanio, Manski, and Sanstad (2022), which generalized the research reported in Manski, Sanstad, and DeCanio (2021).

9.1 THE POLICY PROBLEM

Integrated assessment (IA) models enable quantitative evaluation of alternative climate policies. IA models are long-run (century-scale or more) descriptions of the global economy, including the energy system and its role in economic production. These models also represent the climate and the links between the climatic effects of greenhouse gas (GHG) emissions and their impacts on the economy. IA models have become primary tools for comparing potential policies to reduce GHG emissions.

Policy comparisons have often been performed by considering a planner who seeks to make optimal trade-offs between the costs of carbon abatement and the global economic damages from climate change. The planning problem has been formalized as an optimal-control problem with these components:

(1) equations coupling GHG emissions and abatement to the accumulation of GHGs in the atmosphere and resulting temperature increases.
(2) a damage function quantifying economic effects of climate change as a function of temperature increases.
(3) an abatement cost function that expresses the cost of actions to reduce GHG emissions relative to a stipulated baseline emissions trajectory.

Rather than consider a utilitarian planner, the norm in IA modeling has been to measure costs and damages at a point in time in terms of percentage reductions in gross world product at that time. The control problem is to minimize the present discounted costs of abatement and damages over a time horizon.

Studying climate policy as a problem of optimal control presumes that a planner knows enough about the climate and economic systems to make optimization feasible. Yet uncertainties abound. Physical and economic uncertainties have been handled in different ways.

The physical scientists whose research informs component (1) of IA models have performed *multi-model ensemble* (MME) analysis (Taylor et al., 2012). Lacking a consensus climate model, they have developed multiple distinct models. To cope with what they call inter-model *structural uncertainty*, they compute simple or weighted averages of the outputs of MMEs. Choosing appropriate weights has been problematic.

The economists whose research informs components (2) and (3) have estimated multiple damage functions and abatement cost functions. In general, economists have not performed MME analyses that combine multiple functions by averaging. They have instead reported disparate findings, stemming from their separate studies.

Manski, Sanstad, and DeCanio (2021) (M-S-D hereafter) framed structural uncertainty in climate modeling as a problem of partial identification. The problem is that the underlying mechanisms governing the climate and economic system are not completely known and cannot be credibly modeled definitively, even in the absence of data limitations in the sense of statistical imprecision. We proposed use of the MMR criterion to account for uncertainty in integrated assessment without averaging climate model forecasts. We developed a theoretical framework and applied it computationally with a simple illustrative IA model.

M-S-D studied MMR decision making in the presence only of physical-science uncertainty regarding the correct climate model. However, it is important to recognize uncertainty in both the physical and economic components of IA models. Among the many economic aspects of IA models that have lacked consensus, perhaps the most contentious has been how a planner should assess the costs and benefits of policies across generations. To confront this issue, DeCanio, Manski, and Sanstad (2022) (D-M-S hereafter) studied choice of climate policy that minimizes maximum regret with uncertainty regarding both the correct climate model and the appropriate intergenerational assessment of policy consequences.

Economists have long framed intergenerational policy assessment using a time discount rate. They have evaluated climate policies by the present discounted value of the sum of abatement costs and the corresponding damages. There has been considerable and unresolved debate about what discount rate to use; see, for example, Arrow et al. (2014) and Heal and Milner (2014). The choice is highly consequential. Low discount rates favor policies that reduce GHG emissions aggressively and rapidly (Emmerling et al., 2019). High rates favor policies that act more modestly and slowly. To express uncertainty, D-M-S supposed that the appropriate discount rate lies within an interval that covers the spectrum of rates that have been used in the literature.

Section 9.2 describes how the physical-science and economics literatures have sought to cope with uncertainty about the correct climate model and discount rate, respectively. Section 9.3 formalizes MMR policy choice in an abstract manner. Section 9.4 presents the computational model studied by D-M-S and summarizes the main findings. Section 9.5 discusses the contributions and limitations of this work.

9.2 PREVALENT APPROACHES TO CLIMATE AND DISCOUNT-RATE UNCERTAINTY

9.2.1 Averaging Outputs of Multi-model Ensembles of Climate Models

The climate is a complex system comprising many physical processes occurring at a range of spatial and temporal scales. Climate models aim to represent these processes in a tractable manner. All climate models are based on specific partial differential equations describing large-scale atmospheric dynamics. Uncertainty arises in part because implementation of the equations in particular models is subject to numerous practical choices involving discretization and solution methods. Moreover, some components of the system – such as cloud formation and heat transfer between land surfaces and the atmosphere – are not yet fully understood and must be approximated.

For these reasons, multiple climate models have been developed, each reflecting different but credible choices in model design and implementation. Existing models yield different forecasts of the global climate. Neither a consensus climate model nor definitive quantitative forecasts can be specified with current knowledge (Pindyck, 2022). The range of forecasts produced by different climate models is a gauge of current uncertainty about the climate system.

Virtually all methods of MME analysis combine model outputs into single forecasts of future climate variables. Modelers have perceived policy makers as requiring single forecasts, as functions of particular GHG emissions scenarios, for use in decision making (Parker 2006). However, climate researchers have recognized persistent problems in combining forecasts (Tebaldi and Knutti, 2007; Sanderson, 2018).

A common technique is to take the simple average across model forecasts of policy-relevant variables such as increases in global mean temperature due to anthropogenic carbon emissions. Computation of simple averages of predictions, sometimes called *model democracy*, gives equal weight to each model, an idea lacking a compelling foundation (Knutti, 2016). Researchers may instead compute weighted average forecasts when they believe that models can be ranked with respect to relative accuracy. Unfortunately, dealing with uncertainty about the correct model by averaging model forecasts suffers from difficulties related to those that afflict meta-analysis, studied in Chapters 2 and 3.

Climate scientists recognize that combining climate model ensemble outputs into single projected trajectories of the future global climate remains a challenging and unresolved problem. As summarized in a recent Intergovernmental Panel on Climate Change (IPCC) physical sciences report, "despite some progress, no universal, robust method for weighting a multi-model forecast ensemble is available" (Lee et al., 2021). This poses a quandary for policy makers who rely on climate model forecasts to formulate strategies for GHG emissions abatement and other approaches to address climate change.

9.2.2 Uncertainties and Disagreements Regarding the Discount Rate

IA models are subject to uncertainty in their economic assumptions as well as in their representation of the climate (Heal and Milner, 2014; Weyant, 2017). A leading example is Nordhaus's Dynamic Integrated Climate Economy (DICE) model (Nordhaus, 2019). In DICE and similar models, the economic losses from climate change are represented by damage functions that give the decreases in worldwide output resulting from increases in mean global temperature, as a proportional reduction or in dollar terms. These functions have uncertain theoretical and empirical grounding (Pindyck, 2013).

Economists study dynamic optimization by a planner, which entails discounting to quantify the present value of future economic costs and benefits. The appropriate discount rate is a long-standing and contentious issue in climate change economics (e.g., Ackerman et al., 2009; Arrow et al., 2014; Dasgupta, 2019; Pindyck, 2017; Weisbach and Sunstein, 2009). Controversy persists in part due to the fact that choice of an appropriate discount rate is not only an empirical question regarding the future of the economy. It is also a normative matter, concerning social preferences for equity across future generations which will vary in their time of existence and in their levels of consumption (Dasgupta, 2008).

A simple version of the *Ramsey formula* (Ramsey, 1928) provides a transparent expression of the interplay of normative and empirical considerations in choosing a discount rate. Paraphrasing the exposition in Arrow et al. (2014), let the planner have a utilitarian social welfare function that is additively separable in the welfare of future generations. Let ρ be the rate at which the planner discounts the welfare of future generations. Let the welfare of a representative consumer be an increasing and concave function of consumption, with constant elasticity ($-\eta$) of marginal utility with respect to consumption. Let g be the annual growth rate of consumption between time 0 and a future time t. In this setting, Ramsey showed that it is optimal to discount future consumption between the present (time 0) and time t at the rate:

(9.1) $$\delta = \rho + \eta g.$$

Of the variables on the right-hand side, g describes future consumption growth in the economy. From the perspective of the present, the empirical value of g may be uncertain. Such uncertainty is similar conceptually to the uncertainty that climate modelers face as they attempt to forecast the future trajectory of climate variables.

The time-invariant quantities ρ and η are normative parameters. The value of ρ formalizes how the planner views intergenerational equity, with ρ = 0 if the planner gives equal weight to the welfare of all future generations and ρ > 0 if the planner weights welfare more heavily in the near future than in the distant future. The value of η formalizes how the planner views the desirability of consumption equity. A common utilitarian presumption is that the marginal utility of consumption decreases as consumption increases. Therefore, a larger value of η combined with positive g (i.e., future generations are richer) implies that the planner should use a larger discount rate to evaluate costs and benefits, as expressed in (9.1).

Being normative parameters, ρ and η are not subject to empirical uncertainty in the sense of g or climate forecasts. Nevertheless, a planner may feel normative uncertainty about what values are appropriate to use. Supposing that the planner aims to represent society, a source of this uncertainty may be normative disagreements within the present population. Such disagreements were evident in a highly public dispute between Nordhaus (2007), whose policy analysis used the value ρ = 0.03, and Stern (2007), who used the value ρ = 0.001. This difference was highly consequential. Stern concluded that policy should seek to reduce GHG emissions aggressively and rapidly. Nordhaus favored policies that act more modestly and slowly.

Equation (9.1) gives the simplest version of the Ramsey rule. Other models show that the discount rate may depend on additional factors such as the mean and variance of a stochastic growth rate that is normally distributed (Weitzman, 2007), the risk premium associated with climate policy (Dietz et al., 2018), or the relationship of future damages to output (Dietz and Venmans 2019). Weitzman (2001) suggested use of a weighted average of the discount rates considered in the climate-economics literature, a procedure akin to the weighted averaging performed by climate scientists in MME analysis. Heal and Milner (2014) mentioned other possible ways to obtain a discount rate that a planner might find appropriate to use.

D-M-S did not attempt to derive a discount rate from underlying macroeconomic or normative foundations. We argued against any attempt to cope with empirical and normative uncertainty by choosing a single discount rate. We studied the formation of climate policy recognizing a set of possibly appropriate discount rates.

9.3 MINIMAX REGRET POLICY EVALUATION

The analysis in M-S-D focused on uncertainty in climate modeling. We assumed that the correct physical climate model is one of six prominent models in the literature on climate science, whereas the correct economic model is known. Given the uncertainty about the climate model, we supposed that a planner compares six policies, each of which chooses an emissions abatement path that is optimal under one and only one of the six climate models. Regret is the loss in welfare if the model used in policy making is not correct and, consequently, the chosen abatement path is sub-optimal. The MMR rule chooses a policy that minimizes the maximum regret, or largest degree of sub-optimality, across all six climate models.

D-M-S also supposed that the correct climate model is one of the six models examined in M-S-D. Going further, we characterized uncertainty about the discount rate by supposing that it takes one of the seven values {0.01, 0.02, ..., 0.07}, a range that covers the rates commonly used in IA models. This range reflects both empirical uncertainty about the future of the economy and normative uncertainty, or perhaps disagreement, about how the current population values the welfare of future generations.

Given joint uncertainty about the climate model and the discount rate, we supposed that a planner compares forty-three policies. Forty-two policies entail choosing an abatement path that is optimal under one of the {discount rate, climate model} pairs. The remaining one is a passive policy in which the planner chooses to perform no abatement. The regret of a specified policy in each possible state of the world is the loss in welfare if the abatement path is sub-optimal. The MMR criterion chooses a policy that minimizes maximum regret across the forty-three potential policies.

I summarize the analysis abstractly below, first specifying the optimal-control problem that we assumed a planner would solve in the absence of uncertainty and then stating the MMR criterion. Section 9.4 describes our computational implementation of the abstract analysis.

9.3.1 The Optimal-Control Problem

Let B_t represent baseline GHG emissions at time t, A_t be GHG abatement actions at t under some climate policy, measured in the same units as emissions, $C(A_t)$ be the cost of these actions, and $E_t^{A_t} = B_t - A_t$ be the resulting net emissions. We referred to A_t and $E_t^{A_t}$ as "paths" or "trajectories," and we assumed that abatement paths are chosen from some space of feasible paths.

Emissions paths are used as inputs to a climate model M. We focused on the global mean temperatures forecast by M as a function of these paths. Thus, let $T(E_t^{A_t}, M)$ be the global mean temperature at time t determined by the GHG trajectory $E_t^{A_t}$ when it is enacted in the state with climate model M. Then a damage function, as discussed above, can be written as $D(T(E_t^{A_t}, M))$.

For an abatement path A_t and climate model M, denote the associated total cost (abatement plus damages) at time t as:

$$(9.2) \qquad \mathbb{C}(A_t, M) \equiv C(A_t) + D\left(T\left(E_t^{A_t}, M\right)\right).$$

As has been conventional in IA modeling, we supposed that a planner seeks to minimize the present value of cumulative cost over a planning horizon. As customary in the climate economics literature, we assumed the horizon to be infinite. The optimal control problem given a particular climate model M is to solve:

$$(9.3) \qquad \min_{A_t} \int_0^\infty \mathbb{C}(A_t, M) e^{-\delta t} dt,$$

where δ is a discount rate.

In this problem specification, the optimal A_t is chosen with commitment at time zero; that is, it is not updated over time as new climate or cost information is obtained. As stated, (9.3) is a deterministic optimization problem that has a unique solution given certain technical assumptions regarding the feasible abatement path space and the cost and damage functions. We assumed that such conditions hold.

9.3.2 The Minimax Regret Decision Rule

Let $\Delta = \{\delta_1, \ldots, \delta_K\}$ be a set of possible discount rates and $\mathbf{M} = \{M_1, \ldots, M_N\}$ be a model ensemble. We did not derive the set of possible discount rates from underlying macroeconomic or normative considerations, but took it simply as reflecting the range of values that have been used or proposed in the climate economics literature. The planner now faces the problem of minimizing total present-value cost over the infinite horizon while recognizing joint {discount rate, model} uncertainty. For a particular discount rate δ_i and model M_j, let $A^*_{t;\delta_i,M_j}$ be the abatement path defined by:

$$(9.4) \qquad A^*_{t;\delta_i,M_j} = \arg \min_{A_t} \int_0^\infty \mathbb{C}(A_t, M_j) e^{-\delta_i t} dt.$$

This cost-minimizing A^* is the *optimal* trajectory when the discount rate is δ_i and the model is M_j. Let $\mathbb{C}^*(A^*_{t;\delta_i,M_j}, \delta_i, M_j)$ be the associated minimum cost:

$$(9.5) \qquad \mathbb{C}^*\left(A^*_{t;\delta_i,M_j}, \delta_i, M_j\right) = \int_0^\infty \mathbb{C}\left(A^*_t, M_j\right) e^{-\delta_i t} dt.$$

Note the change in notation. Previously, $\mathbb{C}(A_t, M_j)$ was total cost at time t; now, $\mathbb{C}^*(A^*_{t;\delta_i,M_j}, \delta_i, M_j)$ is total discounted cost; that is, an integral.

Now consider any feasible abatement trajectory A_t. The regret $\mathbb{R}(A_t, \delta_i, M_j)$ associated with A_t, when discount rate δ_i and climate model M_j describe the actual state of the world, is the difference between the cost of A_t in the actual state of the world and the cost of the optimal policy associated with δ_i and M_j:

$$(9.6) \qquad \mathbb{R}\left(A_t, \delta_i, M_j\right) = \int_0^\infty \mathbb{C}\left(A_t, M_j\right) e^{-\delta_i t} dt - \mathbb{C}^*\left(A^*_{t;\delta_i,M_j}, \delta_i, M_j\right).$$

To apply the MMR rule, the planner first considers each feasible abatement path A_t and finds the model and discount rate combination that maximizes regret as defined in (9.6), solving the problem:

$$(9.7) \qquad \max_{\delta_i, M_j} \mathbb{R}\left(A_t, \delta_i, M_j\right) = \max_{\delta_i, M_j} \left[\int_0^\infty \mathbb{C}\left(A_t, M_j\right) e^{-\delta_i t} dt - \mathbb{C}^*\left(A^*_{t;\delta_i,M_j}, \delta_i, M_j\right) \right].$$

The MMR solution is then to find A_t to solve the problem:

$$(9.8) \qquad \min_{A_t} \left[\max_{\delta_i, M_j} \mathbb{R}\left(A_t, \delta_i, M_j\right) \right].$$

9.3.3 Use of Δ to Express Empirical and Normative Uncertainty

In research on decision making under uncertainty, the term "uncertainty" has usually referred to incomplete knowledge of the empirical environment of the decision maker. In the study of climate policy, this interpretation of uncertainty applies to incomplete knowledge of the future global temperature, abatement costs, and damages that will occur if alternative climate policies are chosen. It also applies to uncertainty about the discount rate that stems from difficulty in predicting the future of the economy.

Going further, D-M-S used the MMR rule in (9.8) to embrace normative as well as empirical uncertainty about the appropriate discount rate to use when evaluating climate policy. We needed to consider normative uncertainty (or perhaps disagreement) because, as discussed in Section 9.2.2, debate among economists about the appropriate discount rate has stemmed from more than empirical uncertainty about the future economy.

Our use of the set Δ to express both empirical and normative uncertainty regarding the appropriate discount rate goes beyond the uncertainty, discussed in Chapter 4, that occurs when a utilitarian planner has incomplete knowledge of the preferences of the population. Then the planner's normative uncertainty has an empirical source, namely incomplete knowledge of the population preferences that a utilitarian would seek to maximize. Pushing this idea further, we were concerned that the planner may face the difficult task of representing a population whose members may themselves not be clear about their pure time preferences or willingness to accept intergenerational inequalities.

Social planning using Δ to express normative uncertainty is yet a more radical departure from the decision-theoretic norm if the underlying problem is normative disagreements existing within the present population. That is, a segment of the population may strongly value intergenerational equity whereas another segment may be less concerned with the fate of future generations. In this case, one may think it necessary to abandon the idealization of a planner and replace it with conceptualization of policy making as a noncooperative political game.

We nonetheless found it attractive to study MMR decision making even in this challenging setting. The reason is that the MMR rule has some appeal as a broadly acceptable mechanism for policy choice. Recall that the regret of a policy in a specified state of nature measures its degree of sub-optimality in that state and that maximum regret measures the maximum degree of sub-optimality across all states. Suppose that the members of a heterogeneous present population disagree on what {discount rate, model} should be considered the "true" state of nature. Then use of the MMR rule to choose policy minimizes the maximum degree of sub-optimality that will be experienced across the population.

9.4 ANALYSIS WITH A COMPUTATIONAL MODEL

A number of elaborate computational IA models have been proposed in the literature and are used in climate policy analysis. To show in broad terms the consequences of adoption of the MMR decision rule in this context, we posed a relatively simple IA model that summarizes the essential economic and physical mechanisms at work. While the standard in the IA literature has been to report results only about a century into the future, analyzing the uncertainty associated with discount rates necessitates attention to longer time horizons because phenomena in the more distant future that are negligible in economic terms with high discount rates become salient with low rates.

9.4.1 Model Details

To quantitatively solve the MMR problem (9.8), we specified functional forms and parameters for climate damages, abatement costs, and climate dynamics. To obtain simple reduced forms of complex climate model dynamics, we drew on the work of Matthews et al. (2009). They showed that the "carbon-climate response" (CCR), the change in global mean temperature over periods of decades or longer, varies approximately linearly with the increase in cumulative carbon emissions over the same period. We defined net cumulative emissions as:

$$(9.9) \qquad E_t^{A_t} = \int_0^t \dot{E}_t^{A_t} dt = \int_0^t (B_t - A_t) dt.$$

Note that there is no requirement that $(B_t - A_t)$ be non-negative. Having A_t exceed B_t implies adoption of abatement measures that yield negative net emissions. Doing so may result in declining net cumulative emissions if sustained long enough.

The CCR parameter $m(M_j)$, or m_j for short, associated with each full-scale numerical climate model is estimated by determining the model's projected temperature response when it is driven by a carbon emissions path according to:

$$(9.10) \qquad T_t = m_j E_t^{A_t}, \qquad j = 1,....6,$$

where T henceforth indicates the temperature increase over its initial value at time t = 0. The CCRs vary across climate models, reflecting structural and other forms of uncertainty. The CCR allows incorporating both reduced-form climate dynamics and climate model uncertainty into our simple IA modeling framework.

Our model ensemble **M** was obtained by drawing on results from simulations of six "Earth System Models (ESMs)," which combine physical climate models with representations of biogeochemistry in order to simulate the complete atmospheric, oceanic, and terrestrial carbon cycle. These ESMs were used in the Climate Model Intercomparison Project Phase 5 (CMIP5), a study under the auspices of the World Climate Research Programme. We estimated CCR parameters m_j using historic and projected emissions and temperature data from each of the six ESMs. Our model ensemble can then be described succinctly by $\mathbf{M} = \{m_1, ..., m_6\}$.

Next, we specified abatement cost and climate damage functions in quadratic form to implement the IA model as an optimal control problem, allowing for plausible nonlinearity in these functions as the abatement effort and the temperature increase:

(9.11) $$C(A_t) = \frac{1}{2}\alpha A_t^2$$

(9.12) $$D(T_t) = \frac{1}{2}\beta T_t^2,$$

where α and β are weighting parameters calibrated to numerical estimates in the climate economics literature, and T_t is, as above, global mean temperature increase as of time t. For damages, the quadratic form and the value of β were taken from a statistical survey by Nordhaus and Moffat (2017), and comprise those researchers' preferred regression model for approximating existing empirical damage estimates. For abatement cost, the quadratic form and value of α were derived from Dietz and Venmans' (2019) synthesis of global marginal abatement costs reported in the Intergovernmental Panel on Climate Change's Fifth Assessment Report (Clarke et al., 2014).

A baseline emissions trajectory B_t was derived from the so-called "Representative Concentration Pathway (RCP) 8.5" scenario in its extended version to year 2500, which envisions a relatively high growth rate of global carbon emissions from fossil fuel use through the twenty-first century, followed by a peak plateau period of constant emissions until 2150, and then a decline to a very low level by 2250 (Riahi et al., 2011, Meinshausen et al., 2011). In its original form with a 2100 time horizon, RCP 8.5 reflects an absence of explicit global climate policy. This, and several other extended RCP scenarios assuming different emissions paths, were devised for research purposes, with no explanation given of the policies, technological advances, or other factors that could bring about this peaking, leveling, and decline. See D-M-S, Appendix B for discussion of issues in specifying a realistic baseline trajectory.

A functional form having the same general shape as the RCP 8.5 was fitted by nonlinear least squares. The fitted equation for B_t is:

(9.13) $$B_t = \left(\theta t + \frac{B_0}{\exp(\theta\varphi)}\right)\exp(-\theta(t-\varphi)).$$

This equation smooths connected segments of the extended RCP 8.5, including the plateau during the first half of the twenty-second century, and captures its rapid twenty first century increase and subsequent dramatic decline.

Combining these various components, the optimal control problem is to minimize, for a particular discount rate and model, the present value of abatement costs plus climate damages over an infinite horizon, subject to the dynamic relationship between cumulative emissions and temperature:

(9.14) $$\min_{A_t} \int_0^\infty \frac{1}{2}\left(\alpha A_t^2 + \beta T_t^2\right) e^{-\delta t} dt$$

subject to:

(9.15) $$\frac{d}{dt} E_t^{A_t} = \dot{E}_t^{A_t} = B_t - A_t$$

(9.16) $$T_t = m E_t^{A_t}$$

(9.17) $$E_0^{A_t} = E_0,$$

where the last equation specifies an initial condition for net cumulative emissions. Applying standard solution techniques yields first-order necessary conditions including two coupled differential equations in abatement and the atmospheric greenhouse gas concentration associated with the optimal abatement:

(9.18) $$\frac{dA_t}{dt} = \delta A_t - \frac{\beta m^2}{\alpha} E_t^{A_t}$$

(9.19) $$\frac{dE_t^{A_t}}{dt} = B_t - A_t.$$

These equations can be solved in closed form for A_t and $E_t^{A_t}$. The model satisfies convexity properties implying that the first-order conditions are also sufficient for these to be unique optimal solutions to the problem stated in (9.14) through (9.17), in turn yielding optimal abatement costs and climate damages and the minimum present-value total cost.

For numerical solution of the MMR problem in (9.8), it is also necessary to specify the discount rate set Δ. Following the discussion in Section 9.3.3, we picked seven possible discount rates ranging from a low of 0.01 to a high of 0.07 to represent the extent of empirical and normative uncertainty; these values are in the range of discount rates that have been used in the climate economics literature (Weitzman, 2001; Drupp et al., 2018). For numerical implementation, we pick the seven values {0.01, 0.02, 0.03, 0.04, 0.05, 0.06, 0.07} in this interval. The largest value, 0.07, corresponds to the real, pre-tax return on private investment (Arrow et al., 2013, citing US Office of Management, 2003). The six reduced-form climate models in ensemble **M** are defined by the different values of their CCRs as discussed above. With seven values in the ensemble Δ, there are thus forty-two combinations of δ and m representing the range of the two types of uncertainty we considered.

9.4.2 Findings

The computational model enabled us to quantify the theoretical discussion in Section 9.3. Regrets can be calculated for any feasible abatement path A_t, but to keep the calculations tractable and because a planner may restrict the set of policy choices to ones that are optimal in some state of the world, we focused on paths that are optimal for those combinations of δ and m that are in the Δ and **M** ensembles. There are forty-two such combinations, and a forty-third when the policy of "No Abatement" was included as a further possibility.

The most striking result was that, under a spectrum of combinations of α and β, the discount rate corresponding to the MMR solution was found to be 0.02. Thus, in all cases, the MMR decision rule pointed unambiguously to use of a relatively low discount rate in evaluating the costs and benefits of climate abatement measures.

The computational model also allows for calculation of the maximum temperature increase that will be reached for any policy path, and how long it will take to reach that temperature, two quantities of considerable importance in climate science and policy (Clarke et al. 2014, IPCC, 2021). Once the MMR policy combination of $\{\delta, m\}$ is selected, the abatement and net cumulative emissions paths are determined. The maximum temperature increase given such a path is determined by (9.10), and will occur when net cumulative emissions is at a maximum. However, the value of the CCR parameter in the actual state of the world may be different from that in the MMR policy combination. Because the actual state of the world is unknown, the temperature increase under the MMR policy cannot be known at the time the policy decision is made. What is known is that it will be less than or equal to the maximum for all six models.

We found that for almost all the (α, β) parameter combinations that we considered, the MMR policy keeps the peak temperature increase under 2°C, relative to the global mean surface temperature in the decade 1900–1909. Only for the costliest abatement cases does maximum temperature increase exceed 2°C. We also found that, in the absence of abatement, the maximum temperature increase may be quite high, reaching 14.7°C as time goes to infinity in one scenario.

9.5 DISCUSSION

D-M-S considered the MMR rule to provide a reasonable way to form climate policy with both empirical uncertainty about the physical climate system and normative uncertainty regarding the discount rate. MMR decision making copes with uncertainty without adopting the extreme conservatism of maximin decisions. It enables a planner to deal with heterogeneous populations, who may not themselves be clear about their time preferences or willingness to accept intergenerational inequalities.

The IA model that we studied is relatively simple and tractable, in part because we did not consider all potentially important sources of uncertainty. The appropriate baseline emissions path is highly uncertain. The shapes and parameters of the abatement cost and climate damage functions are also uncertain. We addressed this partially by sensitivity analysis, calculating MMR solutions with various parameters (α, β) characterizing abatement cost and climate damages. It would be desirable to expand our MMR analysis to encompass uncertainty about the correct values for these weights, a formidable computational task.

A strong concern is that our work followed the convention in IA modeling of assuming that present discounted gross world product expresses social welfare. Economists have long been cognizant that this measure of social welfare ignores the distribution of personal welfare in the population. As discussed in Chapter 1, it does not suffice to appeal to the Kaldor–Hicks concept of as-if redistribution, whether across or within generations of persons. IA models should specify social welfare functions that recognize the distributional impacts of climate policy.

Discussions of climate policy often make reference to distributional impacts, but they only do so verbally. Consider, for example, a report on decarbonization policy published by a committee of the National Academies of Science, Engineering, and Medicine (2023). The Committee wrote that society should aim to achieve (p. 4): "a fair, equitable, and just 30-year transition" to decarbonization. Fleshing this out, it specified a predetermined target, being to achieve (p. 51), "the overarching emissions reduction goal of 50 percent by 2030 and net zero by midcentury." It went on to write (p. 51) that, "the objective to reduce emissions to net zero by midcentury (or 50 percent by 2030) can be thought of as a constraint with the goal to minimize cost while maximizing desirable societal objectives of equity, employment, health, and public engagement."

However, the committee did not go beyond this to formalize the terms "fair, equitable, and just." Nor did it assess what society should do if the "objectives of equity, employment, health, and public engagement" should be in tension with one another. The vagueness of the committee's language is similar to that I noted in Chapter 7 when I discussed the arguments made by advocates of removing race from medical risk assessments. Here, as there, verbal allusion to broad goals does not suffice to make coherent policy choices. Analysis grounded in an explicit social welfare function is necessary.

10

Looking Ahead

For a quarter century, I have worked to join welfare economics, decision theory, and econometrics to develop and apply a foundation for credible social planning under uncertainty. Having published numerous focused articles in varied academic journals, I judged this the right time to write the present Discourse, which aims to communicate to a broad scholarly audience and to stimulate further study.

I hope the book will prove useful. I do not claim that it provides a complete template for planning. Indeed, I doubt that the study of planning under uncertainty can ever be fully satisfactory. Optimal decision making under uncertainty is generally infeasible, even when the decision maker is a private entity. One must suffice with some notion of reasonableness. Acting with incredible certitude may yield the illusion of optimization, but not the reality. When a planner represents a population who vary in their perception of social welfare, absence of consensus adds greatly to the difficulty of decision making. Studying planning under uncertainty can help society confront the difficulties, but it cannot make them disappear.

In this concluding chapter, Section 10.1 calls for work that strengthens the foundations for planning under uncertainty in three ways: communicating uncertainty, specifying planning problems, and enhancing the tractability of decision criteria. Among the many substantive problems that warrant study, Section 10.2 cites the immediate need for improved pandemic planning, whose salience society should appreciate following the recent global experience with Covid-19. Section 10.3 concludes with a personal perspective on an existential societal decision, making public a commentary that I wrote forty years ago but have not circulated until now.

10.1 STRENGTHENING THE FOUNDATIONS FOR PLANNING UNDER UNCERTAINTY

10.1.1 Communicating Uncertainty

A prerequisite for credible planning under uncertainty is to appropriately recognize and characterize uncertainty. The prevalence of incredible certitude in research that seeks to inform planning is disheartening. Similarly problematic is the conventional certitude expressed in governmental publication of official statistics. I discussed these matters in Chapter 2 and gave illustrations.

I add here to what I wrote in Chapter 2 regarding publication of official statistics, to give further evidence of how entrenched conventional certitude has been. I mentioned the mid twentieth-century effort of Oskar Morgenstern to argue for regular measurement of error in official economic statistics (Morgenstern, 1950, 1963). Summing up the lessons of his fifteen-chapter study of the many sources and manifestations of error, Morgenstern offered a damning indictment of the agencies of the United States government that report official economic statistics to the public, writing (Morgenstern, 1963, p. 304):

> The process of improving data is an unending one.... There is, however, one area where definite action is possible, though it will take time before desirable results will become visible. That is to stop important government agencies, such as the President's Council of Economic Advisors, the various government departments, the Federal Reserve Board and other agencies, public and private, from presenting to the public economic statistics as if these were free from fault. Statements concerning month-to-month changes in the growth rate of the nation are nothing but absurd and even year-to-year comparisons are not much better. The same applies to variations in price levels, costs of living and many other items. It is for the economists to reject and criticize such statements which are devoid of all scientific value, but it is even more important for them not to participate in their fabrication.

He then called for regular publication of error estimates, stating (pp. 304–305):

> Perhaps the greatest step forward that can be taken, even at short notice, is to insist that economic statistics be only published together with an estimate of their error. Even if only roughly estimated, this would produce a wholesome effect. Makers and users of economic statistics must both refrain from making claims and demands that cannot be supported scientifically. The publication of error estimates would have a profound influence on the whole situation.

When writing my own recent article on communication of uncertainty in official statistics (Manski, 2015a), I was troubled that federal agencies and the economics profession had not paid attention to Morgenstern, so I subtitled my paper: "An Appraisal Fifty Years after Morgenstern." Morgenstern made an important contribution, with a compelling basic message and many specific insights. Although he achieved much recognition through his collaboration with von Neumann in the development of game theory, he was close to a lone voice in his concern with error in official economics statistics. His book attracted notice early on, but it then faded from the attention of economists.

Endorsing Morgenstern's perspective, Manski (2015a) urged federal statistical agencies to measure and communicate important uncertainties in official statistics. I suggested that agencies develop separate strategies for communication of uncertainty in news releases and in technical documentation. News releases are brief and are aimed at a broad audience, so they have only a limited ability to convey nuance. Agencies have more scope for communication of uncertainty in their technical documentation of official statistics.

An open question is how communication of uncertainty would affect policy making. We know little about how the users of official statistics interpret them. Some may mistakenly take the statistics at face value. Others may conjecture that they are prone to errors of varying directions and magnitudes. We know essentially nothing about how planning would change if federal agencies were to communicate uncertainty regularly and transparently. I think it important for behavioral and social scientists to initiate empirical studies that would shed light on these matters.

10.1.2 Specifying Planning Problems

In Chapter 1, I distinguished policy choice when there exists an actual and a hypothetical planner. I observed that decision theory presumes a unitary setting in which a decision maker performs his own research to inform action. The idealized planner of decision theory specifies the social welfare function, the choice set, the state space, and the decision criterion.

I observed that modern democratic societies have created an institutional separation between policy analysis and societal decision making, with researchers reporting findings to planners. With this separation, the primary research task is to perform studies that enable credible formulation of the state space. Researchers also sometimes develop *decision support systems*, which aim in various ways to assist planners to structure social welfare functions, choice sets, and decision criteria. However, specifying these features of planning problems ultimately should remain the responsibility of planners.

In Chapter 1, I wrote that researchers commonly specify pragmatic welfare functions, where "pragmatic" means that researchers combine conjectures regarding societal values, empirical study of population preferences, and concern for analytical tractability. I have specified pragmatic welfare functions in my own work, much of which I summarized in Chapters 5 through 9. Actual planners exist in the settings of each of Chapters 5 through 8. Hence, researchers could in principle replace the pragmatic welfare functions used in those analyses by ones elicited from the relevant planners. In the absence of a world government, the planner of Chapter 9 must be viewed as hypothetical.

I find the notion of a pragmatic welfare function useful, even though it is inevitably subjective. I similarly find the notions of a credible state space and a reasonable decision criterion useful, even though they too are inevitably subjective. I nevertheless worry that when studying planning with a hypothetical rather than actual planner, researchers may use their subjective meta-choices in specifying planning problems to conflate science with advocacy. That is, they may manipulate their analyses to generate predetermined conclusions.

Developing well-motivated ways to interpret the notions of "pragmatic," "credible," and "reasonable" would strengthen the foundations for planning under uncertainty. Of course, the term "well motivated" itself requires interpretation. I discussed in Chapter 6 the prevalent use of hypothesis testing in medical decision making with trial data. Requiring that medical researchers perform conventional calculations of statistical power and report conventional test statistics reduces the subjectivity of their research, but I argued that these practices are not well motivated. I argued that application of statistical decision theory is well motivated.

10.1.3 Enhancing the Tractability of Decision Criteria

A third direction where I see scope to strengthen the foundations for planning under uncertainty is more mundane but still important. This is to perform new methodological research to enhance the mathematical and computational tractability of reasonable decision criteria.

Among the three criteria that I have discussed throughout the book, I see the least need for new work on maximization of subjective expected welfare. This criterion has received sustained attention from the mid twentieth century onward. The primary needs are for expansion of the settings in which the maximin and MMR criteria are tractable. I have argued that the MMR criterion is conceptually appealing. I would be pleased to see new work to enhance its applicability.

The MMR criterion is especially challenging to implement when making decisions with sample data in applications where uncertainty stems from both partial identification and statistical imprecision. I mentioned in Chapter 7 that a few technical studies have been performed that analyze MMR planning with sample data when the planning problem is not separable across covariates. This is an important class of problems that warrants future methodological study. Another is sequential MMR planning, discussed in Chapter 7 in the context of diagnostic testing and treatment.

10.2 PANDEMIC PLANNING

The onset of the Covid-19 pandemic in early 2020 provided an unwelcome but instructive lesson in the importance of credible planning under uncertainty. Many economists, I among them, sought to be of service by directing our research towards subjects related to the pandemic. In my case, this resulted in studies of two identification problems associated with interpretation of data on the Covid infection rate (Manski, 2021a, Manski and Molinari, 2021). I also wrote a journal article (Manski, 2020c) and two blogs (Manski, 2020b, 2020a) on the difficulties that societies faced in choosing Covid policy under uncertainty.

As I write now in 2024, the pandemic appears to have ended. Covid-19 has evolved into a manageable endemic disease, of severity similar to influenza. Nevertheless, the threat of new pandemics has not lessened. Pandemic planning under uncertainty continues to be a subject of great importance. Yet the research to support credible planning has barely begun.

Pandemic planning must cope with substantial uncertainties about the nature of new diseases, the dynamics of transmission, and behavioral responses. These uncertainties limit our ability to predict the impacts of alternative policies. The epidemiological research community has not yet faced up to the fact that prevalent forecasting practices encourage planning with incredible certitude.

Section 10.2.1 documents incredible certitude in modeling that strongly influenced early Covid policy. Section 10.2.2 conveys my early suggestion of adaptive diversification of Covid policy. Looking ahead, Section 10.2.3 calls for a new framing of epidemiological research to provide a firmer basis for confrontation of future pandemics. I draw substantially on material in Manski (2020a, 2020b, 2020c).

10.2.1 Incredible Certitude in Epidemiological Modeling of the Covid-19 Pandemic

At the outset of the Covid-19 pandemic, epidemiological modelers sought to determine policy that would be optimal from a public health perspective if specified models of disease dynamics were accurate and if public health were measured in specified ways. Work by the Imperial College London Covid-19 Response Team and the IHME Covid-19 Health Service Utilization Forecasting Team at the University of Washington was particularly influential. I will discuss an early report by the Imperial College Team to make some general points.

The March 2020 Imperial College Report
On 16 March 2020, the Covid-19 Response Team of Imperial College London made public a report that provided forecasts of the impact of alternative non-pharmaceutical interventions (NPIs) intended to cope with the pandemic in high-income countries, with focus on Great Britain and the United States (Ferguson et al., 2020). The forecasts were made using a modified version of a simulation model previously developed to support pandemic influenza planning. The Response Team distinguished two broad policy alternatives, *mitigation* and *suppression*, which they described as follows (p. 1): "Two fundamental strategies are possible: (a) mitigation, which focuses on slowing but not necessarily stopping epidemic spread – reducing peak healthcare demand while protecting those most at risk of severe disease from infection, and (b) suppression, which aims to reverse epidemic growth, reducing case numbers to low levels and maintaining that situation indefinitely."

Drawing implications from their forecasts, they recommended suppression as the preferred policy option. Media coverage indicated that the report immediately affected policy formation in the United Kingdom and the United States, influencing both nations to shift sharply from mitigation strategies to suppression.

Should this policy change have occurred? I would confidently say yes if there were reason to think that the Imperial College report provided a credible integrated assessment of the impacts of alternative policies. But the report did not make an integrated assessment. Moreover, there is much reason to question the credibility of the forecasts that it offered.

Integrated benefit–cost analysis of Covid-19 policy would consider the full impacts on society of alternative policy options. The Imperial College report did not do this. Comparing mitigation and suppression, the Response Team wrote (p. 2): "We do not consider the ethical or economic implications of either strategy ... Instead we focus on feasibility, with a specific focus on what the likely healthcare system impact of the two approaches would be." Considering the impacts on the healthcare system is obviously important. Nevertheless, it is difficult to understand how the Response Team could justify drawing policy conclusions based only on consideration of the healthcare system.

From the beginning of the pandemic onward, the public sought to learn the broad impacts of policy on social welfare, which requires joint consideration of healthcare, the economy, education, and other matters. While some believed that suppression is the best policy from all perspectives, others argued the contrary. Potential tension between health and other objectives became apparent. For example, criteria for school reopening in fall 2020 became controversial.

Why didn't the Imperial College Response Team perform an integrated assessment of the broad impacts of Covid-19 policy? The basic answer is that epidemiological modeling has, since its inception more than a century ago, mainly been performed by researchers with backgrounds in medicine and public health. Researchers with these backgrounds have found it natural to focus on health concerns, viewing other aspects of social welfare as matters that may be important but are beyond their purview.

Hence, the Response Team mentioned in passing that (p. 2): "Suppression ... carries with it enormous social and economic costs which may themselves have significant impact on health and well-being in the short and longer-term." Yet they made no attempt to quantify social and economic costs. They effectively ignored them when reaching their policy conclusion.

Indeed, the epidemiological model used by the Response Team did not consider how a pandemic may generate behavioral responses within the population. The Response Team acknowledged verbally that behavioral response may be an important determinant of outcomes, stating (p. 1): "the impact of many of the NPIs detailed here depends critically on how people respond to their introduction, which is highly likely to vary between countries and even communities. Last, it is highly likely that there would be significant spontaneous changes in population behaviour even in the absence of government-mandated interventions." This statement acknowledged that the dynamics of epidemics depend on the decisions that individuals make to protect themselves from infection. Nevertheless, the Response Team did not model behavioral responses. Instead, they invoked assumptions about the fractions of households who would comply with alternative policies, without justifying the assumptions.

I should note that modeling and analysis of behavioral responses to epidemics has been a central concern of a separate literature on economic epidemiology, whose contributors are primarily health economists rather than researchers with backgrounds in medicine and public health. See Philipson (2000).

Combining Epidemiological and Macroeconomic Modeling
Recognizing that the Covid-19 pandemic may have serious economic as well as health impacts, macroeconomists sought to expand the scope of optimal policy analysis by joining epidemiological models with models of macroeconomic dynamics and by specifying welfare functions that consider both health and economic outcomes. Examples included Eichenbaum et al. (2021) and Acemoglu et al. (2021). Research of this type was potentially welcome, but there was little basis to assess the realism of the models that were developed.

A serious problem in the modeling by epidemiologists and macroeconomists was the dearth of evidence available to inform model specification and estimation. As discussed in Chapters 3 and 8, social interactions in treatment response imply that studies of infectious disease are largely unable to perform the randomized trials that have been considered the so-called "gold standard" for medical research. Modeling necessarily relies on the limited available observational data. Lacking much evidence, epidemiologists and macroeconomists developed models of the Covid-19 pandemic that were mathematically sophisticated but that had little grounding.

10.2.2 Adaptive Diversification of Covid-19 Policy

During the pandemic, there were frequent calls for adoption of a uniform policy across locations, particularly across the fifty states of the United States. For example, an editorial in the *Washington Post* (2020) was titled, "The Patchwork of State Reopenings Is a Deadly Game of Trial and Error." The text referred to "the peril posed by the hodgepodge of state decisions to reopen quickly, gradually or not at all yet." The editorial did not propose what a uniform national policy should be.

Calling for a uniform Covid-19 policy across states would have been justified if it were clear what constitutes optimal policy and if it were known that the optimal policy is invariant across states. Then each state should adhere to that policy. However, we did not know optimal policy. It may have been that continued suppression was better for some states and that some version of reopening was better for others, depending on their characteristics.

Thus, there was no well-grounded case for making policy uniform across states. I suggested that policy diversification, with some locations implementing suppression and others implementing mitigation, would protect against making a gross error in policy choice and would enable learning of policy impacts.

10.2.3 The Pressing Need for Credible Integrated Assessment of Pandemic Impacts

Looking ahead, I see an urgent need for epidemiologists, economists, education researchers and others to join forces to develop credible integrated assessment models of epidemics. Even with the best intentions, this will take considerable time. There is reason to hope that epidemiologists and macroeconomists may be able to communicate with one another because they share a common language for mathematical modeling of dynamic processes, used to formalize epidemiological models and dynamic stochastic general equilibrium models, respectively. However, each group has in the past exhibited considerable insularity, which may impede collaboration. Moreover, neither discipline has shown willingness to face up to uncertainty when developing and applying models.

I see lessons to be learned from research on climate policy. Climate research was at first a subject for study by earth scientists, who seek to forecast the impact of emissions on the atmosphere and oceans. Having backgrounds in the physical sciences, these researchers find it natural to focus on the physics of climate change rather than behavioral responses and social impacts. Over the past thirty years, the study of climate policy has broadened with the development of integrated assessment models, with major contributions by economists. As a result, we now have some perspective on how our planet and our social systems interact with one another. However, this progress has been more qualitative than quantitative. As discussed in Chapter 9, existing integrated assessment models make quantitative forecasts with limited credibility. Climate scientists and epidemiologists both need to improve the credibility of their modeling.

10.3 PLANNING TO BOLDLY GO

In the early 1980s, deeply concerned with the future of humanity, I wrote but did not distribute a commentary calling for permanent human expansion beyond this Earth and, indeed, beyond our solar system. My motivation was pragmatic rather than visionary. I did not use the word "diversification" in the commentary, but I did use the related word "dis-integrate."

In the mid 2000s, when I began to perform research on treatment diversification, I recognized that this concept underlay what I had written twenty years earlier. Writing now, another twenty years later and still being deeply concerned with the future of humanity, I see this book to provide an appropriate venue to go public. I view the theme of my commentary to be as relevant now as it was forty years, perhaps more so. To close the book, I present the commentary below, verbatim as drafted in 1984.

SOME OF US MUST LEAVE HOME: A Plea for Colonization in Space (April 1984)
The American space program is continually called upon to justify itself as a prudent investment of national resources. The usual response is to cite various tangible benefits including contributions to science, technological spinoffs, commercial applications, and defense missions. On occasion, it is argued that the exploration of space fills man's psychological need for a frontier to conquer.

Those committed to some form of space program debate the proper mix of activities. NASA has recently proposed that the construction of a permanent orbiting space station should be our next major project. Many disagree, preferring to see funds allocated to unmanned exploration. For example, an editorial in the *New York Times* of January 29, 1984 termed the proposed space station, "An Expensive Yawn in Space." The *Times* wrote, "Almost every proposed use for the manned space station could be better accomplished without man." Going on, the editorial asked, "As for using the space station as a base from which to send humans to other planets, what could a man do on Mars that robots could not do far better?"

The *Times* obviously sees no good reason for human colonization in space. Indeed, colonization is only rarely proposed as a goal for our space program. When the idea has been discussed, the arguments offered have been either too mundane or too romantic to arouse a national commitment. Colonization has seemed too grand a project, too distant in feasibility, and too uncertain in its benefits to be taken seriously. I believe there to be a most compelling case for colonization. That is, colonization in space is insurance for the survival of mankind.

How is it that man has survived thus far in the face of all the cataclysms that could occur? Confined to one world, we have always been vulnerable to a range of natural disasters. We should, I think, simply consider ourselves fortunate. It has been our luck that thus far, the Sun's energy output has remained relatively stable, that no large asteroid has impacted the Earth, that no virus has proved universally fatal.

We should also recognize that historically, the primitiveness of our technology has protected us. The mountains and oceans have provided barriers to movement which have impeded the transmission of disease. The destructiveness of our wars has been constrained by the limited effectiveness of our weapons. Dispersed across a large and resilient planet, men have died, but mankind has survived.

Here is the rub. As a consequence of the technological advances of the last century, humanity has become increasingly integrated; in many respects, a single world civilization has emerged. The material benefits of our progress are clear. Equally clear is that our capacity to limit damage has diminished. In particular, our advances have grossly enlarged the scope of our wars. Our civilization has become powerful and simultaneously fragile.

How have we responded to this consequence of our evolution? I would characterize our policies as those of the sophisticated and sensitive manager. We know that proposed solutions to perceived problems may generate new problems, so we attempt to anticipate these. We recognize that an attempt to improve one aspect of the functioning of society may affect other aspects, so we try to predict the indirect effects. We admit that we cannot always avoid crises but we are confident that with enough analysis and planning, we can at least contain them. Thus, we are cautious but ultimately optimistic that we can manage our civilization and direct its progress.

I believe that careful management is necessary but not sufficient if man is to survive much longer. Our management efforts must be complemented by a reduction in the fragility of our civilization. We need to reorganize human society so that a failure in some part no longer threatens a breakdown of the whole.

To see that management alone cannot suffice, consider the threat that most haunts us, nuclear war. To cope with this danger, we have developed a management strategy with three subtly interacting components. First, we have designed weapons which we hope will deter an intentional nuclear strike by the other side. Second, we have built into our deterrent weapons systems procedures intended to lower the probability of accidental or unauthorized launch. Third, we have sought to reach arms controls agreements in an attempt to reconcile the other side's deterrence objectives with our own.

Given the situation we face, the logic of our strategy seems impeccable. At the same time, it would be foolish to think that it can succeed forever. As we are painfully aware, it is very difficult to construct a deterrent weapon that does not simultaneously imply an offensive capability. Moreover, no weapon can be made truly failsafe.

Finally, it seems clear that arms control efforts may mitigate but will not eliminate the risks we now face. One must conclude that with non-negligible probability, our intricately woven strategy to prevent nuclear war will someday fail.

What can we do to ensure that if nuclear war or some other global catastrophe should occur, nevertheless mankind will survive? I see only one course. We must dis-integrate our civilization through expansion into space. We must use the vastness of space to restore the barrier to transmission of risks once provided by the mountains and oceans of Earth.

Only space offers the buffer of distance and time we need if we are to contain the damage we can inflict on ourselves and if we are to limit our vulnerability to the vagaries of natures. With self-sufficient colonies spread across the universe, man would be no more at risk from the explosion of a sun than he now is from the eruption of a volcano. We could no more destroy ourselves with hydrogen bombs than with gunpowder. The point is not, of course, that risks would disappear. The point is that risks would be contained. Whatever our luck vis a vis the environment and whatever our own failures, somewhere life would go on.

Colonization in space should be thought of as an open-ended process each step along which confers further security. The first step has already been taken with the development of the space shuttle. NASA's proposed Earth-orbiting station follows logically. We should then envision a sequence of projects including construction of a Moon-orbiting station, development of Moon colonies, and then colonies on Mars. It is not enough to talk about the feasibility of these projects. We must commit ourselves today and begin the work. Humanity is most at risk right now.

We should also understand that we must eventually plan beyond Mars colonies, in fact beyond our solar system. For at least two reasons, colonization within our solar system can offer only a limited increment to the survivability of man. First, the distances between the planets, which may now seem enormous, will eventually become less a barrier to communication and travel. The solar system will someday be too small to provide the buffer we require.

Second, given what we know about the environments of the other planets and moons, it is not clear that any colony within the solar system can be self-sufficient. It is even less clear that our first colonies will have the indigenous resources needed to support further colonization. But it is crucial to our survival that Earth's colonies be capable of creating their own progeny. A breed which produces sterile offspring is doomed.

Eventually then, we must look to the stars. It is too early to begin the construction of starships. It is not, however, too soon to begin the process of identifying potentially hospitable destinations for such ships. The recently announced telescopic evidence that some stars have planetary systems should be considered the start of our explorations. Much more research of this kind should be supported. We should increase our support of research on space propulsion methods. And we should begin work on the design of unmanned deep-space probes capable of reporting back on the suitability for human life of candidate planets.

If we agree on the goals set here, then we need to face the practical question of establishing a program for colonization in space. In an ideal world, extraterrestrial settlement would be a cooperative enterprise of all mankind. Unfortunately, it is precisely man's inability to cooperate that makes colonization urgent. We cannot afford to wait the years that may be needed for an international proposal to be formulated and acted on. It seems to me more prudent to work through existing channels. In particular, colonization in space should be made a cornerstone of the American space program.

Once an American colonization program is announced, other nations will undoubtedly feel compelled to initiate their own competing programs. The prospect of humanity carrying its Earthborn chauvinism into space is not appealing.

Nevertheless, competition in space may have a positive side. A race to the stars is likely to be run faster.

Does man deserve to survive? It is sometimes easy to feel that our species should be confined to Earth, that we should not be allowed to pollute the universe with our pettiness. I reject this suggestion although I am not sure why. Perhaps I am genetically programmed to want the survival of my own kind. I prefer to believe that the good in humanity outweighs the bad and that we can mature as a race. To do so, we must first survive.

It is ironic that the invention of nuclear weapons has occurred almost simultaneously with the perfection of a capability for space flight. The former may destroy man, the latter may save us. This coincidence of timing is not accidental. Our advances in science and technology have led to both developments. It is reasonable to speculate that every intelligent species must some time reach such a critical phase in its evolution.

References

Acemoglu, D., V. Chernozhukov, I. Werning, and M. Whinston (2021), "Optimal Targeted Lockdowns in a Multi-Group SIR Model," *American Economic Review: Insights*, 3, 487–502.

Ackerman, F., S. DeCanio, R. Howarth, and K. Sheeran (2009), "Limitations of Integrated Assessment Models of Climate Change," *Climatic Change*, 95, 297–315.

Afriat, S. (1967), "The Construction of Utility Functions from Expenditure Data," *International Economic Review*, 8, 67–77.

Aikman D, P. Barrett, S. Kapadia, M. King, J. Proudman, T. Taylor, I. de Weymarn, and T. Yates (2011), "Uncertainty in Macroeconomic Policy-Making: Art or Science," *Philosophical Transactions of the Royal Society*, 369, 4798–4817.

Akerlof, G. and W. Dickens (1982), "The Economic Consequences of Cognitive Dissonance," *American Economic Review*, 72, 307–319.

Althouse, B., T. Bergstrom, and C. Bergstrom (2010), "A Public Choice Framework for Controlling Transmissible and Evolving Diseases," *Proceedings of the National Academy of Sciences*, 107, 1696–1701.

Anderson, R. and R. May (1991), *Infectious Diseases of Humans: Dynamics and Control*, Oxford: Oxford University Press.

Aneja, A., J. Donohue, and A. Zhang (2011), "The Impact of Right-to-Carry Laws and the NRC Report: Lessons for the Empirical Evaluation of Law and Policy," *American Law and Economic Review*, 13, 565–632.

Angrist, J., G. Imbens, and D. Rubin (1996), "Identification of Causal Effects Using Instrumental Variables," *Journal of the American Statistical Association*, 91, 444–455.

Armantier, O., W. Bruine de Bruin, S. Potter, G. Topa, W. van der Klaauw, and B. Zafar (2013), "Measuring Inflation Expectations," *Annual Review of Economics*, 5, 273–301.

Arrow, K. J. (1950), "A Difficulty in the Concept of Social Welfare," *Journal of Political Economy*, 58, 328–346.

Arrow, K. J. (1973a), "Some Ordinalist-Utilitarian Notes on Rawls's Theory of Justice," *Journal of Philosophy*, 70, 245–263.

Arrow, K. J. (1973b), "The Theory of Discrimination," in O. Ashenfelter and A. Rees (eds.), *Discrimination in Labor Markets*, Princeton, NJ: Princeton University Press, 3–33.

Arrow, K. J. et al. (2013), "Determining Benefits and Costs for Future Generations," *Science*, 341, July 26, 349–350.

Arrow, K. J. et al. (2014), "Should Governments Use a Declining Discount Rate in Project Analysis?" *Review of Environmental Economics and Policy*, 8, 145–163.

Atkinson, A. and J. Stiglitz (1980), *Lectures on Public Economics*, Princeton, NJ: Princeton University Press.

Bachmann, R., G. Topa, and W. Van der Klaauw (eds.) (2023), *Handbook of Economic Expectations*, Amsterdam: Elsevier.

Backhouse, R., A. Baujard, and T. Nishizawa (eds.) (2021), *Welfare Theory, Public Action, and Ethical Values*, Cambridge: Cambridge University Press.

Balke, A. and J. Pearl (1997), "Bounds on Treatment Effects from Studies with Imperfect Compliance," *Journal of the American Statistical Association*, 92, 1171–1176.

Ball, F. and O. Lyne (2002), "Optimal Vaccination Policies for Stochastic Epidemics among a Population of Households," *Mathematical Biosciences*, 177&178, 333–354.

Bar–Anan, Y., T. Wilson, and D. Gilbert (2009), "The Feeling of Uncertainty Intensifies Affective Reactions," *Emotion*, 9, 123–127.

Barlevy, G. (2011), "Robustness and Macroeconomic Policy," *Annual Review of Economics*, 3, 1–24.

Barro, R. (1990), "Government Spending in a Simple Model of Endogenous Growth," *Journal of Political Economy*, 98, S103–S125.

Barseghyan, L., M. Coughlin, F. Molinari, and J. Teitelbaum (2021), "Heterogeneous Choice Sets and Preferences," *Econometrica*, 89, 2015–2048.

Barsky, R. (1998), *Noam Chomsky: A Life of Dissent*, Cambridge, MA: MIT Press.

Basu, A. and D. Meltzer (2007), "Value of Information on Preference Heterogeneity and Individualized Care," *Medical Decision Making*, 27, 112–127.

Becker, N. and D. Starczak (1997), "Optimal Vaccination Strategies for a Community of Households," *Mathematical Biosciences*, 139, 117–132.

Ben Akiva, M., D. McFadden, and K. Train (2019), "Foundations of Stated Preference Elicitation: Consumer Behavior and Choice-Based Conjoint Analysis," *Foundations and Trends® in Econometrics*, 10, 1–144.

Bénabou, R. and J. Tirole (2016), "Mindful Economics: The Production, Consumption, and Value of Beliefs," *Journal of Economic Perspectives*, 30, 141–164.

Bentham, J. (1776), *A Fragment on Government*, London: Payne.

Berger, J. (1985), *Statistical Decision Theory and Bayesian Analysis*, 2nd ed., New York: Springer.

Berger, J. (2006), "The Case for Objective Bayesian Analysis," *Bayesian Analysis*, 1, 385–402.

Berkson, J. (1958), "Smoking and Lung Cancer: Some Observations on Two Recent Reports," *Journal of the American Statistical Association*, 53, 28–38.

Bhattacharya, J., A. Shaikh, and E. Vytlacil (2012), "Treatment Effect Bounds: An Application to Swan–Ganz Catheterization," *Journal of Econometrics*, 168, 223–243.

Binmore, K. (2009), *Rational Decisions*, Princeton, NJ: Princeton University Press.

Black, D. and D. Nagin (1998), "Do Right-to-Carry Laws Deter Violent Crime?" *Journal of Legal Studies*, 27, 209–219.

Blackstone, W. (1769), *Commentaries on the Laws of England*, republished in 2016 by Oxford: Oxford University Press.

Blass, A., S. Lach, and C. Manski (2010), "Using Elicited Choice Probabilities to Estimate Random Utility Models: Preferences for Electricity Reliability," *International Economic Review*, 51, 421–440.

Blumstein, A., J. Cohen, and D. Nagin (1978), *Deterrence and Incapacitation: Estimating the Effects of Criminal Sanctions on Crime Rates*, Washington, DC: National Academy Press.

Blundell, R. and T. MaCurdy (1999), "Labor Supply: A Review of Alternative Approaches," in O. Ashenfelter and D. Card (eds.), *Handbook of Labor Economics*, Vol. 3, Amsterdam: North-Holland, 1559–1695.

Boulier, B., T. Datta, and R. Goldfarb (2007), "Vaccination Externalities," *B.E. Journal of Economic Analysis & Policy*, 7(1), article 23.

Brief, R. (1975), "The Accountant's Responsibility in Historical Perspective," *Accounting Review*, 50, 285–297.

Briggs, A. (2022), "Healing the Past, Reimagining the Present, Investing in the Future: What Should Be the Role of Race As a Proxy Covariate in Health Economics Informed Health Care Policy?" *Health Economics*, 31, 2115–2119.

Brito, D., E. Sheshinski, and M. Intriligator (1991), "Externalities and Compulsory Vaccinations," *Journal of Public Economics*, 45, 69–90.

Brunnermeier, M. and J. Parker (2005), "Optimal Expectations," *American Economic Review*, 95, 1092–1118.

Budescu, D. and T. Wallsten (1987), "Subjective Estimation of Precise and Vague Uncertainties," in G. Wright and P. Ayton (eds.), *Judgmental Forecasting*, Wiley, 63–81.

Buhr, K. and M. Dugas (2009), "The Role of Fear of Anxiety and Intolerance of Uncertainty in Worry: An Experimental Manipulation," *Behaviour Research and Therapy*, 47, 215 223.

Burtis, M., J. Gelbach, and B. Kobayashi (2018), "Error Costs, Legal Standards of Proof, and Statistical Significance," *Supreme Court Economic Review*, 25, 1–57.

Campbell, D. (1984), "Can We Be Scientific in Applied Social Science?" *Evaluation Studies Review Annual*, 9, 26–48.

Campbell, D., and J. Stanley (1963), *Experimental and Quasi-experimental Designs for Research*, Chicago, IL: Rand McNally.

Cao, B. et al. (2020), "A Trial of Lopinavir–Ritonavir in Adults Hospitalized with Severe Covid-19," *New England Journal of Medicine*, 382, 1787–1799.

Caplin, A. and J. Leahy (2001), "Psychological Expected Utility Theory and Anticipatory Feelings," *Quarterly Journal of Economics*, 116, 55–80.

Cassidy, R. and C. Manski (2019), "Tuberculosis Diagnosis and Treatment under Uncertainty," *Proceedings of the National Academy of Sciences*, 116, 22990–22997.

Centers for Disease Control and Prevention (2006), *Principles of Epidemiology in Public Health Practice*, 3rd ed., https://stacks.cdc.gov/view/cdc/6914, accessed December 20, 2023.

Cerdeña, J., M. Plaisime, and J. Tsai (2020), "From Race-Based to Race-Conscious Medicine: How Anti-racist Uprisings Call Us to Act," *Lancet*, 396, 1125–1128.

Chavel, C. (1967), *Maimonides the Commandments*, London: Soncino Press.

Chen, F. and F. Toxvaerd (2014), "The Economics of Vaccination," *Journal of Theoretical Biology*, 363, 105–117.

Chernoff, H. (1954), "Rational Selection of Decision Functions," *Econometrica*, 22, 422–443.

Cheville, A., M. Almoza, J. Courmier, and J. Basford (2010), "A Prospective Cohort Study Defining Utilities Using Time Trade-Offs and the Euroqol-5D to Assess the Impact of Cancer-Related Lymphedema," *Cancer*, 116, 3722–3731.

Chipman, J. and J. Moore (1978), "The New Welfare Economics 1939–1974," *International Economic Review*, 19, 547–584.

Clarke, L. et al. (2014), "Assessing Transformation Pathways," in O. Edenhofer et al. (eds.), *Climate Change 2014: Mitigation of Climate Change*. Contribution of Working Group III to the Fifth Assessment Report of the Intergovernmental Panel on Climate Change. Cambridge: Cambridge University Press.

Congressional Budget Office (2007), "The Effect of Tax Changes on Labor Supply in CBO's Microsimulation Tax Model," Congress of the United States, Congressional Budget Office.

Connors, A. et al. (1996), "The Effectiveness of Right Heart Catheterization in the Initial Care of Critically Ill Patients," *Journal of the American Medical Association*, 276, 889–897.

Cornfield, J. (1951), "A Method of Estimating Comparative Rates from Clinical Data. Applications to Cancer of the Lung, Breast, and Cervix," *Journal of the National Cancer Institute*, 11, 1269–1275.

Cox, D. (1958), *Planning of Experiments*, New York: Wiley.

Crane, B, A. Rivolo, and G. Comfort (1997), *An Empirical Examination of Counterdrug Interdiction Program Effectiveness*. IDA Paper P-3219, Alexandria, VA: Institute for Defense Analyses.

Craske, M. and M. Stein (2016), "Anxiety," *Lancet*, 388, 3048–3059.

Cross, P. and C. Manski (2002), "Regressions, Short and Long," *Econometrica*, 70, 357–368.

Croushore, D. (2011), "Frontiers of Real-Time Data Analysis," *Journal of Economic Literature*, 49, 72–100.

Dasgupta, P. (2008), "Discounting Climate Change," *Journal of Risk and Uncertainty*, 37, 141–169.

Dasgupta, P. (2019), "Ramsey and Intergenerational Welfare Economics," *Stanford Encyclopedia of Philosophy*, https://plato.stanford.edu/entries/ramsey-economics/, 1–15, accessed June 3, 2024.

Deaton, A. (2009), "Instruments of Development: Randomization in the Tropics, and the Search for the Elusive Keys to Economic Development," National Bureau of Economic Research Working Paper 14690.

DeCanio, S., C. Manski, and A. Sanstad (2022), "Minimax-Regret Climate Policy with Deep Uncertainty in Climate Modeling and Intergenerational Discounting," *Ecological Economics*, 201, https://doi.org/10.1016/j.ecolecon.2022.107552.

DeGroot, M. (1970), *Optimal Statistical Decisions*, New York: McGraw-Hill.

Delavande, A. (2008), "Pill, Patch, or Shot? Subjective Expectations and Birth Control Choice," *International Economic Review*, 49, 999–1042.

Delavande, A. (2014), "Probabilistic Expectations in Developing Countries," *Annual Review of Economics*, 6, 1–20.

Delavande, A. and C. Manski (2015), "Using Elicited Choice Probabilities in Hypothetical Elections to Study Decisions to Vote," *Electoral Studies*, 38, 28–37.

Delgado, C. et al. (2021), "A Unifying approach for GFR Estimation: Recommendations of the NKF-ASN Task Force on Reassessing the Inclusion of Race in Diagnosing Kidney Disease," *Journal of the American Society of Nephrology*, 32, 2994–3015.

Dempster, A. (1968), "A Generalization of Bayesian Inference," *Journal of the Royal Statistical Society, Series B*, 30, 205–247.

DerSimonian, R., and N. Laird (1986), "Meta-analysis in Clinical Trials," *Controlled Clinical Trials*, 7, 177–188.

Dietz, S. and F. Venmans (2019), "Cumulative Carbon Emissions and Economic Policy: In Search of General Principles," *Journal of Environmental Economics and Management*, 96, 108–129.

Dietz, S., C. Gollier, and L. Kessler (2018), "The Climate Beta," *Journal of Environmental Economics and Management*, 87, 258–274.

Domınguez-Rivera, P. and S. Raphael (2015), "The Role of the Cost-of-Crime Literature in Bridging the Gap between Social Science Research and Policy Making: Potentials and Limitations," *Criminology & Public Policy*, 14, 589–632.

Dominitz, J. (2003), "How Do the Laws of Probability Constrain Legislative and Judicial Efforts to Stop Racial Profiling?" *American Law and Economics Review*, 5, 412–432.

Drupp, M., M. Freeman, B. Groom, and F. Nesje (2018), "Discounting Disentangled," *American Economic Journal: Economic Policy*, 10, 109–134.

Dubin, J. and D. Rivers (1993), "Experimental Estimates of the Impact of Wage Subsidies," *Journal of Econometrics*, 56, 219–242.

Dugas, M., K. Buhr, and R. Ladouceur (2004), "The Role of Intolerance of Uncertainty in the Etiology and Maintenance of Generalized Anxiety Disorder," in R. Heimberg, C. Turk, and D. Mennin (eds.), *Generalized Anxiety Disorder: Advances in Research and Practice*, New York: Guilford Press, 143–163.

Duggan, M. (2001), "More Guns, More Crime," *Journal of Political Economy*, 109, 1086–1114.

Duignan, B. (2023), "Occam's Razor," *Encyclopædia Britannica*, www.britannica.com/topic/Occams-razor, accessed July 8, 2023.

Durlauf, S. (2006), "Racial Profiling," *Economic Journal*, 116, F402–F426.

Durlauf, S., S. Navarro, and D. Rivers (2016), "Model Uncertainty and the Effect of Shall-Issue Right-to-Carry Laws on Crime," *European Economic Review*, 81, 32–67.

Eichenbaum, M., S. Rebelo, and M. Trabandt (2021), "The Macroeconomics of Epidemics," *Review of Financial Studies*, 34, 5149–5187.

Ellsberg, D. (1961), "Risk, Ambiguity, and the Savage Axioms," *Quarterly Journal of Economics*, 75, 643–669.

Elmendorf, D. (2010) Letter to Honorable Nancy Pelosi, Speaker, U.S. House of Representatives, Congressional Budget Office, housedocs.house.gov/energycommerce/hr4872_CBO.pdf, accessed July 5, 2023.

Emmerling, J., L. Drouet, K. van der Wijst, D. van Vuuren, V. Bosetti, and M. Tavoni (2019), "The Role of the Discount Rate tor Emission Pathways and Negative Emissions," *Environmental Research Letters*, 14, 104008.

Epps, D. (2015), "The Consequences of Error in Criminal Justice," *Harvard Law Review*, 128, 1065–1151.

Faries, M. (2018), "Completing the Dissection in Melanoma: Increasing Decision Precision," *Annals of Surgical Oncology*, https://doi.org/10.1245/s10434-017-6330-4.

Faries, M. et al. (2017), "Completion Dissection or Surveillance for Sentinel-Node Metastasis in Melanoma," *New England Journal of Medicine*, 376, 2211–2222.

Fenichel, E. et al. (2011), "Adaptive Human Behavior in Epidemiological Models," *Proceedings of the National Academy of Sciences*, 108, 6306–6311.

Ferguson, N. et al. (2020), "Report 9: Impact of Non-pharmaceutical Interventions (NPIs) to Reduce COVID-19 Mortality and Healthcare Demand," Imperial College London, www.imperial.ac.uk/media/imperial-college/medicine/mrc-gida/2020-03-16-COVID19-Report-9.pdf, accessed December 23, 2023.

Ferguson, T. (1967), *Mathematical Statistics: A Decision Theoretic Approach*, San Diego, CA: Academic Press.

Financial Accounting Standards Board (2018), *Statement of Financial Accounting Concepts* No. 8, As Amended; Norwalk, CT: Financial Accounting Standards Board.

Fine, P. (1993), "Herd Immunity: History, Theory, Practice," *Epidemiological Reviews*, 15, 265–302.

Fine, P, K. Eames, and D. Heymann (2011), "'Herd Immunity': A Rough Guide," *Clinical Infectious Diseases*, 52, 911–916.

Fischhoff, B. and D. MacGregor (1982), "Subjective Confidence in Forecasts," *Journal of Forecasting*, 1, 155–172.

Fixler, D., R. Greenaway-McGrevy, and B. Grimm (2011), "Revisions to GDP, GDI, and Their Major Components," *Survey of Current Business*, 91, 9–31.

Fixler, D., R. Greenaway-McGrevy, and B. Grimm (2014), "Revisions to GDP, GDI, and Their Major Components," *Survey of Current Business*, 94, 1–23.

Fleiss, J. (1981), *Statistical Methods for Rates and Proportions*, New York: Wiley.

Fleurbaey, M. (2018), "Welfare Economics, Risk and Uncertainty," *Canadian Journal of Economics*, 51, 5–40.

Foley, D. (1967), "Resource Allocation and the Public Sector," *Yale Economic Essays*, 7, 45–98.

Francis, P. (1997), "Dynamic Epidemiology and the Market for Vaccinations," *Journal of Public Economics*, 63, 383–406.

Friedman, M. (1953), *Essays in Positive Economics*. Chicago, IL: University of Chicago Press.

Gigerenzer, G., U. Hoffrage, and H. Kleinbölting (1991), "Probabilistic Mental Models: A Brunswikian Theory of Confidence," *Psychological Review*, 98, 506–528.

Gilbert, F. and R. Pfouts (1958), "A Theory of the Responsiveness of Hours of Work to Changes in Wage Rates," *Review of Economics and Statistics*, 40, 116–121.

Gilboa, I. and D. Schmeidler (1989), "Maxmin Expected Utility with Non-unique Prior," *Journal of Mathematical Economics*, 18, 141–153.

Giustinelli, P. (2016), "Group Decision Making with Uncertain Outcomes: Unpacking Child–Parent Choice of the High School Track," *International Economic Review*, 57, 573–602.

Giustinelli, P., C. Manski, and F. Molinari (2022), "Precise or Imprecise Probabilities? Evidence from Survey Response on Late-Onset Dementia," *Journal of the European Economic Association*, 20, 187–221.

Glass, G. (1977), "Integrating Findings: The Meta-analysis of Research," *Review of Research in Education*, 5, 351–379.

Goldberger, A. (1972), "Structural Equation Methods in the Social Sciences," *Econometrica*, 40, 979–1001.

Goldberger, A. (1991), *A Course in Econometrics*, Cambridge, MA: Harvard University Press.

Gollier, C. and A. Muermann (2010), "Optimal Choice and Beliefs with Ex Ante Savoring and Ex Post Disappointment," *Management Science*, 56, 1272–1284.

Good, I. (1967), "On the Principle of Total Evidence," *British Journal for the Philosophy of Science*, 17, 319–321.

Gul, F. and W. Pesendorfer (2008), "The Case for Mindless Economics," in A. Caplan and A. Schotter (eds.), *The Foundations of Positive and Normative Economics*, New York: Oxford University Press.

Haavelmo, T. (1944), "The Probability Approach in Econometrics," *Econometrica*, 12, Supplement, iii–vi and 1–115.

Hale, M. (1736), *Historia Placitorum Coronæ: The History of The Pleas of The Crown*, republished in 2004 by Clark, NJ: The Lawbook Exchange.

Halpern, S., J. Karlawish, and J. Berlin (2002), "The Continued Unethical Conduct of Underpowered Clinical Trials," *Journal of the American Medical Association*, 288, 358–362.

Hampel, F., E. Ronchetti, P. Rousseeuw, and A. Werner (1986), *Robust Statistics*, New York: Wiley.

Hansen, L. and T. Sargent (2008), *Robustness*, Princeton, NJ: Princeton University Press.

Harmon, R. (2012), "The Problem of Policing," *Michigan Law Review*, 110, 761–818.

Harsanyi, J. (1955), "Cardinal Welfare, Individualistic Ethics, and Interpersonal Comparisons of Utility," *Journal of Political Economy*, 63, 309–321.

Heal, G. and A. Milner (2014), "Uncertainty and Decision Making in Climate Change Economics," *Review of Environmental Economics and Policy*, 8, 120–137.

Heckman, J. and S. Urzua (2009), "Comparing IV with Structural Models: What Simple IV Can and Cannot Identify," National Bureau of Economic Research Working Paper 14706.

Hicks, J. (1939), "The Foundations of Welfare Economics," *Economic Journal*, 49, 696–712.

Higgins, J. and S. Green (eds.) (2011), *Cochrane Handbook for Systematic Reviews of Interventions*, Version 5.1.0, The Cochrane Collaboration, https://handbook-5-1.cochrane.org/, accessed February 16, 2024.

Hill, A. and I. Longini (2003), "The Critical Vaccination Fraction for Heterogeneous Epidemic Models," *Mathematical Biosciences*, 181, 85–106.

Horowitz, J., and C. Manski (2000), "Nonparametric Analysis of Randomized Experiments with Missing Attribute and Outcome Data," *Journal of the American Statistical Association*, 95, 77–84.

Hsieh, D., C. Manski, and D. McFadden (1985), "Estimation of Response Probabilities from Augmented Retrospective Observations," *Journal of the American Statistical Association*, 80, 651–662.

Huber, P. (1981), *Robust Statistics*, New York: Wiley.

Hudgens, M. and E. Halloran (2008), "Toward Causal Inference with Interference," *Journal of the American Statistical Association*, 103, 832–842.

Hurd, M. (2009), "Subjective Probabilities in Household Surveys," *Annual Review of Economics*, 1, 543–564.

Hurd, M., J. Smith, and J. Zissimopoulos (2004), "The Effects of Subjective Survival on Retirement and Social Security Claiming," *Journal of Applied Econometrics*, 19, 761–775.

Hurwicz, L. (1951), "Some Specification Problems and Applications to Econometric Models," *Econometrica*, 19, 343–344.

IHME COVID-19 Health Service Utilization Forecasting Team (2020). "Forecasting COVID-19 Impact on Hospital Bed-Days, ICU-Days, Ventilator Days and Deaths by US State in the Next 4 Months," Institute for Health Metrics and Evaluation (IHME), Seattle: University of Washington, www.medrxiv.org/content/10.1101/2020.03.27.20043752v1.full.pdf, accessed February 16, 2024.

Imbens, G. and J. Angrist (1994), "Identification and Estimation of Local Average Treatment Effects," *Econometrica*, 62, 467–476.

Immunization Action Coalition (2023), "Vaccine Specific Requirements: State Laws and Mandates by Vaccine," www.immunize.org/official-guidance/state-policies/requirements/, accessed December 20, 2023.

Institute of Medicine (2011), *Clinical Practice Guidelines We Can Trust*, Washington, DC: National Academies Press.

International Conference on Harmonisation (1999), "ICH E9 Expert Working Group. Statistical Principles for Clinical Trials: ICH Harmonized Tripartite Guideline," *Statistics in Medicine*, 18, 1905–1942.

Ioannidis, J. (2005), "Why Most Published Research Findings Are False," *PLoS Medicine*, 2, 696–701.

IPCC (2018), *Global Warming of 1.5°C. An IPCC Special Report on the impacts of global warming of 1.5°C above pre-industrial levels and related global greenhouse gas emission pathways, in the context of strengthening the global response to the threat of climate change, sustainable development, and efforts to eradicate poverty* (V. Masson-Delmotte et al., eds.), Geneva: Intergovernmental Panel on Climate Change (IPCC).

IPCC (2021), *Climate Change 2021: The Physical Science Basis. Contribution of Working Group I to the Sixth Assessment Report of the Intergovernmental Panel on Climate Change*, ed. V. Masson-Delmotte, P. Zhai, A. Pirani, S. L. Connors, C. Péan, S. Berger, N. Caud, Y. Chen, L. Goldfarb, M. I. Gomis, M. Huang, K. Leitzell, E. Lonnoy, J. B. R. Matthews, T. K. Maycock, T. Waterfield, O. Yelekçi, R. Yu, and B. Zhos, Cambridge: Cambridge University Press.

IPCC (2022), *Climate Change 2022: Mitigation of Climate Change. Working Group III Contribution to the Sixth Assessment Report of the Intergovernmental Panel on Climate Change* [J. Shea et al., drafting authors], Geneva: IPCC, www.ipcc.ch/report/sixth-assessment-report-working-group-3/., accessed June 3, 2024.

Johansen, L. (1978), *Lectures on Macroeconomic Planning, Part 2*, Amsterdam: North-Holland.

Kadane, J., M. Shervish, and T. Seidenfeld (2008), "Is Ignorance Bliss?" *Journal of Philosophy*, 105, 5–36.

Kaldor, N. (1939), "Welfare Propositions in Economics and Interpersonal Comparisons of Utility," *Economic Journal*, 49, 549–552.

Kaplan, J. (1967), "Decision Theory and the Factfinding Process," *Stanford Law Review*, 20, 1065–1092.

Kaplow, L. (2011), "Burden of Proof," *Yale Law Journal*, 121, 738–859.

Karlin, S. and H. Rubin (1956), "The Theory of Decision Procedures for Distributions with Monotone Likelihood Ratio," *Annals of Mathematical Statistics*, 27, 272–299.

Keane, M. (2011), "Labor Supply and Taxes: A Survey," *Journal of Economic Literature*, 49, 961–1075.

Keeling, M. and A. Shattock (2012), "Optimal but Unequitable Prophylactic Distribution of Vaccine," *Epidemics*, 4, 75–85.

Kessler, R. and H. Wittchen (2002), "Patterns and Correlates of Generalized Anxiety Disorder in Community Samples," *Journal of Clinical Psychiatry*, 63, 4–10.

Kitagawa, T. (2021), "The Identification Region of the Potential Outcome Distributions under Instrument Independence," *Journal of Econometrics*, 225, 231–253.

Kitagawa, T. and A. Tetenov (2018), "Who Should Be Treated? Empirical Welfare Maximization Methods for Treatment Choice," *Econometrica*, 86, 591–616.

Knowles, J., N. Persico, and P. Todd (2001), "Racial Bias in Motor Vehicle Searches: Theory and Evidence," *Journal of Political Economy*, 109, 203–229.

Knutti, R. (2016), "The End of Model Democracy?" *Climatic Change*, 102, 395–404.

Knutti, R., R. Furrer, C. Tebaldi, J. Cermak, and G. Meehl (2010), "Challenges in Combining Projections from Multiple Climate Models," *Journal of Climate*, 23, 2739–2758.

Koopmans, T. (1949), "Identification Problems in Economic Model Construction," *Econometrica*, 17, 125–144.
Kreps, D. (1988), *Notes on the Theory of Choice*. Boulder, CO: Westview Press.
Kunda, Z. (1990), "The Case for Motivated Reasoning," *Psychological Bulletin*, 108, 480–498.
Kuznets, S. (1948), "Discussion of the New Department of Commerce Income Series," *Review of Economics and Statistics*, 30, 151–179.
Lee, J. et al. (2021), "Future Global Climate: Scenario-Based Projections and Near-Term Information," *Climate Change 2021: The Physical Science Basis. Contribution of Working Group I to the Sixth Assessment Report of the Intergovernmental Panel on Climate Change*, ed. V. Masson-Delmotte, P. Zhai, A. Pirani, S. L. Connors, C. Péan, S. Berger, N. Caud, Y. Chen, L. Goldfarb, M. I. Gomis, M. Huang, K. Leitzell, E. Lonnoy, J. B. R. Matthews, T. K. Maycock, T. Waterfield, O. Yelekçi, R. Yu, B. Zhou, Cambridge: Cambridge University Press., 553–672.
Li, S., V. Litvin, and C. Manski (2023), "Partial Identification of Personalized Treatment Response with Trial-Reported Analyses of Binary Subgroups," *Epidemiology*, 34, 319–324.
Lochner, L. (2007), "Individual Perceptions of the Criminal Justice System," *American Economic Review*, 97, 444–460.
Loeb, M. et al. (2010), "Effect of Influenza Vaccination of Children on Infection Rates in Hutterite Communities: A Randomized Trial," *Journal of the American Medical Association*, 303, 943–950.
Lott, J. (2010), *More Guns, Less Crime: Understanding Crime and Gun-Control Laws*, Chicago, IL: University of Chicago Press.
Lott, J. and D. Mustard (1997), "Crime, Deterrence and Right-to-Carry Concealed Handguns," *Journal of Legal Studies*, 26, 1–68.
Manski, C. (1988), "Ordinal Utility Models of Decision Making under Uncertainty," *Theory and Decision*, 25, 79–104.
Manski, C. (1990), "Nonparametric Bounds on Treatment Effects," *American Economic Review Papers and Proceedings*, 80, 319–323.
Manski, C. (1993), "Adolescent Econometricians: How Do Youth Infer the Returns to Schooling?" in C. Clotfelter and M. Rothschild (eds.), *Studies of Supply and Demand in Higher Education*, Chicago, IL: University of Chicago Press, 43–57.
Manski, C. (1995), *Identification Problems in the Social Sciences*, Cambridge, MA: Harvard University Press.
Manski, C. (1996), "Learning about Treatment Effects from Experiments with Random Assignment of Treatments," *Journal of Human Resources*, 31, 707–733.
Manski, C. (1997), "Monotone Treatment Response," *Econometrica*, 65, 1311–1334.
Manski, C. (1999), "Analysis of Choice Expectations in Incomplete Scenarios," *Journal of Risk and Uncertainty*, 19, 49–65.
Manski, C. (2000), "Identification Problems and Decisions under Ambiguity: Empirical Analysis of Treatment Response and Normative Analysis of Treatment Choice," *Journal of Econometrics*, 95, 415–442.

Manski, C. (2003), *Partial Identification of Probability Distributions*, New York: Springer-Verlag.
Manski, C. (2004a), "Measuring Expectations," *Econometrica*, 72, 1329–1376.
Manski, C. (2004b), "Statistical Treatment Rules for Heterogeneous Populations," *Econometrica*, 72, 221–246.
Manski, C. (2005a), "Optimal Search Profiling with Linear Deterrence." *American Economic Review Papers and Proceedings*, 95, 122–126.
Manski, C. (2005b), *Social Choice with Partial Knowledge of Treatment Response*, Princeton, NJ: Princeton University Press.
Manski, C. (2006), "Search Profiling with Partial Knowledge of Deterrence," *Economic Journal*, 116, F385–F401.
Manski, C. (2007a), *Identification for Prediction and Decision*, Cambridge, MA: Harvard University Press.
Manski, C. (2007b), "Minimax-Regret Treatment Choice with Missing Outcome Data," *Journal of Econometrics*, 139, 105–115.
Manski, C. (2007c), "Partial Identification of Counterfactual Choice Probabilities," *International Economic Review*, 48, 1393–1410.
Manski, C. (2008), "Studying Treatment Response to Inform Treatment Choice," *Annales D'Économie et de Statistique*, 91–92, 93–105.
Manski, C. (2009), "Diversified Treatment under Ambiguity," *International Economic Review*, 50, 1013–1041.
Manski, C. (2010), "Vaccination with Partial Knowledge of External Effectiveness," *Proceedings of the National Academy of Sciences*, 107, 3953–3960.
Manski, C. (2011a), "Actualist Rationality," *Theory and Decision*, 71, 195–210.
Manski, C. (2011b), "Policy Analysis with Incredible Certitude," *Economic Journal*, 121, F261–F289.
Manski, C. (2013a), "Diagnostic Testing and Treatment under Ambiguity: Using Decision Analysis to Inform Clinical Practice," *Proceedings of the National Academy of Sciences*, 110, 2064–2069.
Manski, C. (2013b), "Identification of Treatment Response with Social Interactions," *Econometrics Journal*, 16, S1–S23.
Manski, C. (2013c), *Public Policy in an Uncertain World: Analysis and Decisions*, Cambridge, MA: Harvard University Press.
Manski, C. (2014a), "Choosing Size of Government under Ambiguity: Infrastructure Spending and Income Taxation," *Economic Journal*, 124, 359–376.
Manski, C. (2014b), "Identification of Income-Leisure Preferences and Evaluation of Income Tax Policy," *Quantitative Economics*, 5, 145–174.
Manski, C. (2015a), "Communicating Uncertainty in Official Economic Statistics: An Appraisal Fifty Years after Morgenstern," *Journal of Economic Literature*, 53, 631–653.
Manski, C. (2015b), "Narrow or Broad Cost-Benefit Analysis?" *Criminology and Public Policy*, 14, 647–651.
Manski, C. (2015c), "Randomizing Regulatory Approval for Diversification and Deterrence," *Journal of Legal Studies*, 44, S367–S385.
Manski, C. (2016), "Credible Interval Estimates for Official Statistics with Survey Nonresponse," *Journal of Econometrics*, 191, 293–301.

Manski, C. (2017), "Mandating Vaccination with Unknown Indirect Effects," *Journal of Public Economics Theory*, 19, 603–619.

Manski, C. (2018a), "Credible Ecological Inference for Medical Decisions with Personalized Risk Assessment," *Quantitative Economics*, 9, 541–569.

Manski, C. (2018b), "Survey Measurement of Probabilistic Macroeconomic Expectations: Progress and Promise," *NBER Macroeconomics Annual*, 32, 411–471.

Manski, C. (2019a), "Communicating Uncertainty in Policy Analysis," *Proceedings of the National Academy of Sciences*, 116, 7634–7641.

Manski, C. (2019b), *Patient Care under Uncertainty*, Princeton, NJ: Princeton University Press.

Manski, C. (2019c), "Treatment Choice with Trial Data: Statistical Decision Theory Should Supplant Hypothesis Testing," *American Statistician*, 73, 296–304.

Manski, C. (2020a), "Adaptive Diversification of COVID-19 Policy," @ *VoxEU*, June 12, https://cepr.org/voxeu/columns/adaptive-diversification-covid-19-policy, accessed December 23, 2023.

Manski, C. (2020b), "COVID-19 Policy Must Take *All* Impacts into Account," *Scientific American*, March 28, https://blogs.scientificamerican.com/observations/covid-19-policy-must-take-all-impacts-into-account/, accessed December 23, 2023.

Manski, C. (2020c), "Forming COVID-19 Policy under Uncertainty," *Journal of Benefit-Cost Analysis*, 11, 341–356.

Manski, C. (2020d), "Judicial and Clinical Decision Making under Uncertainty," *Journal of Institutional and Theoretical Economics*, 176, 33–43.

Manski, C. (2020e), "The Lure of Incredible Certitude," *Economics and Philosophy*, 36, 216–245.

Manski, C. (2020f), "Towards Credible Patient-Centered Meta-Analysis," *Epidemiology*, 31, 345–352.

Manski, C. (2021a), "Bounding the Accuracy of Diagnostic Tests, with Application to COVID-19 Antibody Tests," *Epidemiology*, 32, 162–167.

Manski, C. (2021b), "Econometrics for Decision Making: Building Foundations Sketched by Haavelmo and Wald," *Econometrica*, 89, 2827–2853.

Manski, C. (2022), "Patient-Centered Appraisal of Race-Free Clinical Risk Assessment," *Health Economics*, 31, 2109–2114.

Manski, C. (2023), "Probabilistic Prediction for Binary Treatment Choice: With Focus on Personalized Medicine," *Journal of Econometrics*, 234, 647–663.

Manski, C. (2024), "Inference with Missing Data: The Allure of Making Stuff Up," *Journal of Labor Economics*.

Manski, C. and S. Lerman (1977), "The Estimation of Choice Probabilities from Choice Based Samples," *Econometrica*, 45, 1977–1988.

Manski, C. and F. Molinari (2010), "Rounding Probabilistic Expectations in Surveys," *Journal of Business and Economic Statistics*, 28, 219–231.

Manski, C. and F. Molinari (2021), "Estimating the COVID-19 Infection Rate: Anatomy of an Inference Problem," *Journal of Econometrics*, 220, 181–192.

Manski, C. and D. Nagin (1998), "Bounding Disagreements about Treatment Effects: A Case Study of Sentencing and Recidivism," *Sociological Methodology*, 28, 99–137.

Manski, C. and D. Nagin (2017), "Assessing Benefits, Costs, and Disparate Racial Impacts of Confrontational Proactive Policing," *Proceedings of the National Academy of Sciences*, 114, 9308–9313.

Manski, C. and J. Pepper (2000), "Monotone Instrumental Variables: With an Application to the Returns to Schooling," *Econometrica*, 68, 997–1010.

Manski, C. and J. Pepper (2013), "Deterrence and the Death Penalty: Partial Identification Analysis Using Repeated Cross Sections," *Journal of Quantitative Criminology*, 29, 123–141.

Manski, C. and J. Pepper (2018), "How Do Right-to-Carry Laws Affect Crime Rates? Coping with Ambiguity Using Bounded-Variation Assumptions," *Review of Economics and Statistics*, 100, 232–244.

Manski, C. and E. Sheshinski (2023), "Optimal Paternalism in a Population with Bounded Rationality: With Focus on Discrete Choice," *National Bureau of Economic Research Working Paper* 31349, October.

Manski, C. and A. Tetenov (2007), "Admissible Treatment Rules for a Risk-Averse Planner with Experimental Data on an Innovation," *Journal of Statistical Planning and Inference*, 137, 1998–2010.

Manski, C. and A. Tetenov (2016), "Sufficient Trial Size to Inform Clinical Practice," *Proceedings of the National Academy of Sciences*, 113, 10518–10523.

Manski, C. and A. Tetenov (2019), "Trial Size for Near-Optimal Treatment: Reconsidering MSLT-II," *American Statistician*, 73, 305–311.

Manski, C. and A. Tetenov (2021), "Statistical Decision Properties of Imprecise Trials Assessing Coronavirus 2019 (COVID-19) Drugs," *Value in Health*, 24, 641–647.

Manski, C. and A. Tetenov (2023), "Statistical Decision Theory Respecting Stochastic Dominance," *Japanese Economic Review*, 74, 447–469.

Manski, C., J. Mullahy, and A. Venkataramani (2023), "Using Measures of Race to Make Clinical Predictions: Decision Making, Patient Health, and Fairness," *Proceedings of the National Academy of Sciences*, 120, www.pnas.org/doi/10.1073/pnas.2303370120.

Manski, C., A. Sanstad, and S. DeCanio (2021), "Addressing Partial Identification in Climate Modeling and Policy Analysis," *Proceedings of the National Academy of Sciences*, 118, doi:10.1073/pnas.2022886118.

Manski, C., A. Tambur, and M. Gmeiner (2019), "Predicting Kidney Transplant Outcomes with Partial Knowledge of HLA Mismatch," *Proceedings of the National Academy of Sciences*, 116, 20339–20345.

Marshall, A. (1890), *Principles of Economics*, London: Macmillan & Co.

Materson, B. et al. (1993), "Single-Drug Therapy for Hypertension in Men: A Comparison of Six Antihypertensive Agents with Placebo," *New England Journal of Medicine*, 328, 914–921.

Matthews, H., N. Gillett, P. Stott, and K. Zickfeld (2009), "The Proportionality of Global Warming to Cumulative Carbon Emissions," *Nature*, 459, 829–832.

May, T. and R. Silverman (2005), "Free-Riding, Fairness, and the Rights of Minority Groups in Exemption from Mandatory Childhood Vaccination," *Human Vaccines*, 1, 12–15.

McFadden, D. (1974), "Conditional Logit Analysis of Qualitative Choice Behavior," in P. Zarembka (ed.), *Frontiers in Econometrics*, New York: Academic Press, 105–142.

Meghir, C. and D. Phillips (2010), "Labour Supply and Taxes," in T. Besley, R. Blundell, M. Gammie, and J. Poterba (eds.), *Dimensions of Tax Design: The Mirrlees Review*, Oxford: Oxford University Press, 202–274.

Meinshausen, M. et al. (2011), "The RCP Greenhouse Gas Concentrations and Their Extensions from 1765 to 2300," *Climatic Change*, 109, 213–241.

Mirrlees, J. (1971), "An Exploration in the Theory of Optimal Income Taxation," *Review of Economic Studies*, 38, 175–208.

Molinari, F. (2020), "Microeconometrics with Partial Identification," in S. Durlauf, L. Hansen, J. Heckman, and R. Matzkin(eds.), *Handbook of Econometrics*, Vol. 7A, Amsterdam: Elsevier, 355–486.

Mongin, P. and M. Pivato (2016), "Social Evaluation under Risk and Uncertainty," in M. Adler and M. Fleurbaey (eds.), *The Oxford Handbook of Well-Being and Public Policy*, Oxford: Oxford University Press, 711–745.

Morgenstern, O. (1950), *On the Accuracy of Economic Observations*. Princeton, NJ: Princeton University Press.

Morgenstern, O. (1963), *On the Accuracy of Economic Observations: Second Edition*. Princeton, NJ: Princeton University Press.

Natapoff, A. (2012), "Misdemeanors," *Southern California Law Review*, 85, 101–163.

National Academies of Sciences, Engineering, and Medicine (2023), *Accelerating Decarbonization in the United States: Technology, Policy, and Societal Dimensions*, Washington, DC: National Academies Press, https://doi.org/10.17226/25931.

National Research Council (1999), *Assessment of Two Cost-Effectiveness Studies on Cocaine Control Policy*, Committee on Data and Research for Policy on Illegal Drugs, C. F. Manski, J. V. Pepper, and Y. Thomas (eds.), Committee on Law and Justice and Committee on National Statistics, Commission on Behavioral and Social Sciences and Education, Washington, DC: National Academy Press.

National Research Council (2005), *Firearms and Violence: A Critical Review*, ed. C. Wellford, J. Pepper, and C. Petrie, Washington, DC: National Academy Press.

National Research Council (2012), *Deterrence and the Death Penalty*, Washington, DC: National Academies Press.

National Research Council (2013), *Principles and Practices for a Federal Statistical Agency: Fifth Edition*, Washington, DC: National Academies Press.

Nordhaus, W. (1991), "To Slow or Not to Slow: The Economics of the Greenhouse Effect," *Economic Journal*, 101, 920–937.

Nordhaus, W. (1994), *Managing the Global Commons: The Economics of Climate Change*, Cambridge, MA: MIT Press.

Nordhaus, W. (2007), "A Review of the *Stern Review on the Economics of Climate Change*," *Journal of Economic Literature*, 45, 686–702.

Nordhaus, W. (2008), *A Question of Balance: Weighing the Options on Global Warming Policy*, New Haven, CT: Yale University Press.

Nordhaus, W. (2019), "Climate Change: The Ultimate Challenge for Economics," *American Economic Review*, 109, 1991–2014.

Nordhaus, W. and A. Moffat (2017), A Survey of Global Impacts of Climate Change: Replication, Survey Methods, and a Statistical Analysis. NBER Working Paper No. 23646.

Nyarko, Y. and A. Schotter (2002), "An Experimental Study of Belief Learning Using Elicited Beliefs," *Econometrica*, 70, 971–1005.

O'Donoghue, T. and M. Rabin (2003), "Studying Optimal Paternalism, Illustrated by a Model of Sin Taxes," *American Economic Review (Papers and Proceedings)*, 93, 186–191.

Parker, W. (2006), "Understanding Pluralism in Climate Modeling," *Foundations of Science*, 11, 349–368.

Parmigiani, G. and L. Inoue (2009), *Decision Theory: Principles and Approaches*, New York: Wiley.

Patel, R., I. Longini, and E. Halloran (2005), "Finding Optimal Vaccination Strategies for Pandemic Influenza Using Genetic Algorithms," *Journal of Theoretical Biology*, 234, 201–212.

Persico, N. (2002), "Racial Profiling, Fairness, and the Effectiveness of Policing," *American Economic Review*, 92, 1472–1497.

Phelps, C. and A. Mushlin (1988), "Focusing Technology Assessment Using Medical Decision Theory," *Medical Decision Making*, 8, 279–289.

Philipson, T. (2000), "Economic Epidemiology and Infectious Diseases," in A. Culyer and J. Newhouse (eds.), *Handbook of Health Economics*, Vol. 1, Amsterdam, North-Holland: Elsevier, 1761–1799.

Pindyck, R. (2013), "Climate Change Policy: What Do the Models Tell Us?" *Journal of Economic Literature*, 51, 860–872.

Pindyck, R. (2017), "The Use and Misuse of Models for Climate Policy," *Review of Environmental Economics and Policy*, 11, 100–114.

Pindyck, R. (2022), *Climate Future: Averting and Adapting to Climate Change*, Oxford: Oxford University Press.

Ramsey, F. (1928), "A Mathematical Theory of Saving," *Economic Journal*, 38, 543–559.

Rawls, J. (1971), *A Theory of Justice*, Cambridge, MA: Harvard University Press.

Reiersol, O. (1945), "Confluence Analysis by Means of Instrumental Sets of Variables," *Arkiv fur Matematik, Astronomi Och Fysik*, 32A(4), 1–119.

Reiss, D. and A. Caplan (2020), "Considerations in Mandating a New Covid-19 Vaccine in the USA for Children and Adults," *Journal of Law and the Biosciences*, 7, 1–9, https://doi.org/10.1093/jlb/lsaa025.

Riahi, K. et al., (2011), "RCP 8.5 – A Scenario of Comparatively High Greenhouse Gas Emission," *Climatic Change*, 109, 33–57.

Robbins, L. (1930), "On the Elasticity of Demand for Income in Terms of Effort," *Economica*, 29, 123–129.

Robins, J. (1989), "The Analysis of Randomized and Non-randomized AIDS Treatment Trials Using a New Approach to Causal Inference in Longitudinal Studies," in L. Sechrest, H. Freeman, and A. Mulley (eds.), *Health Service Research Methodology: A Focus on AIDS*, Washington, DC: NCHSR, U.S. Public Health Service, 113–159.

Roosevelt, T. (1912), "Introduction," in C. McCarthy (ed.), *The Wisconsin Idea*, New York: Macmillan, vii–xi.

Rothenberg, J. (1961), *The Measurement of Social Welfare*, Englewood Cliffs, NJ: Prentice-Hall.

Rubin, D. (1978), "Bayesian Inference for Causal Effects: The Role of Randomization," *Annals of Statistics*, 6, 34–58.

Rydell, C. and S. Everingham (1994), *Controlling Cocaine*, Report prepared for the Office of National Drug Control Policy and the U.S. Army, Santa Monica, CA: RAND Corporation.

Samuelson, P. (1938), "A Note on the Pure Theory of Consumer Behavior," *Economica*, 5, 61–71.

Samuelson, P. (1948), "Consumption Theory in Terms of Revealed Preferences," *Economica*, 15, 243–253.

Sanderson, B. (2018), "Uncertainty Quantification in Multi-model Ensembles," *Oxford Research Encyclopedia of Climate Science*, doi:10.1093/acrefore/9780190228620.013.707.

Savage, L. (1951), "The Theory of Statistical Decision," *Journal of the American Statistical Association*, 46, 55–67.

Savage, L. (1954), *The Foundations of Statistics*, New York: Wiley.

Schlag, K. (2006), "Eleven – Tests Needed for a Recommendation," *European University Institute Working Paper* ECO No. 2006/2.

Schotter, A., and I. Trevino (2014), "Belief Elicitation in the Laboratory," *Annual Review of Economics*, 6, 103–128.

Scuffham, P. and P. West (2002), "Economic Evaluation of Strategies for the Control and Management of Influenza in Europe," *Vaccine*, 20, 2562–2578.

Seeskin, Z. and B. Spencer (2015), "Effects of Census Accuracy on Apportionment of Congress and Allocations of Federal Funds," Working Paper Series 15-05, Evanston, IL: Institute for Policy Research, Northwestern University.

Sen, A. (1973), "Behaviour and the Concept of Preference," *Economica*, 40, 241–259.

Sen, A. (1977), "On Weights and Measures: Informational Constraints in Social Welfare Analysis," *Econometrica*, 45, 1539–1572.

Sen, A. (1993), "Internal Consistency of Choice," *Econometrica*, 61, 495–521.

Sen, A. (2002), "Why Health Equity?" *Health Economics*, 11, 659–666.

Simon, H. (1955), "A Behavioral Model of Rational Choice," *Quarterly Journal of Economics*, 69, 99–118.

Smith, D. and R. Paternoster (1990), "Formal Processing and Future Delinquency: Deviance Amplification as Selection Artifact," *Law and Society Review*, 24, 1109–1131.

Spiegelhalter D., L. Freedman, and M. Parmar (1994), "Bayesian Approaches to Randomized Trials" (with discussion), *Journal of the Royal Statistics Society Series A*, 157, 357–416.

Stern, N. (1986), "On the Specification of Labour Supply Functions," in R. Blundell and I. Walker (eds.), *Unemployment, Search and Labour Supply*, Cambridge: Cambridge University Press, 143–189.

Stern, N. (2007), *The Economics of Climate Change: The Stern Review*, Cambridge: Cambridge University Press.

Stewart, A. (2009), "Mandatory Vaccination of Health Care Workers." *New England Journal of Medicine*, 361, 2015–2017.

Stoye, J. (2009), "Minimax Regret Treatment Choice with Finite Samples," *Journal of Econometrics*, 151, 70–81.

Stoye, J. (2012), "Minimax Regret Treatment Choice with Covariates or with Limited Validity of Experiments," *Journal of Econometrics*, 166, 138–156.

Subcommittee on National Security, International Affairs, and Criminal Justice (1996), *Hearing before the Committee on Governmental Reform and Oversight*. U.S. House of Representatives, Washington, DC: U.S. Government Printing Office.

Subcommittee on National Security, International Affairs, and Criminal Justice (1998), *Hearing before the Committee on Governmental Reform and Oversight*. U.S. House of Representatives, Washington, DC: U.S. Government Printing Office.

Sugden, R. (1990), "Rational Choice: A Survey of Contributions from Economics and Philosophy," *Economic Journal*, 101, 751–785.

Swinburne, R. (1997), *Simplicity as Evidence for Truth*, Milwaukee, WI: Marquette University Press.

Tamer, E. (2010), "Partial Identification in Econometrics," *Annual Review of Economics*, 2, 167–195.

Taylor, K., R. Stouffer, and G. Meehl (2012), "An Overview of CMIP5 and the Experimental Design," *Bulletin of the American Meteorological Society*, 93, 485–498.

Tebaldi, C. and R. Knutti (2007), "The Use of the Multi-model Ensemble in Probabilistic Climate Projections," *Philosophical Transactions of the Royal Society A*, 365, 2053–2075.

Thaler, R. and C. Sunstein (2003), "Libertarian Paternalism," *American Economic Review (Papers and Proceedings)*, 93, 175–179.

Tittle, C. (1980), "Labelling and Crime: An Empirical Evaluation," in W. Gove (ed.), *The Labelling of Deviance*, 2nd ed., Beverly Hill, CA: Sage Publications.

Tobin, J. (1970), "On Limiting the Domain of Inequality," *Journal of Law & Economics*, 13, 263–278.

Tukey, J. (1962), "The Future of Data Analysis," *Annals of Mathematical Statistics*, 33, 1–67.

Tversky, A. and D. Kahneman (1974), "Judgment under Uncertainty: Heuristics and Biases," *Science*, 185, 1124–1131.

U.S. Bureau of Labor Statistics (2023), "Employment Situation Technical Note," www.bls.gov/news.release/empsit.tn.htm, accessed July 8, 2023.

US Census Bureau (2011), *Current Housing Reports, Series H150/09, American Housing Survey for the United States: 2009*, Washington, DC: U.S. Government Printing Office.

U.S. Department of Transportation (2023), "What Is a Benefit-Cost Analysis," www.transportation.gov/grants/dot-navigator/what-is-a-benefit-cost-analysis, accessed July 16, 2023.

U.S. Food and Drug Administration (2010), Guidance for the Use of Bayesian Statistics in Medical Device Clinical Trials, www.fda.gov/regulatory-information/search-fda-guidance-documents/guidance-use-bayesian-statistics-medical-device-clinical-trials, accessed January 21, 2024.

U.S. Food and Drug Administration (2013), *Structured Approach to Benefit-Risk Assessment in Drug Regulatory Decision-Making*, www.fda.gov/downloads/forindustry/userfees/prescriptiondruguserfee/ucm329758.pdf, accessed February 16, 2024.

U.S. Food and Drug Administration (2017), "The FDA's Drug Review Process: Ensuring Drugs Are Safe and Effective," www.fda.gov/drugs/information-consumers-and-patients-drugs/fdas-drug-review-process-ensuring-drugs-are-safe-and-effective, accessed February 16, 2024.

U.S. Food and Drug Administration (2020), "Postmarketing Surveillance Programs," www.fda.gov/drugs/surveillance/postmarketing-surveillance-programs, accessed February 16, 2024.

U.S. Office of Management and Budget (2003), "U.S. Office of Management and Budget Circular A-4: Regulatory Analysis," https://obamawhitehouse.archives.gov/omb/circulars_a004_a-4/, accessed June 3, 2024.

Vamos, C., R. McDermott, and E. Daley (2008), "The HPV Vaccine: Framing the Arguments FOR and AGAINST Mandatory Vaccination of All Middle School Girls," *Journal of School Health*, 78, 302–309.

Van der Heiden, C., P. Muris, and H. van der Molen (2012), "Randomized Controlled Trial on the Effectiveness of Metacognitive Therapy and Intolerance-of-Uncertainty Therapy for Generalized Anxiety Disorder," *Behaviour Research and Therapy*, 50, 100–109.

van der Klaauw, W. (2012), "On the Use of Expectations Data in Estimating Structural Dynamic Models," *Journal of Labor Economics*, 30, 521–554.

van der Klaauw, W. and K. Wolpin (2008), "Social Security and the Retirement and Savings Behavior of Low-Income Households," *Journal of Econometrics*, 145, 21–42.

Varian, H. (1974), "Equity, Envy, and Efficiency," *Journal of Economic Theory*, 9, 63–91.

Varian, H. (1982), "The Nonparametric Approach to Demand Analysis," *Econometrica*, 50, 945–973.

Von Neumann, J. and O. Morgenstern (1944), *Theory of Games and Economic Behavior*, Princeton, NJ: Princeton University Press.

Vyas, D., L. Eisenstein, and D. Jones (2020), "Hidden in Plain Sight – Reconsidering the Use of Race Correction in Clinical Algorithms," *New England Journal of Medicine*, 383, 874–882.

Wald, A. (1950), *Statistical Decision Functions*, New York: Wiley.

Walley, P. (1991), *Statistical Reasoning with Imprecise Probabilities*, New York: Chapman & Hall.

Wallsten, T., B. Forsythe, and D. Budescu (1983), "Stability and Coherence of Health Experts' Upper and Lower Subjective Probabilities about Dose-response Functions," *Organizational Behavior and Human Performance*, 31, 227–302.

Washington Post (2020), "The Patchwork of State Reopenings Is a Deadly Game of Trial and Error," May 11, www.washingtonpost.com/opinions/the-patchwork-of-state-reopenings-is-a-deadly-game-of-trial-and-error/2020/05/11/5e255288-9179-11ea-a0bc-4e9ad4866d21_story.html, accessed June 3, 2024.

Washington State Board of Health (2006), *Immunization Advisory Committee: Criteria for Reviewing Antigens for Potential Inclusion in WAC 246-100-166*, https://sboh.wa.gov/sites/default/files/2022-01/ImmunizationCriteria-Update2017-Final.pdf, accessed February 16, 2024.

Wasserstein, R. and N. Lazar (2016), "The ASA's Statement on p-Values: Context, Process, and Purpose," *American Statistician*, 70, 129–133.

Watson, J. and C. Holmes (2016), "Approximate Models and Robust Decisions," *Statistical Science*, 31, 465–489.

Weisbach, D. and C. Sunstein (2009), "Climate Change and Discounting the Future: A Guide for the Perplexed," *Yale Law and Policy Review*, 27, 433.

Weitzman, M. (2001), "Gamma Discounting," *American Economic Review*, 91, 260–271.

Weitzman, M. (2007), "A Review of *The Stern Review on the Economics of Climate Change*," *Journal of Economic Literature*, 45, 703–724.

Weyant, J. (2017), "Some Contributions of Integrated Assessment Models of Global Climate Change," *Review of Environmental Economics and Policy*, 11, 115–137.

Whitchurch, E., T. Wilson, and D. Gilbert (2011), "He Loves Me, He Loves Me Not ...: Uncertainty Can Increase Romantic Attraction," *Psychological Science*, 22, 172–175.

Wilson, T., D. Centerbar, D. Kermer, and D. Gilbert (2005), "The Pleasures of Uncertainty: Prolonging Positive Moods in Ways People Do Not Anticipate," *Journal of Personality and Social Psychology*, 88, 5–21.

Wiswall, M. and B. Zafar (2015), "Determinants of College Major Choice: Identification Using an Information Experiment," *Review of Economic Studies*, 82, 791–824.

Woodbury, S. and R. Spiegelman (1987), "Bonuses to Workers and Employers to Reduce Unemployment: Randomized Trials in Illinois," *American Economic Review*, 77, 513–530.

Wright, J. (2013), "Unseasonal Seasonals?" *Brookings Papers on Economic Activity*, Fall, 65–126.

Zafar, B. (2013), "College Major Choice and the Gender Gap," *Journal of Human Resources*, 48, 545–595.

Zhou, K., J. Doyle, and K. Glover (1996), *Robust and Optimal Control*, Englewood Cliffs, NJ: Prentice Hall.

Zinman, B. et al. (2015), "Empagliflozin, Cardiovascular Outcomes, and Mortality in Type 2 Diabetes," *New England Journal of Medicine*, 373, 2117–2128.

Index

ε-optimal rule, 141

Acemoglu, D., 219
actual choice behavior, 11
actualist rationality, 11
adaptive diversification
　AMR, 127
　by Bayesian planning, 127
　implementation of, 127
　life-threatening disease, 127–129
　regulatory approval, 129–130
adaptive minimax regret (AMR), 127, 128
Administrative Procedure Act (APA), 129
Afriat, S., 96
Aikman, D., 41
Akerlof, G., 60
Althouse, B., 182
American Progressive movement, 126
AMR. *See* adaptive minimax regret (AMR)
Anderson, R., 186
Aneja, A., 51
Angrist, J., 58
APA. *See* Administrative Procedure Act (APA)
Armantier, O., 62, 111
Arrow, K., 25, 29, 151, 198, 200
as-if optimization, 62–63
　financial accounting, 63–64
ATEs. *See* average treatment effects (ATEs)
Atkinson, A., 5
attributable risk, 56
average treatment effect (ATE), 69, 71, 137, 139

axiomatic decision theory, 8–10
axiomatic theory, 7, 10, 11
　planning, 11–13

Backhouse, R., A., 31
Balke, A., 73, 82
Ball, F., 182
Bar-Anan, Y., 60
Barlevy, G., 4
Barro, R., 32
basic revealed preference analysis. *See also* revealed-preference analysis
　absence of assumptions, 103
　labor supply, 104–105
　preference distribution, restrictions, 105–107
　proposed tax schedule, 104–105
　status quo tax policy, 103
　utilitarian policy evaluation, 107
Basu, A., 153
Bayes rules, 140
Bayesian analysis, 134–135
Bayesian planning
　mean treatment response, 170
　x-pox, 121
BEA. *See* Bureau of Economic Analysis (BEA)
Becker, N., 182
before-and-after analysis, 49
Ben Akiva, M., 114
Bénabou, R., 60
benefit–cost analysis, 4, 5
benefit-risk assessment, 149
　qualitative *vs*. quantitative, 149

Index

Bentham, J., 25
Berger, J., 10, 11, 134, 135, 171
Bergstrom, C., 182
Bergstrom, T., 182
Berkson, J., 57
Berlin, J., 132
Bhattacharya, J., 74, 75
Binmore, K., 8, 12, 20
Black, D., 51
Blackstone, W., 160
Blass, A., 114
Blumstein, A., 48
Blundell, R., 102
Boulier, B., 182
bounded rationality, 29–30
bounded-variation assumptions, 50, 86–88
Brief, R., 63
Briggs, A., 161
Brito, D., 182, 184
broken windows policing, 165
Brown, E. C., xiv
Brunnermeier, M., 60
Bureau of Economic Analysis (BEA), 39, 40
Bureau of Labor Statistics, 39
Burtis, M., 159

Campbell, D., 58
Cao, B., 145, 146
Caplan, A., 183
Caplin, A., 60
carbon-climate response (CCR), 206
Cassidy, R., 117, 173, 175, 178, 179
CBO. *See* Congressional Budget Office (CBO)
CCR. *See* carbon-climate response (CCR)
Census Bureau, 39
Cerdeña, J., 161
CES. *See* Constant-Elasticity-of-Substitution (CES)
Chavel, C., 160
Chen, F., 184
Chernoff, H., 20
Chipman, J., 25
choice axioms, 12
choice behavior, analysis of, 7, 8, 93
choice set, 14
choice-based sampling, 56
Chomsky, N., 55
classical economic approach, 30
Climate Model Intercomparison Project Phase 5 (CMIP5), 206
climate models, 198–199

CMIP5. *See* Climate Model Intercomparison Project Phase 5 (CMIP5)
cocaine-control policy, 46–48
Cochrane system, 131
Cohen, J., 48
communicating uncertainty, 213–214
complete class theorems, 17
computational model
 details of, 206–208
 findings, 209
conceptual uncertainty, 43–44
confrontational proactive policing, 163–167
Congressional Budget Act of 1974, 38
Congressional Budget Office (CBO), 38–39
Connors, A., 74, 75
consequentialism, 125
consequentialist decision theory, 7
 choice set, 14
 decision criteria, 15–17
 minimax regret planning, 19–21
 state space, 14
 statistical decision theory, 17–19
 welfare function, 14
constant treatment response (CTR), 89–90
Constant-Elasticity-of-Substitution (CES), 101
conventional certitude, in official economic statistics
 CBO, 38–39
 conceptual uncertainty, 43–44
 economic statistics, 39–40
 permanent statistical uncertainty, 41–43
 statistical agencies, 45
 transitory statistical uncertainty, 40–41
conventional inference, 24
convicted juvenile offenders, 122–123
Cornfield, J., 57
covariate data, 78–81
covariate information, value of, 154–156
COVID-19 pandemic, 145–146, 183
 adoption policy, 219
 epidemiological and macroeconomic modeling, 219
 integrated assessment models, 220
 Response Team of Imperial College London, 217–219
Cox, D., 88
CPS. *See* Current Population Survey (CPS)
Craske, M., 59

credibility, 11, 12, 14, 30, 35, 43, 47, 66, 72, 75, 78, 81, 83, 99, 109, 146, 220
credible meta-analysis, 91–92
crime commission, rates of, 159
 frequentist risk assessment, 159
 legal precedents, 159–160
Cross P., 85
Croushore, D., 41
CTR. *See* constant treatment response (CTR)
Current Population Survey (CPS), 41–43

Daley, E., 183
data-invariant rules, 140
Datta, T., 182
DBP. *See* diastolic blood pressure (DBP)
death penalty, 48–50
Deaton, A., 58
DeCanio, S., 196, 197
decision criteria, 15–17
decision support systems, 214
decision theory, 6–7. *See also* axiomatic decision theory; consequentialist decision theory
 axiomatic theorists, 8–10
 consequentialist, 7
 consequentialist structure, 14–21
 institutional separation of research, 13–14
deep uncertainty, 22
DeGroot, M., 134
Delavande, A., 62, 111, 112
Delgado, C., 161
demand-control policy, 46
Dempster, A., 16
deontological ethics, 125
Department of Veteran Affairs (DVA), 79
 hypertension trial, 80
DerSimonian, R., 91
deterrent effect
 capital punishment, 50
 death penalty, 48–50
diagnostic testing and treatment
 ambiguity, 178–180
 two-stage optimization problem, 174–178
Diamond, P., xiv
diastolic blood pressure (DBP), 79
Dickens, W., 60
DID. *See* difference-in-difference (DID)
Dietz, S., 207
difference-in-difference (DID), 49

discount-rate uncertainty, 200–201
disparity aversion, 31
diversification of treatments. *See also* equal treatment of equals
 adaptive diversification, 126–130
 consequentialism, 125
 deontological ethics, 125
 ex ante, 124–125
 ex post equal treatment, 124–125
Domínguez-Rivera, P., 26
Dominitz, J., 163
Dubin, J., 82, 84
dueling certitudes, in criminal justice research
 deterrent effect of death penalty, 48–50
 IDA studies, 46–48
 RAND, 46–48
 RTC, 50–52
Duggan, M., 51
Duignan, B., 37
Durlauf, S., 51
DVA. *See* Department of Veteran Affairs (DVA)
Dynamic Integrated Climate Economy (DICE), 200

Eames, K., 182, 186
Earth System Models (ESMs), 206
effective reproduction rate, 185
effective vaccination rate, 187
eGFR. *See* estimated glomerular filtration rate (eGFR)
Eichenbaum, M., 219
Ellsberg, D., 9, 22
empirical research
 identification analysis, 21–23
empirical success (ES) rule, 135, 140
Environmental Protection Agency, 129
envy-free allocations of resources, 31
Epps, D., 160
equal treatment of equals, 31, 124–126
ESMs. *See* Earth System Models (ESMs)
ES rule. *See* empirical success (ES) rule
estimated glomerular filtration rate (eGFR), 161
ex ante treatment, 124–125
ex post equal treatment, 124–125
expression of uncertainty, 61–62
external validity, 53

fair allocations of resources, 31
Faries, M., 143

federal statistical agencies, 39–40
Ferguson, T., 134
financial accounting, 63–64
Financial Accounting Standards Board (2018), 64
Fine, P., 182, 186
Fischhoff, B., 61
Fisher, F., xiv
Fixler, D., 40
Fleiss, J., 56, 57
Fleurbaey, M., 10
Foley, D., 31
Food and Drug Administration Safety and Innovation Act of 2012, 148
fractional monotone rule, 139
Francis, P., 184
Freedman, L., 135
Friedman, M., 37, 38
Furman v. *Georgia* case, 48

GAD. *See* generalized anxiety disorder (GAD)
Gelbach, J., 159
generalized anxiety disorder (GAD), 59–60
GHG emissions. *See* greenhouse gas (GHG) emissions
Gigerenzer, G., 61
Gilbert, D., 60, 61
Gilbert, F., 102
Giustinelli, P., 112, 113
Gmeiner, M., 87
Goldberger, A., 72, 85
Goldfarb, R., 182
Gollier C., 60
Good, I., 170
greenhouse gas (GHG) emissions, 196
Gregg v. *Georgia* case, 48
Gul, F., 11

Hale, M., 160
Halloran, E., 182
Halpern, S., 132
Hansen, L., 4
Harsanyi, J.
  initial position arguments of, 27–29
Hausman, J., 35
Heal, G., 198, 201
Heckman, J., 58
herd immunity threshold (HIT), 186
heterogeneous decision makers
  conditional choice probabilities, 98–100

incomplete data, 98–100
utility theory, 97
Heymann, D., 182, 186
Hicks, J., 25
Hill, A., 182
HIT. *See* herd immunity threshold (HIT)
Hoffrage, U., 61
Holmes, C., 19
Horowitz, J., 78, 81
Hsieh, D., 57
Hudgens, M., 182
Hurd, M., 62, 111, 112
Hurwicz, L., 16
hypertension, trial comparing treatments for, 79–81
hypothesis tests
  medical decisions, 132–133
  Type I error, 132
  Type II error, 132
hypothetical choice behavior, 11, 12

IDA. *See* Institute for Defense Analyses (IDA)
identification analysis, concepts of, 21–23, 65
identification region, 66
identified set, 66
IIA. *See* independence of irrelevant alternatives (IIA)
illinois unemployment insurance (UI), 82–83
Imbens, G., 58
Immunization Action Coalition, 183
imprecise probabilities, 112–113
income-leisure preference, 100
income tax policy
  basic revealed preference analysis, 103–105
  labor supply, 100–103
  taxation, 100–103
incredible certitude
  as-if optimization, 62–64
  in philosophy, 36–38
  psychological rationales for, 59–62
  in religion, 36–38
  statistical agencies, 45
  study planning with, 4–6
independence of irrelevant alternatives (IIA), 20
individualistic treatment response (ITR), 88
initial position, 27–29
Inoue, L., 134
Institute for Defense Analyses (IDA), 46–48

Index

Institute of Medicine (IOM), 1, 149
institutional separation, 13–14
instrumental variables (IV), 72–75
integrated assessment (IA), 196
intention-to-treat, 83–84
Intergovernmental Panel on Climate
    Change (IPCC), 199
internal validity, 53
International Conference on
    Harmonisation, 132, 141
intersection bound, 73
intolerance of uncertainty (IU), 59–60
intolerance of uncertainty therapy (IUT), 60
Intriligator, M., 182, 184
Ioannidis, J., 133
IOM. *See* Institute of Medicine (IOM)
ITR. *See* individualistic treatment
    response (ITR)
IU. *See* intolerance of uncertainty (IU)
IUT. *See* intolerance of uncertainty
    therapy (IUT)
IV. *See* instrumental variables (IV)

Johnson, L. B., 35
Joint Committee on Taxation (JCT), 38
juvenile justice system, 69

Kadane, J., 170
Kahneman, D., 7, 61
Kaldor, N., 25
Kaldor-Hicks efficiency, 26–27
Kaplan, J., 158–160
Kaplow, L., 159
Karlawish, J., 132
Karlin, S., 139
Keane, M., 101
Kessler, R., 59
Kitagawa, T., 73, 82, 171
Kleinbölting, H., 61
Knightian uncertainty, 22
Knowles, J., 163
Kobayashi, B., 159
Koopmans, T., 21
Kreps, D., 8
Kunda, Z., 60
Kuznets, S., 45

labeling theory, 70
labor supply, 100–103
    proposed tax schedule, 104–105
laboratories of democracy, 126
Lach, S., 114

Laird, N., 91
LATE. *See* local average treatment
    effect (LATE)
Lazar, N., 133
Leahy, J., 60
Li, S., 84, 170
Litvin, V., 84, 170
local average treatment effect (LATE), 58
Lochner, L., 112
Loeb, M., 182
long term care (LTC), 113
Longini, I., 182
Lott, J., 51
LTC. *See* long term care (LTC)
lymph node dissection
    (lymphadenectomy), 143
Lyne, O., 182

MacGregor, D., 61
macroeconomic planning, 3
MaCurdy, T., 102
Manski, C., 2, 11, 13, 15, 18, 20, 22, 30,
    31, 36, 40, 42, 43, 48, 50, 52, 55,
    57, 58, 62, 63, 65–67, 69, 70, 72,
    73, 76–78, 81, 82, 84, 85, 87, 113,
    114, 117, 122, 123, 131, 132, 139,
    141–143, 145, 154, 162, 163, 165,
    167, 170, 171, 173, 175, 178, 179,
    196, 197
Marshall, A., 1
Materson, B., 79, 81
Matthews, H., 206
maximin criterion, 15, 16, 20, 123, 135,
    172. *See also* maximin rule
maximin rule, 136, 140. *See also*
    maximin criterion
maximin welfare, 27–29
May, R., 186
May, T., 183
McDermott, R., 183
McFadden, D., xiv, 57, 114
mean treatment response
    Bayesian planning, 170
    maximin problem, 168
    MMR planning, 169
    with data from trials
        missing outcome/covariate data, 78–81
        partial compliance, 81–84
        trial-reported findings, 84–88
    with observational data
        counterfactual outcomes, 67–69
        instrumental variables, 72–75

mean treatment response (cont.)
   monotone instrumental variables, 75–77
   monotone treatment response, 77–78
   recidivism, 69–71
   sentencing, 69–71
The Measurement of Social Welfare (Rothenberg), xiv
Meghir, C., 101
Meltzer, D., 153
meta-analysis, 54–55
Milner, A., 198, 201
minimax regret, 20, 63, 118, 119, 126, 140, 180, 194
minimax regret (MMR) criteria, 15, 16, 62, 119, 120, 122, 124, 127, 135, 179. *See also* minimax-regret rule
minimax regret (MMR) decisions
   consequentialist decision theory, 19–21
   decision rule, 203–204
   empirical and normative uncertainty, 204–205
   mean treatment response, 168, 169
   optimal-control problem, 202–203
   piecemeal decision making, 179–180
   SDF, 135–137
   surveillance/aggressive treatment, 172–173
   x-pox, 122–123
minimax regret rule, 140, 141. *See also* minimax regret criterion
Mirrlees, J., xiv, 26, 27, 31, 100
missing data, 35, 42, 66, 78–81
missing outcome, 78–81
MIV. *See* monotone instrumental variable (MIV)
MME. *See* multi-model ensemble (MME)
MMR decisions. *See* minimax regret (MMR) decisions
model democracy, 199
Molinari, F., 22, 113
Mongin, P., 5, 10
monotone instrumental variable (MIV), 75–77, 87
monotone treatment response (MTR), 77–78
monotone treatment rules, 139
monotone treatment selection (MTS), 76, 77
Moore, J., 25
Morgenstern, O., 8, 45
motivated reasoning, 60–61
MSLT-II. *See* Multicenter Selective Lymphadenectomy Trial II (MSLT-II)

MTR. *See* monotone treatment response (MTR)
MTS. *See* monotone treatment selection (MTS)
Muermann, A., 60
Mullahy, J., 31, 154, 162
Multicenter Selective Lymphadenectomy Trial II (MSLT-II), 143–145
multi-model ensemble (MME) analysis, 197, 199, 201
Mushlin, A., 153, 174, 175
Mustard, D., 51

Nagin, D., 48, 51, 69, 70, 73, 122, 123, 163, 165, 167
NASA, 221, 223
National Academies of Science, Engineering, and Medicine, 210
National Research Council (2012), 48
National Research Council (2013), 45
National Research Council Committee on Data and Research for Policy on Illegal Drugs, 47
near-optimal treatment choice, 141–142
new welfare economics, 25
New York State Ice Co. v. Liebmann, 126
nodal observation, 143
non personalist welfare functions, 30–31
non-pharmaceutical interventions (NPIs), 217, 218
non-sampling errors, 42
Nordhaus, W., 32, 201, 207
NPIs. *See* non-pharmaceutical interventions (NPIs)
Nyarko, Y., 111

O'Donoghue, T., 30
odds ratio, 56–58
Office of National Drug Control Policy (ONDCP), 46, 47
optimal paternalism, in populations, 29–30
optimal treatment
   choice between two treatments, 153–154
   confrontational proactive policing, 163–167
   covariate information, value of, 154–156
   crime commission, rates of, 157–160
   race as covariate risk prediction, 161–162
   surveillance/aggressive treatment, 156–157
   utilitarian treatment choice, 167–172
overconfidence bias, 61

Parker, J., 60
Parmar, M., 135
Parmigiani, G., 134
partial identification, 22–23
Patel, R., 182
Paternoster, R., 70
Patient Care under Uncertainty (Manski), xv
Patient Protection and Affordable Care Act of 2010, 38
Pearl, J., 73, 82
Pepper, J., 48, 50, 52, 76, 78, 87
permanent uncertainty, 41–43
Persico, N., 163
personal welfare, 93
personalism, 31
Pesendorfer, W., 11
Pfouts, R., 102
p-hacking, 133
Phelps, C., 153, 174, 175
Phillips, D., 101
philosophy of science, 37
piecemeal MMR decision making, 179–180
Pivato, M., 5, 10
policy problem, 196–198
pragmatic welfare, 31–32
predict behavior, 2
primacy of internal validity, 59–60
Principles of Economics (Marshall), 1
proactive policing, 164
probabilistic expectations, 110–112
The Probability Approach in Econometrics (Haavelmo), 21
psychological necessity, incredible certitude
  expression of uncertainty, 61–62
  intolerance of uncertainty, 59–60
  motivated reasoning, 60–61
public health, 56–58
Public Policy in an Uncertain World: Analysis and Decisions (Manski), xv

quality-adjusted life years (QALYS), 32

Rabin, M., 30
race
  confrontational proactive policing, impacts of, 163–167
  as covariate in risk prediction, 161–62
Ramsey formula, 200
RAND study, 46–48
random expected-utility models
  rational expectations assumptions, 109
  returns to schooling of youth, 109–110

random-effects model, 54
random utility, 96–100, 108, 112–114
randomized trials, 58
Raphael, S. 26
rational expectations assumptions, 109
Rawls, J., 27
  initial position arguments of, 27–29
RCP 8.5. *See* Representative Concentration Pathway (RCP) 8.5
recidivism, 69–71
Reconciliation Act of 2010, 38
reference groups, 90
regulatory approval, adaptive diversification of, 129–130
Reiersol, O., 72
Reiss, D., 183
relative risk, 57
reliability of the estimates, 42
religious dogma, 36–38
representation theorems, 7, 10–11
Representative Concentration Pathway (RCP) 8.5, 207
research on planning and actual planning, 13–14
response-based sampling, 56
retrospective studies, 56
revealed preference analysis
  classical consumer
    multiple choice settings, 95–96
    single choice setting, 94–95
  heterogeneous decision makers
    conditional choice probabilities, 98–100
    incomplete data, 98–100
    utility theory, 97
right-to-carry (RTC), 50–52
Rivers, D., 82, 84
Robbins, L., 100, 101
Robins, J., 82
robust decisions, 18–19
Rothenberg, J. xiii, xiv
RTC. *See* right-to-carry (RTC)
Rubin, D., 58, 88
Rubin, H., 139

sacrificing relevance, certitude
  odds ratio, 56–58
  primacy of internal validity, 58
  public health, 56–58
  randomized trials, 58
Samuelson, P., 94, 103–105
Sanstad, A., 196, 197

Sargent, T., 4
Savage, L., 8–13, 135, 136
Schlag, K., 136
Schotter, A., 62, 111
Scuffham, P., 182
SDF. *See* statistical decision function (SDF)
seasonal adjustment of statistics, 43–44
Seeskin, Z., 63
Seidenfeld, T., 170
semi-monotone treatment response (SMTR), 89–90
Sen, A., 11, 20, 30, 162
sentencing, 69–71
SEW. *See* subjective expected welfare (SEW)
Shervish, M., 170
Sheshinski, E., 30, 182, 184
Silverman, R., 183
Simon, H., 29, 45, 62
SIR. *See* susceptible-infectious-removed (SIR)
SMTR. *See* semi-monotone treatment response (SMTR)
skepticism, 70, 149
Smith, A., 4
Smith, D., 70
Smith, J., 112
social cost minimization, 185–186
social welfare, 2–5
  bounded rationality, 29–30
  maximin welfare, 27–29
  new welfare economics, 25
  non personalist welfare functions, 30–31
  optimal paternalism in populations, 29–30
  pragmatic welfare, 31–32
  utilitarian welfare, 25–27
  x-pox, 123–124
social choice theory, 5
specific egalitarianism., 31
Spencer, B., 63
Spiegelhalter, D., 135
Spiegelman, R., 83
SQF. *See* stop, question, and frisk (SQF)
Stable Unit Treatment Value Assumption, 88
Starczak, D., 182
state of nature, 6
state space, 6, 14
statistical decision function (SDF), 17, 18, 24

Bayes decisions, 134–135
MMR, 135–137
STR, 137
statistical decision theory, 17–19
statistical discrimination, 151
statistical imprecision, 23–24
statistical treatment rule (STR), 137–139
status quo treatment, 132, 138–141
Stein, M., 59
Stern, N., 101, 102, 201
Stewart, A., 183
Stiglitz, J., 5
stop, question, and frisk (SQF), 163, 165
Stoye, J., 136, 171
STR. *See* statistical treatment rule (STR)
subjective data analysis
  hypothetical choice scenarios, 113–114
  imprecise probabilities, 112–113
  probabilistic expectations, 110–112
subjective expected welfare (SEW), 15–18, 119
Sugden, R., 12
Sunstein, C., 30
supply-control policy, 46
surveillance/aggressive treatment, 156–157, 172–173
susceptible-infectious-removed (SIR), 185
Swan–Ganz catheterization, 74–75
Swinburne, R., 37

Tambur, A., 87
Tamer, E., 22, 65
tax schedules, 104–105
taxation, 100–103
TB. *See* tuberculosis (TB)
Tetenov, A., 18, 131, 132, 139, 141–143, 145, 171
Thaler, R., 29
Tirole, J., 60
Tobin, J., 31
Todd, P., 163
Toxvaerd, F., 184
Train, K., 114
transitory uncertainty, 40–41
treatment choice
  COVID-19 pandemic, 145–146
  mean treatment response, 167–169
  near-optimal treatment choices, 141–142
  observed covariates, 170–171
  with primary and secondary outcomes, 142–145

with sample data, 171–172
with trial data, 137–141
treatment response, identification of.
    See also mean treatment response
    concepts and notation, 88–89
    CTR, 89–90
    SMTR, 89–90
Trevino, I., 62, 111
trial-reported findings, binary categorical
        variable, 84–85
    bounded-variation assumptions, 86–88
    short trial findings, 85–86
tuberculosis (TB), 173, 174, 176, 178, 179
Tukey, J., 55
Tversky, A., 7, 61
two-stage optimization problem, 174–175
    optimization with utilitarian welfare,
        175–177
    threshold risk assessments, 177–178
Type I error, 18, 132, 133, 136, 142,
    147, 150
Type II error, 18, 132, 133, 136, 142,
    147, 150

UI. *See* unemployment insurance (UI)
US Census Bureau (2011), 42
US Food and Drug Administration (FDA)
    adaptive partial drug approval, 150
    drug approval process, 147–148
    rejection of formal decision analysis,
        148–150
uncertainty
    communication of, 213–214
    decision making, 22
    in decision theory, 6–7
    in empirical research, 21–24
    in epidemiological models, 2
    macroeconomic planning, 3
    in physical-science climate models, 2
    planning problems, 214–215
    tractability of decision criteria, 215–216
unemployment insurance (UI), 82–83
universal mandate
    in heterogeneous population
        optimization problem, 192
        policy choice without knowledge,
            193–194
    with representative agent
        optimization problem, 187–188
        policy choice without knowledge,
            188–191

Urzua, S., 58
utilitarian social welfare function, 107
utilitarian welfare, 25–27
utility models
    expectations and choice data,
        111–112
utility theory, 97

vaccination
    of children and young adults, 183
    direct effect of, 182
    of health care workers, 183
    policy, 181, 184
    rates, 182, 183
    policy, 2
    studied choice of, 184
Vamos, C., 183
van der Klaauw, W., 112
Varian, H., 31, 96
Venkataramani, A., 31, 154, 162
Venmans, F., 207
Von Neumann and Morgenstern (VN-M),
    8, 10, 11, 13
Von Neumann, J., 8
Vyas, D., 161

Wald, A., 17, 19, 131, 134
    ex ante evaluation, 134
    SDF, 134
    theory, 17, 18, 23–24
Walley, P., 16
Washington Post, 219
Wasserstein, R., 133
Watson, J., 19
welfare economics, 4
    fundamental theorems of, 4
welfare function, 14
welfarism, 30
wellbeing, 1
West, P., 182
Whitchurch, E., 61
willingness to pay, 26–27
Wilson, T., 60, 61
wishful extrapolation
    experimental treatments to clinical
        treatments, 53–54
    meta-analysis, 54–55
    study populations to patient
        populations, 52–53
    systematic review, 54
Wiswall, M., 112

Wittchen, H., 59
Wolpin, K., 112
Woodbury, S., 83
Wright, J., 44

X-12-ARIMA method, 44
x-pox, 118–120
   Bayesian planning, 121
   maximin planning, 122
   minimax regret planning, 122–123
   social welfare functions, 123–124
   treatments of, 120–121

Zafar, B., 112
Zinman, B., 84, 88
Zissimopoulos, J., 112